THE FASHION ASSISTANT

For the past, present, and future fashion assistants of London—may your stories be seen and your voices heard.

The Fashion Assistant

ISBN: 978-1-9194507-0-4

Edited by Bianka Walter
Layout design by Tl Mason
Cover design by Zsofi N Peto

In order to protect the privacy of individuals and the confidentiality of certain institutions, some names, dates, and identifying details have been changed.

September 2010

Welcome to my chaotic yet strangely charming living situation. Imagine walking into a place that feels like a crime scene from a quirky detective show. There are bloodstains on the mattress (fingers crossed it's just red wine), dusty footprints playing detective on the floor, and the wardrobe doors swinging like they've got a secret to spill. Oh, and don't even get me started on the Thujas outside—let's just say they didn't survive London's unpredictable weather. And the suspect? Mice. Lots of them. It's like they're hosting a tiny rave in the walls every night. Note to self: invest in mouse traps and maybe some earplugs.

Living in London has turned me into a detective of sorts. People randomly buzz the doorbell like they're playing ding-dong ditch. Cheap thrills, I guess. Not so thrilling for me, especially when it's 2 a.m. It took me a while to decode the buzzes; turns out, not everyone wants to have a chat through the intercom at odd hours. On the plus side, the walls of my room are cheery sun yellow—I've always been a fan of sunshine vibes—although somewhat stained and in need of a touch-up.

Let's talk about the great London shuffle—moving. I've become a relocation expert since landing in this whirlwind of a city. Crash at the airport? Check. House-hunt like it's a full-time job? Double-check. London's like a fast-paced game of musical chairs, and I'm just trying to snag a seat before the music stops. I used to have a pretty stable life. Same home, same friends. But in London, everything changes rapidly and in unapologetic ways. Even me. Although I prefer to think of the changes I experience as growth.

My new home on Hackney Road is a room in a ramshackle 3-bed flat. The flat opens onto a wide, spacious roof terrace, which is very cool! There are two other small flats in the block; we share the same entry door and the roof paradise. We must keep our windows and doors closed at all times, or someone might break in.

This area, as it turns out, attracts athletic robbers who climb onto the roofs. The girl who lives in the top one-bed flat told me that her laptop and camera were stolen by someone who climbed in through her roof window. She warns everyone to keep the doors and windows locked when we are not at home.

Now, let me introduce you to the cast of characters in my sit-com-esque life: Lena and Eric. Lena is my partner in crime from university—we bailed on film school together, chasing different dreams. We turned our backs on the diploma that seemed pointless to us at the time. I wanted to learn on the job, while she wanted to save the planet. "More and more people are waking up, questioning the system, looking for meaning... looking for themselves." I over-heard someone saying this on the bus. Lena is the yin to my yang, the Rachel to my Monica who joins me for tennis matches in front of the striptease bar down the road and bingo sessions with the el-derly on Saturdays. And then there's Eric... uh, I'll tell you about him later.

Oh, and according to Sean, my neighbouring drama king, "Shoreditch ended two years ago." He and his girlfriend provide the live soundtrack through the thin walls with their epic arguments. Popcorn, anyone? Spoiler alert: they're moving out soon. Maybe Shoreditch has ended for Sean but it is just beginning for me.

***

I'd been emailing numerous fashion stylists and editors whose names I snapped with my phone from magazines at Wardour News. My friend Flora and I frequented the place to browse through magazine pages for inspiration until the man behind the counter yelled, "If you don't buy anything, you have to go!" So, we left. Until the next month rolled around, and this time Flora purchased a copy of W magazine and a pack of menthol cigarettes.

"Since when have you been into menthol cigarettes?" I inquired.

"Since I got a sore throat," she replied.

"Really?"

"No! I just wanted a different flavour," she chuckled.

"Variety is the spice of life," I quipped. "Can I taste it?" I took a small menthol drag, surprisingly enjoying it.

Thursday, 16th September

I lost my nanny job. It's okay. I admit, I secretly manifested it so that I could follow my dream and start working in fashion instead.

Studio D.I.

I arrived at the door of an up-and-coming creative agency after sending numerous unanswered emails in response to their Gumtree ad. They were on the lookout for interns. Determined not to let this opportunity slip away, I even went to the extent of tracking down the studio's location—thank you, Google!—and on a rare sunny morning, I summoned the courage to visit the address armed with my home-printed portfolio.

Inside the narrow building, halfway up the stairs, I spotted a woman at the top of the staircase.

"Hello!" I waved.

"Hello! Are you here for the internship?" she asked.

"Yes, I'd love to find out more about it and also... ask for your advice regarding my portfolio."

"Did I send you an email?" she inquired.

"No, you didn't. That's why I am here."

She seemed surprised but managed a polite smile and directed me to wait in the room on the right before hurrying off to the room on the left. In the room, in an armchair, sat a man in his thirties wearing a black leather jacket, engrossed with an i-D magazine in his lap. He didn't acknowledge my presence, so I confidently exclaimed, "Hi!" towards him.

"Hey, how are you?" He glanced up, swiftly scanning me from head to toe before tossing the magazine onto the table. Then, silence.

"Do you work here?" I broke the silence.

"Sort of."

He bent over to inspect his shoes.

"What do you do?"

"I am a photographer," he replied, still focused on his shoes. "You?"

"I came to find out about the internship and to show my portfolio."

"Is that your portfolio?" He gestured towards the black folder I held. "Let me see!"

I handed it over and moved closer to the chair next to him.

"You a photographer?" he inquired.

"No. I am into styling, graphics, and post-production. My friend was the photographer."

"Interesting stuff. I like the graphics! Edgy," he remarked while flipping through the pages.

"Thanks. Do you think I can do something with it in fashion?"

"What do you want to do? Styling or graphics? You have to choose one direction to start with."

"I guess, styling."

"Have you assisted stylists before?"

"No. I haven't got professional experience yet, and I don't know anybody."

"The best way to build contacts is to start assisting, y' know, doing internships, volunteering."

"Is this how you started?"

The answer never arrived because the woman I saw earlier entered the room.

"Hi, I am Grace! Sorry for keeping you waiting!"

"Zsofi. Nice to meet you." I reached out for a handshake.

She squinted her eyes in confusion upon hearing the foreign sound of my name, but she didn't inquire about my origins, which relieved me. I often feel scrutinised because of my Eastern European background, a sentiment shared by my expat friends from Southern and Northern Europe. Perhaps because the UK and Ireland are the westernmost countries on the continent, to them, all other European countries are eastern. Only a few of them know that the most westerly point of Europe is actually Cabo da Roca in Portugal.

"So, you are here for the internship. Where did you hear about it?" Grace asked.

"Gumtree," I replied. "Do you mind having a quick look at my portfolio?" I asked politely.

She reached out for my folder and examined my work.

"What are you interested in doing? Are you into fashion or arts?" she inquired, "Your work is quite different... editorial stuff."

"Styling. Do you know any stylists I could start building work experience with? I am new to the scene."

Grace finished looking at my photos and turned away to retrieve something—a business card.

"We don't give out contacts but... try this girl. Io Miura is one of the stylists I have recently met. She works on editorials. She may need assistants." Grace handed me the card.

"Cool. Thank you. I appreciate it."

"When you get in touch with Io, let her know that you got her contact from Grace at Studio D.I."

"I will. Thank you! It was nice meeting you both!"

"Good luck!" Grace smiled.

October 2010

Tuesday, 5th October

I can't pay my rent. I am mortified. I have submitted my applications for Jobseeker's Allowance and Housing Benefit. In the meantime, I'm becoming more and more stressed out about my life. Everything's going downhill. My food cupboard is empty, and I have started to eat the hard icing that Lena has been keeping on the kitchen shelf since last Christmas. Then I am advised to sign up for a Crisis Loan.

Friday, 8th October

Lena took me to Hackney Library, where I registered for a membership card. After that, I started coming here more often just to spend a few hours of the day away from home, and because the library is well-heated inside. We often rent DVDs to watch movies or listen to music when Lena is not at work or at the Bethnal Green Working Men's Club. I have to admit that going through the benefits process would be less fun without her lightheartedness.

Tuesday, 19th October

I contacted Io on the same day I went to Studio D.I., and she wrote back to me in thirty minutes.

> "*hi*
> *thank you very much for your e-mail*
> *what sort of thing are you looking to assist?*
> *are you flexible?*

i am on editorial shoot so i wont be able to pay you anything. is that ok?
speak you soon
x"

Over the next two days we discussed my availability, her upcoming projects, and the compensation. I requested my travel costs be covered, and she agreed. Then, this morning she dropped me an email with her phone number and a list of pickups that needed to be done. However, I didn't check my emails until much later, at 7 p.m. Oops! I immediately sent Io my apologies, but I haven't heard back from her yet.

November 2010

Music Video Shoot

Io sent me an email asking if I am available on Friday for a music video shoot. I thought she had written me off after our miscommunication, and I felt lucky that she was giving me another chance.

"hi
sorry it didnt work out last time as i dont know if i need assistant until very last minutes also its so chaotic that its hard to manege sometime.
anyhow i am doing music video shoot this friday are you free to help me out?
i can't pay you on this but lunch provided and a day travel card
let me know what you think
the shoot would be in hackney
thanks
x"

The call time for the shoot was 7 a.m., and the location was in Hackney Downs, not too far from where I lived. I decided to save the last coins from my crisis loan, so I opted not to take the bus. After checking the map, I figured it'd take me about an hour to walk there. So, I dragged myself out of bed at 5 a.m. and hit the road by 5:40 a.m., giving myself an extra 20 minutes just in case I got lost—which, I did end up doing a bit. Despite that, I managed to arrive right on the dot at 7 a.m. But guess what? Io was nowhere to be found! So, there I was, just chilling outside in the dawn, observing a bunch of guys unloading a van and lugging these huge boxes into the pub where we were shooting. I had absolutely no clue what the project entailed; Io didn't fill me in on the details. All I managed to gather yesterday were three pairs of shoes, two garments, and a necklace—all snugly packed in my trusty blue IKEA carrier bag slung over my shoulder. And now, here I was, waiting. Then, out of the blue, this dude—cigarette dangling from his mouth—sauntered over.

"Hiya, are ya 'ere for the shoot?" he asked with his Cockney accent.

"Yes, I assist Io. I'm the stylist assistant," I proudly informed him.

He gave me that particular look that only British people give when they realise I'm not British, and they start wondering about my accent or why I don't speak "correct" English. That split second of puzzlement on their faces makes living in London worthwhile!

"Assist who?" he interjected.

Normally, after the puzzled look, the next question would be "Where are you from?" But the loader skipped this step. I'm pretty sure if I had said I was from Hungary, he would have cracked the classic joke "Are you hungry?", a tired line I've heard so many times it just makes me yawn.

"Io Miura, fashion stylist," I repeated and showed him my printed call sheet. He didn't seem to have a clue who Io was.

"Go inside if you want, ya can sit down in there," he said, barely glancing at the paper in my hand.

Io rocked up half an hour late, and although I'd never seen her before, I recognised her instantly from the garment bags and the mountain of hangers she wrestled through the door. As soon as I spotted her and hurried over, she started barking orders for me to help haul everything from the cab. In that moment, I wasn't sure if we'd ever manage to create the *senpai-kohai* dynamic—a Japanese relationship between seniors and juniors, where the senpai benefits from the growth and contribution of the kohai, and the kohai learns from the experience and guidance of the senpai. Even though it was her cultural background, she didn't seem the type to care much about mutual exchange—she clearly preferred giving orders.

She was short, with straight black hair, dressed head-to-toe in black, no jewellery, no make-up except for her eyeliner. Her short legs moved fast as she carried the tightly packed bags from the door to the stylist's area, and I found myself matching her pace, eager to prove I could keep up. She seemed stressed, determined to make up for the time she'd lost by being late.

We kicked things off by setting up the clothing rails and decking them out with all the outfits from the oversized suitcase and other smaller bags.

Io communicated with me using short, sharp commands, almost like we were in the army. For instance, "Sophie! My scissor!" meant "Please bring my scissors here," or "Sophie! Water!" translated to "Please fill the tank of the steamer with water," or "Sophie! Where my pen?" simply meant "Sophie, can you look for my pen?". I was too excited about the gig to sweat the small stuff like her communication style or her not-so-perfect English—I just got on with it and flashed a smile. By the way, I still had no clue whose music video we were working on.

We grabbed a table and a couple of chairs, scooting them closer to the rail, and carefully lay out the accessories on the flat surfaces like they were priceless treasures. We covered the table with a sheet for the rings, earrings, and necklaces but kept the headwear separate, displayed for all to see. One standout piece was this intricate black and white origami-style accessory that we left partly wrapped to shield it from dust. It was thrilling to unpack the bags and boxes and get a first look at all these different styles of outfits and jewellery—it was like Christmas came early, with a lot of presents! While I was steaming the garments (my first time using a hand steamer, and Io showed me how to do it with a cloth tied at the mouth to prevent drips), I got a closer look at all the pieces and marvelled at the designs. We had loads of DIY, pop culture-inspired, dance-style outfits, many of them taped or pinned together. They looked like stage outfits. I didn't recognise any of the designers or labels. They must have been small indie brands.

There was this stunning long silk dress that we layered over a folded garment bag to keep it off the grubby floor. It was terribly creased, and despite my meticulous steaming for twenty minutes, those creases were stubborn as ever. Io finally told me to ease off. "Don't stress too much about it!" So, I decided it was time for a breather and headed for some breakfast. When I got to the kitchen, all I saw were some unripe bananas, a squashed croissant, and sandwiches with bites taken out of them left on crumb-filled trays. I settled for the squashed croissant and a bland banana, washing it down with a cup of hot mint tea.

Not long after, a young woman strutted in wearing a fur coat and a massive grin, followed by her posse of girlfriends. She was beaming as she greeted crew members, and when she swung by the stylist station, I introduced myself, saying, "Hi, I'm just an assistant," to which she kindly responded, "Assistants are important too! We never have enough." I reckoned she was the VIP we were all here for.

Soon enough, Io rushed over and started getting her to try on various outfits and footwear before she headed to the makeup chair. Many dresses and tops didn't fit her, so we moved those pieces to the end of the rail. Personally, I was relieved—it meant less headache deciding what she should wear. I later found out her name was Rachel, thanks to others calling out to her.

From then until the end of the shoot, my main responsibilities were keeping the stylist station spick and span and guarding the pricey bling. I perched on a chair next to our accessory desk, passing the time by observing everything around me. I watched the dancers practicing their moves in front of the big mirror, and the crew buzzing up and down the stairs. I watched the walls, the floor, and even my worn-out black sneakers. I took in the glitter on one of the outfits catching sunlight through the shutter slits, making it twinkle in my eyes. Was I bored or just sleepy? Definitely cold—I downed countless cups of hot peppermint tea. I had a brief chat with the makeup assistant, but nothing memorable—except for her mentioning that Rachel was an X Factor contestant.

The song we were shooting the video for played on a loop from the upstairs speakers, and I heard the shuffle of feet overhead where they were filming the party scene. I could also hear the entry door's loud creak at noon that announced the arrival of the catering company's food delivery. They laid everything out neatly in the kitchen, but I was too disciplined (or shy?) to dive in first, so I hung around the jewellery desk until Io walked to me with a bowl of pasta salad in her hands and gave me permission to leave. "Sophie, eat!" she said, and we changed guards.

I nibbled on a bit of everything: salad, salmon, chicken, rice, bagel, biscuit, fruit—and stashed away a piece of apple for later. Seeing food was such a relief! At least that day, I didn't have to worry about what to eat. Still no news on my housing benefit application—I was surviving on a crisis loan and whatever Lena shared with me.

Later that afternoon, we packed up the expensive bling, and Io invited me to join her upstairs to watch the rest of the shoot. But the music was too blaring for my liking, so I stationed myself at the top of the stairs in the narrow corridor with the runners and crew members. I took in the scene with awe and excitement, from Rachel to the dancers, set designer, extras, and runners. Eventually, I sidled up to the Bud Spencer-lookalike cameraman, who seemed worn out but friendly. During a five-minute break, he let me perch in his chair and peer through the camera lens. We then dove back into retakes until one of the dancers slipped and fell. She was okay, thankfully, but the embellished helmet she was wearing had cracked slightly, leading to a minor panic as Io rushed over to assess the damage. We wrapped up at seven in the evening, and I embarked on the journey home with the items that the stylist had asked me to return to various showrooms and designers. Carrying three enormously packed bags made me stop and catch my breath four times along the way. I had initially offered to help Io with these bags, convincing her it wouldn't be an issue, but my arms and shoulders ached terribly, and I still felt the pain the next day when I set out to do the returns.

Since most of the showrooms in East London were in the vicinity of where I lived, I managed to do the returns on foot. However, due to the size of one bag, I had to dip into my emergency money for a bus ride to Farringdon. I paid for a one-way ticket and walked back the 40 minutes, bundled up warmly in my winter coat and scarf. I finished up the deliveries with the cracked helmet. Io immediately called the designer on the spot with apologies and agreed to pay the damage fee. My job now was just to return the helmet to the designer who lived above the Vietnamese takeaway on Kingsland Road. I was delighted she lived close to my house but less thrilled with her greeting when I arrived with the damaged headpiece.

"What a fuck happened to my helmet? Who did this? Where is Io? Why did she send you? Who are you? You have to pay me for this! I'm going to call her..." she fired off in rapid succession in one breath. She was probably in her late teens or early twenties, was clad in just panties and a T-shirt as she stood at her door, barely 25 cm away from my face, spitting her attitude all over me.

Oblivious to my discomfort, she didn't notice as I scanned her semi-dark flat with a racing heart. The room was a chaotic mess, filled with piles of clothes, beer cans, wine bottles, pizza boxes, and more. A tall, skinny guy appeared from a mattress on the floor, his eyes half-shut, seemingly to be under the influence of some drugs or alcohol. Fearing being attacked by a teenager-looking redneck designer and her unpredictable friend, I turned toward the stairs and hastened away, urging her to contact Io to address her concerns since I wasn't responsible for the damage.

I was happy that I didn't have to walk far to get home but I ended up almost running until I reached my street, checking over my shoulder to ensure she didn't follow. In the evening Io called me to check if everything went well with the returns. I recounted my experience with the helmet designer, and she revealed that many others had complained about her attitude. It left me wondering why she hadn't prepared me, and just like the designer questioned me, I found myself asking the same: "Why did Io send *me*?"

I've googled the designer, I really want to say her name but I can't because of privacy protection, so I can't pull the joke that rhymes with her name, unfortunately, but I've found out that the meaning of the name behind her clothing label is "eager to fight" and "uncooperative".

Wednesday, 10th November

I'm on the edge of a nervous breakdown, feeling like I'm in the midst of a midlife crisis as a result of chasing my dream career. These days, tears come easily due to the overwhelming pressure and uncertainty I face. I've lost control of my life's direction and have plunged deep into despair. Each new challenge leaves me emotionally and mentally drained, reaching a point where I simply let things unfold. Why must I endure this? Flora, in her sympathy, says, "I understand how you feel. Sometimes you think you've hit rock bottom, only to realise it goes deeper." *Thanks for the support, eh?*

Recently, I struck up a conversation with a woman at the Jobcentre who shared similar aspirations for life changes. However, unlike me, she was unsure of her next steps. Our exchange unexpectedly lifted my spirits. Despite feeling like a wreck on many fronts, I am young, driven, and passionate about my goals—qualities she admired. Yet, I couldn't shake the feeling of being in crisis, so, I asked her, "Is it possible to go through a midlife crisis at the age of 28?" Her response? "Honey, this is London; anything is possible!"

Starworks Press Day

After wrapping up the 12-hour music video shoot, we were busy packing everything back into bags when Io received a text message. She turned to me with a deep, exhausted sigh and asked, "Do you wanna do this?"

"Do what?" I wondered, squeezing the silk dress into its garment bag.

She explained that a designer from New York she used to work for needed help for "*Stawokpesdi*". I had no idea what that was, but I screamed yes when she mentioned the £100 payment. Having lived so poorly recently, this amount meant a lot to me!

Over the next couple of days, I exchanged emails with the people in New York to confirm the details. The event was called Starworks Press Day that I had misheard as "*Stawokpesdi*" from Io's accent. I googled the designer's name to study her work but found limited information, except that she collaborated with one of Calvin Klein's designers for her S/S collection.

They asked me to dress up, preferably in a skirt or dress. I didn't own skirts, but I had a dress from GAP, which I later discovered was from the maternity department.

I don't have a lot of clothes, but with my smile, I can look attractive in a simple T-shirt and jeans too. I have been in London for just over three years and haven't succumbed to the shopping fever that many people call a sport.

So, I wore the black maternity dress, adding my homemade pins—circle badges with eye details—on the belt, and matched it with my black hairy ankle boots. They might have expected me in heels, but I only had two pairs of shoes: the boots and sneakers. Boots it was. It was very cold outside and I wore them with two pairs of socks over the black tights.

On the day of the event, I was expected at Daniel's, the designer's partner's, home at 7:45 a.m. in Notting Hill. I arrived very early, unwilling to risk being late. I took the tube from Liverpool Street Station despite the fact that it meant I had to endure a 1.5 km walk in the morning frost. However, catching the tube directly to West London was both cheaper and faster than coming with two buses, even though the bus stop was only a stone's throw away from home. I arrived at 7:15 a.m., finding Notting Hill dark and freezing with no one around, quite unusual for such a busy area.

After some waiting, I rang the doorbell at 7:30 a.m., but there was no answer. I rang again and again but still got no response. I even took a stroll before returning and ringing again. Finally, after repeated attempts, a man opened the door. It was Daniel, a rich-looking gentleman in a white shirt and ironed trousers with no smile on his clean-shaven face. It felt to me that he purposefully didn't answer the door because it was not time yet. He ushered me into his museum-like living room and offered tea, but the atmosphere felt uncomfortable to me, almost mysterious, with a lifeless and chilly aura mirroring the wintry weather outside, so I politely declined the offer. I tried to strike up a conversation to break the ice, asking about his connection to fashion, the designer's whereabouts, and today's plan. My natural, smiley attitude thawed the room slightly, making me feel less uncomfortable. I learned that the designer had arrived from NY the previous night, battling jet lag. It turned out I would have to go to the event alone, set up the garment racks, unpack the collection, and wait for the designer to join later. Glancing at the wheeled suitcases and the large box of hangers in the hallway, I almost panicked.

"Are you taking me to the venue or…" I asked hesitantly, fearing I might have to carry everything myself.

"No! The taxi will take you there," he said firmly.

"Ah, good! I'm relieved," *Phew.*

When the taxi arrived, Daniel assisted me in bringing out the suitcases to the car, and he placed them in the boot with the driver. It was a black private taxi with a very young chauffeur. I mean VERY young, like 17 years old. He looked sharp in his uniform of a black suit, a white shirt, and a tie. He spoke with an East London accent, wore a cunning smile, and his eyes seemed glassy, as if he had just jumped out of bed and was not fully awake yet. It was evident he disliked wearing the chauffeur dress code.

As I sat in the car, a strange feeling washed over me, reminiscent of scenes from Sin City. In the eerily quiet, dark morning, a chauffeur had been hired to transport the innocent fashion assistant to a secret location through the dark, misty, soulless streets. The setting felt remarkably cinematic.

Anyway, upon arriving at the venue in Fitzroy Square, I was led to a room set up as the designer's showroom space. My task was to immediately unpack the outfits and hang them on the rails, but I encountered a problem—I couldn't open the luggage. "OH MY GOD!!! I CAN'T OPEN THE LUGGAGE!" Panic set in as I tried repeatedly and failed. I was scared to reach out to Daniel for help, the stoic rich man, but I was left with no other option. There was no time to waste. I kept trying for a little while longer with no luck, then I mustered the courage to make the dreaded call. After three rings, Daniel picked up and patiently guided me through the trick to unlock the luggage. Despite following his instructions, I was still struggling. Determined not to call him again, I rushed down the corridor to seek help from the well-built security man I had seen earlier at the entry. He assisted me promptly, and within minutes, we managed to unlock the luggage. Relieved, I proceeded to hang the neoprene tops and bikinis on the rail, stowed away the luggage and the box into the cupboard, and then my job shifted to standing by the collection until 7 pm, welcoming and introducing it to buyers, stylists, fashion editors, writers, and bloggers who visit. With no formal training, I relied on information gathered online. The designer added two more sentences when she dropped by at noon, and the rest of the interactions between me and the VERY IMPORTANT fashion people were improvised. Despite the long hours, I found joy in this job and derived satisfaction from seeing the designs displayed cohesively on the hangers. It took a bit of time to build confidence in engaging with the diverse visitors, from those dressed quite averagely to others with more groovy or extraordinary styles. The designer provided a notebook for collecting contact details from visitors, and I discreetly saved some of these contacts for myself too. Wouldn't you have done the same?

When the British Vogue editor entered the room, she didn't arrive alone but with a retinue of women trailing behind her. While I was unaware of their affiliation with Vogue, their aura of importance was palpable. They carried themselves with such esteem that everyone around them transitioned from normal to nervous. As the woman in the blue shirtdress, presumably the editor, requested two samples from the collection, I fumbled awkwardly to take note. Politely, I inquired about her name, prompting an exclamation from the entourage of women. The air stopped moving. Eventually, the Vogue editor provided her name, which I inadvertently misspelled on the note, and a big sweaty woman from behind me grabbed the pen out of my hand to finish the note on my behalf. Before leaving the room, the editor noticed the eye badges pinned to my dress and engaged in a friendly chat with me.

"Those eyes are intriguing! What are they?" she inquired.

"They are circle badges," I responded, removing one to show her.

"Where did you find them?" she probed further.

"I make them at home using a badge-making kit. I cut out pictures and press them into the badges. They can enhance simple outfits," I explained eagerly.

"I can see that. Do you sell them?" she asked, her smile encouraging.

"I would love to! Currently, I've only made a few for myself and friends, but I aspire to turn it into a business in the future," I shared excitedly.

"Good luck with that!" she bade farewell with a supportive smile, and proceeded to explore the other rooms of the event.

At around 2 p.m., I became very hungry and was dying for a coffee since I hadn't eaten anything yet that day. Daniel was there, sitting comfortably in the only armchair we had. I wasn't allowed to sit down, so I rested by leaning against the wall when there were no visitors in the room. He mentioned that he was going out to buy some coffee and asked if I wanted anything. Uncertain whether I had to pay him back, I declined and said I would just grab something from the kitchen. I had heard other assistants mention something about lunch in the kitchen, so I assumed I could get a coffee and maybe some food there. Daniel wanted to buy me a piece of chocolate at least, but I was reluctant to accept. My gut feeling picked up on something malicious about this man, and I wanted no connection or communication with him whatsoever. He insisted on buying me a piece of chocolate, so I hesitantly agreed just to shut him up and let him get me a bar of Snickers.

Later during my break, I went to the restroom to splash some cold water on my face before finding the kitchen, where I made an instant coffee and finally sat down. Boy, did it feel good to sit! I took my time, grabbing a napkin and laying down a triangle sandwich, a chocolate muffin, and a croissant that I grabbed from the tray. Being very hungry, the sandwich went down my throat in two bites, which I rinsed down with some coffee. The croissant disappeared in three bites, and I was comfortably nibbling on the chocolate muffin when a girl came around the food table to pour some orange juice into her cup. I asked her if it was okay for me to sit there and eat. She told me that the kitchen was only for Starworks staff to use but she was cool and didn't mind me being there. I should have been more assertive and helped myself to more food, after all, I had been up since 6 a.m., but that would have been rude. I enjoyed what I had and then headed back to our room. Just one more coffee and back to work.

At the end of the day, Daniel gave me a lift in his car to the tube station. I agreed to the lift only because the designer was coming with us in the car. I turned to her for some advice and asked her how she started her career. She was kind and honest in her answers, which gave me a good end to the day, along with the £100 cash she withdrew from the ATM next to the station. She mentioned that it took about 10 years to establish herself in the industry, and this sentence stuck in my head for many years to come.

I arrived home late in the evening, dead tired and with back pain from standing all day. Despite the physical strain, the experience was worth it! As soon as I was in bed, I fell asleep quickly but woke up in the middle of the night from a terrible dream in which Daniel raped me.

Sunday, 14th November

I am delving into the law of attraction and the insightful teachings of oracle cards, all thanks to Lena, who gifted me a deck of angel cards. We make it a daily practice to draw cards and contemplate their messages deeply. I frequently encounter cards like "Let your past go," "Blessing in disguise," and "Entrepreneur," each offering profound insights into my journey and mindset.

Simultaneously, I am actively cultivating trust in my inner wisdom and embracing the power of my authentic voice. The more I align with my true self, the more fulfilled I become, and the less I am swayed by external opinions. This introspective journey has led me to reassess my life choices and relationships across all aspects of my life—family, friends, and most importantly, my relationship with myself. I've utilised this time for self-reinvention and goal-setting, shedding the layers of conformity that once dictated my actions. The old Zsofi often pursued desires dictated by external pressures, leaving her disconnected from her true passions. I am now embracing my uniqueness and peeling off layers of conditioning and societal expectations that no longer serve my growth. I comfort myself by admitting that it's okay to be lost. As the saying goes, "If you're lost, you can be found." In those moments of uncertainty lies the potential to rediscover and redefine oneself.

According to Dictionary.com the definition of authentic is "not false or copied; genuine; real; representing one's true nature or beliefs."

> "*To be authentic, we must cultivate the courage to be imperfect—and vulnerable. We have to believe that we are fundamentally worthy of love and acceptance, just as we are.*" Brené Brown

> "*Authenticity is about presence, living in the moment with conviction and confidence, and staying true to yourself. An authentic person puts the people around them at ease, like a comforting, old friend who welcomes us in and makes us feel at home.*" Christopher D. Connors

Friday, 19th November

Eric is dead.

Okay, he is not. Lena feared he might be. She called me on the phone and asked me to come home ASAP because Eric was unusually quiet in his room, and his door was open, which was abnormal since he always kept it shut whether he was home or not, adding to the mystery of London living. Initially, Lena didn't think anything was wrong, despite knowing a bit about Eric's troubled past and his connection to drugs. However, after an hour of no movement or sound from his room, she started to freak out.

"Are you absolutely sure he's in his room?" I asked Lena, trying to assess the situation.

"Yes, I can see his legs at the end of the bed," Lena replied, her voice filled with worry.

"Can you try to peek in a bit more to check on him?" I suggested, hoping for a clearer view.

"I don't want to," Lena hesitated, clearly distressed.

"Maybe gently knock on his door again," I suggested, trying to remain calm.

"I did, but there's been no response. I don't want to be here alone. Please come home quickly," Lena urged, her concern growing evident.

"Okay," I said. "Meet me at Liverpool Street Station in half an hour and let's walk back to the house together to assess the remains of Eric," I added half-jokingly.

Upon arriving home, we found Eric's door still open, and there was still no sign of movement or sound from his room. And finally, there was quiet, without the loud music blaring from his room, a rarity akin to finding a unicorn at a petting zoo. Determined to savour the serenity of a music-free home, I revelled in the silence like a detective uncovering a clue. Then Lena and I exchanged worried whispers, contemplating our next steps. Peering cautiously into Eric's room, I noticed a syringe on the floor, and only half of Eric was visible on the bed. I refrained from entering further, feeling a mix of concern and dread. I was just a fashion assistant, after all, not a detective.

"I don't want to deal with this," I whispered to Lena, my anxiety growing.

"Okay, I'll do it," Lena decided, bravely stepping forward to check on him.

After a tense moment, Lena confirmed that Eric was indeed breathing, and she gently closed his door. Just as we started to relax, Eric emerged from his room, visibly annoyed. He scolded Lena for entering his room without permission, oblivious to the fear and concern we had experienced moments earlier. And...that's what you get when you want to help.

Blanche Magazine

I assisted Io again, this time for a photo shoot editorial for Blanche magazine, and I couldn't have been more excited. The location was on Kingsland Road, the same road where the "uncooperative" designer lived, and I silently hoped that I wouldn't bump into her. I had to meet Io at her flat in Stoke Newington, prompting me to wake up super early once again to ensure I arrived on time on foot. I walked the length of Kingsland Road, passing by the current shoot location, until the road changed names to Stoke Newington Road, where I continued a bit further. The walk was good exercise for my legs. Upon reaching the flat, I had to tread quietly as Io's partner was still asleep. We settled in the kitchen, which was almost the size of my wardrobe, and enjoyed a morning tea until the cab arrived. Our conversation ranged from London housing to fashion styling opportunities and my future plans. Io was kind and attentive but appeared quite exhausted, not necessarily from the job but perhaps from London itself. She shared insights about the industry, cautioning me that I would likely encounter many stylists and unpaid work if I was serious about becoming a fashion stylist. She also warned me, saying, "Not everybody is going to be as nice as me." I assured her that I could handle it; while I was humble and kind-natured, there was a fighter inside me that pushed to reach my goals. We then lugged bags of outfits, oversized hats, hangers, and clothing rails in pieces down the stairs, squeezing everything into the car while leaving just enough space for both of us to sit.

The shoot took place inside a fantastic top-floor flat with a built-in studio, or perhaps the spacious living room had been cleverly transformed into one—I couldn't quite tell, but it looked really cool. The atmosphere was intimate, with only a handful of people present including the photographer, the director of photography (DOP), the makeup artist (MUA), the model, the stylist, and me. The windows were covered with thick black fabric around the frames, casting the room in a soft, artificial glow from the studio lamps and the computer screen. Soft music filled the air from the iMac speakers as the MUA delicately worked on the model's face and hair. Meanwhile, the DOP meticulously tested the lights, and I focused on organising the outfits on the rack, identifying pieces that could benefit from steaming. Io was present one moment and then off assisting the photographer, who was also from Japan, conversing with each other in their native language. Despite the various tasks, the atmosphere remained friendly and laid-back. The shoot proceeded smoothly and swiftly thanks to everyone's focus and preparation.

I found inspiration in the Japanese work ethic and their dedication to order, cleanliness, punctuality, and speed. In Hungary, the emphasis is more on multitasking and shut up. You usually receive instructions and are expected to work independently, even managing multiple roles under one title. If you refuse to take on additional tasks, maybe even outside of your regular working hours and without compensation, you might face the threat of being fired. On the other hand, in London (or is it just in fashion?), employees are encouraged to be self-motivated and proactive. Rather than explicit instructions, British colleagues expect you to figure things out independently, but then they call you out or make you re-do your task if you don't do it the way they expected.

At midday, I was entrusted with £40 and asked to pop down to Sainsbury's to purchase snacks and soft drinks. I picked up some croissants, fruits, chocolate, and a packet of biscuits. For drinks, I opted for a high-quality bottle of orange juice, not the cheap Sainsbury's type, along with two bottles of water. Upon my return, everyone immediately reached for the water, and nobody touched the juice.

On the shoot, my primary responsibility was to assist the model in changing between looks and to arrange the outfits neatly at the end of the rack while Io chose the next ensemble.

The outfits were predominantly abstract black-and-white pieces, leaning toward a unique, avant-garde aesthetic compared to what we had worked on for the music video. One outfit in particular stood out for being *almost too abstract*—the kind of design that made you wonder how it was even meant to be worn—and Io asked for my opinion on it. I appreciated her effort to involve me in the creative process and valued the freedom I had when she let me choose the next outfit and accessory. That sense of collaboration made me feel like a genuinely valued member of the team. *This* was what a true senpai-kohai relationship was meant to be.

The model, resembling Sasha Pivovarova, exuded a sweet and optimistic aura. She shared her plans to travel to New York the next month and try signing with overseas model agencies, believing she had better prospects there than in the UK. She was creative and confident in front of the camera, which was evident in her dynamic yet playful poses, swiftly adjusting with each click of the camera shutter. It was a joy to watch her work, and I drank in every moment of it.

At the end of the shoot, Io gave me £10 to thank me for my help. We divided the returns, and as we did the first time, I would let her know in a message when I delivered everything successfully.

Friday, 26th November

Observing a touching moment today, I witnessed an African woman cradling a baby boy in her arms at the council office. As they patiently waited to be called, the woman fed the baby a banana that she had pre-chewed for him.

A concept store and...

... a mess. A big mess. I decided to step into concept stores in East London to showcase and sell the pins I craft. Engaging in my badge-making hobby brings out my creativity and productivity, allowing me to sidestep the anxiety of unemployment. With ample free time, I've turned my badge-making into a serious endeavour, churning them out like a factory. If it caught the attention of the Vogue editor, surely it will captivate the entire city. *Always dream big.*

After my “Tour de Sale”, only one shop—selling a well-known alternative British brand—showed interest in the self-made badges, but the creative director requested me to pin them on clothes; otherwise, she wouldn't take them in. What kind of clothes, though? I didn’t have spare funds to buy new pieces. Eventually I could find something in my wardrobe that I didn’t wear and presented the badges on them. Two days later, I emailed a mood board with DIY punk-style designs I randomly put together, and the creative director sent me back a quick response:

> “*looks interesting and, god, the things with eyes are just AMAZING!!!!!! come to see me, give me ur number and I call u as soon as I m back to fix a meeting during the weekend. see u supersoon*”

When we met again in the store, we dressed the fragile mannequins in my designs and placed them in the display window. To my surprise, I made £20 on the spot when an Asian girl purchased one of my designs, the shortcut tights. It amazed me how smoothly someone was willing to pay for something I created on a whim.

I inquired with the creative director about payment terms and the percentage they deducted from sales. She explained that they would call me when they made a sale and then pay me, taking a 50% cut. There was no contract, no written agreement, and no certainty. While I was unsure about placing my trust in her, I was willing to take the risk. I wanted to gauge people's reactions to my designs and see if I could turn my ideas into a revenue stream. Exploring opportunities with this shop and potential collaborations excited me. The creative director's enthusiasm and the prospect of a video project further intrigued me. As a newcomer designer, I was ready to experience the highs and lows, balancing childlike curiosity with cautious vigilance. I quieted my apprehensions to embrace the learning journey ahead.

For the next couple of weeks, I continued making badges for the shop, earning little cash and not selling much. However, one of my designs stood out—an outfit embellished with nearly a hundred badges pinned on it attracted a lot of attention in the display window. Passersby often stopped to take photos of it.

The creative director began suggesting other tasks for me that were unrelated to my trademark designs. At first, I enjoyed the idea of new challenges, such as experimenting with new ways to deconstruct and reconstruct outfits that she provided. However, when she asked me to create a collection using a lamination technique without compensation for my work, I felt the need to set boundaries. While the dresses I reconstructed are intended for sale in the shop, allowing me to earn a certain percentage, the lamination work would benefit only her brand. Therefore, I passed.

Soon after this incident, my relationship with the shop took a downturn. The creative director decided to alter my designs without seeking my permission first. I strongly felt that she should respect my creations, and if she had any issues with them, she should discuss them with me before making changes. During our meeting, I brought up this concern for discussion, and it became evident that she didn't value my feelings or opinions in this matter.

We experienced another clash when I visited the shop to collect my payment. The creative director had instructed me to come in on Friday, but she was absent, and the temporary sales assistant was unable to locate the money. I called her, and she advised me to return on a day when she would be present. So, I came back a few days later, and she handed me £23, including £13 in pennies. To add to my frustration, I did not receive the full amount; there were some missing pennies. That day, I left the shop with a bad feeling and decided to end our collaboration before the situation deteriorated further. The next day, I went back to the shop to retrieve my design. There were three individuals in the shop behind the counter: (1) the creative director, (2) an elderly man who happened to be the owner of the concept store—I recognised him from an interview I watched on YouTube, and (3) a super skinny girl with very bad teeth and dark circles under her eyes (the sales assistant or old man's lover?). I began by discussing with the creative director to explore possibilities of improving communication between us and inquired about the potential of drafting a written agreement if we decided to continue our collaboration. Unfortunately, my attempt only worsened the situation. The creative director insisted that "we had an unspoken agreement" and expected me to be content with that. Initially,

I was fine with the arrangement until I witnessed her inconsistent behaviour, making me realise that I had nothing tangible to rely on or to hold her accountable for in case of any damage or loss to my designs. A silent agreement felt more like a promise, not a guarantee.

Here's a useful quote from the book "The Gift of Fear" written by Gavin De Becker:

> "*Promises are used to convince us of an intention, but they are not guarantees. A guarantee is a promise that offers some compensation if the speaker fails to deliver. But promises offer no such collateral. They are the very hollowest instrument of speech, showing nothing more than the speaker's desire to convince you of something.*"

She informed me that a customer was interested in purchasing one of my outfits for £400.

"Don't you want the money?" she asked, her tone turning bitter.

I affirmed that I preferred to take my designs home.

"Go ahead!" she snapped, retreating behind the screen of her laptop.

The old man appeared bewildered. He questioned my presence. I politely introduced myself to him then the creative director stepped in, mentioning that I crafted the pins showcased in their store.

"What pins? Who is she? What stuff does she have in the shop?" he demanded more information, hinting that the communication issues weren't just with me.

When the creative director mentioned the potential £400 sale involving my outfit, the old man and the skinny girl with bad teeth reacted strongly. The old man called me a stupid bitch and sent me to business school—*I think I was attending one right in that moment.* The skinny girl with the bad teeth started to bark at me like a chihuahua on ecstasy calling me all sorts of names, while the creative director continued to hide behind her laptop screen, feigning detachment from the situation.

I was taken aback by this hostile attitude. Hastily, I started removing my designs from the hangers, desperate to leave as soon as possible. The skinny girl with bad teeth stepped forward, attempting to grab the outfits from my grasp. She screamed into my ears that I was a whore—*hello everyone!*—and that what pieces of shit design I made, and if I removed more stuff, she would call the police. *I would love her to call the police!* She was jumping around me without understanding why she was doing it, perhaps under the influence of something. There was clearly something off about her, and she could be a story all on her own. I stole a glance at the creative director, hoping for intervention against the abusive behaviour, but she remained passive. It became clear that it was not me but the money, specifically the £400 they had never seen, that was at the root of their aggression. There might have been other underlying issues, possibly secrets the creative director was concealing, now bubbling to the surface.

"*We don't see things as they are, we see them as we are.*" Anais Nin

Encountering aggression for the second time in a few weeks, following the meeting with the "uncooperative" designer, felt like a scene out of a movie turned reality. I was let down, I was shamed, I was misunderstood, I was verbally abused, I was thrown out. I knew I would recover from the bad experience and humiliation but to tell you the truth, it was difficult to sleep well that night.

December 2010

Thursday, 2nd December

I cry a lot these days, almost every day. I feel lonely.

Sunday, 5th December

I decided to try out the "cigarette and chocolate milk" combination inspired by Rufus Wainwright's song. I bought a small pack of cigarettes and a box of chocolate milk, then sat on the roof terrace beneath the neighbouring billboard advertisement. And that was all I consumed today. Although this habit didn't become my new favourite, it was an interesting experiment.

Moreover, I stumbled upon a budget-friendly yet healthy food option: a banana for £0.20, perfect for breakfast. For an extra £0.10, I could indulge in a less healthy packet of pink biscuits available at Costcutter. However, I prefer to avoid unhealthy food as much as possible. Some might question this choice, given my circumstances, but I firmly believe we always have choices. I choose to prioritise eating less but healthier foods over consuming more unhealthy options.

Friday, 10th December

Finally, my Housing Benefit has arrived! It's an immense relief to know that I won't face homelessness. The past two months involved weekly visits to the council office to submit more and more documents each time, which was incredibly draining. To qualify for housing benefits, I had to sort out my jobseeker's allowance first, which significantly slowed down the process. While submitting the applications was quick, receiving actual assistance took much longer.

What turned the tide for me was a moment of vulnerability. Under the pressure and the hunger I was experiencing at the time, I couldn't hold back my tears and broke down in front of the Jobcentre consultant. Fortunately, the man took pity on me and made a crucial phone call to the main office to locate my application, which was then approved on the spot. He provided me with a stamped document bearing his name and contact number, instructing me to call him if I didn't receive the approval letter within the next fourteen days.

By the time I received the benefits, I'd lost 6 kg, missed my period once (likely due to low-calorie intake or stress), and fallen behind on two months' rent with an impatient landlord.

On the positive side, I had ample time to work on my portfolio and have become creatively very productive. I've also started to establish relationships with model agencies to collaborate with new face models. Knowing that Io is moving back to Japan before Christmas, I asked her to share some of her contacts with me to continue building professional experience. Simultaneously, I've sent out my CV to stylists whose contacts I either scribbled from magazine pages or found on LinkedIn, where I recently joined for this purpose.

While I tried not to worry, some days it was challenging, and I fell into fear, developing headaches from my own thoughts. However, I've learned that shifting my focus away from things I can't control and towards actionable tasks helps me stay positive and hopeful. Essentially, redirecting my focus from the lacks towards what I do have, keeps me grounded. I hold the belief that everything unfolds for a reason, following its necessary course rather than the way I desire it to happen. Sometimes I just have to trust the process instead of doubting it.

Surviving in London with no income was a challenge, but I found creative ways to manage. Inspired by a documentary on poverty in China, where orphans survived on a bowl of rice daily, I decided to adopt a similar strategy. I chose to buy the healthier, fibre-rich brown rice over refined white rice. Occasionally, I would enhance my meals with fried onions, peas, or both on a good day.

To meet my protein needs affordably, I purchased chicken drumsticks, and I even ate the skin, even though I usually dislike it, and scraped off all the gooey and chunky bits from the bones to consume more calories.

Every second week after signing up at the Jobcentre, I treated myself to the best chocolate brownie from a nearby organic shop. It became a ritual, a small reward to acknowledge my resilience and ability to cope with the adversities I faced.

I developed a routine of waking up late in the mornings and going to bed early at night to shorten my days, reducing the time I felt hungry during the day. I limited physical activities to conserve energy, occasionally taking short walks, albeit limited due to the cold weather and lack of proper shoes. Overall, it wasn't too bad to manage.

My daily routines haven't changed much since I received the housing benefit, except that now I include a wider variety of vegetables and fruits in my diet. I remain cautious about my expenses until I feel more secure and balanced with the regular monthly financial support.

A day in Paris

Earlier, in September, I decided to go to Paris for a day using the last £50 I had in my bank account. When you have such little money, you might as well enjoy spending it. It happened to be fashion week in Paris, and I thought it would be too bold to hope to see the Rick Owens show—or catch a glimpse of him at all, really. Instead, I figured I could at least find out his studio address to send him a copy of my portfolio which contained graphics and video art. I am a huge fan of his design and am inspired by his work and journey. as a designer, so collaborating with him would be a dream come true. I pulled the "GO FOR IT" oracle angel card, taking it as a sign of confirmation for my plan to go to Paris. The whole idea was insane, but I felt I had to do it, and taking the risk seemed fun, especially with my good friend Flora joining me on the trip!

We took the night bus with the ferry crossing from Dover. It was a double-decker, and as soon as we got on the bus, I headed for the two front seats on the top deck to enjoy the view. However, Flora quickly pulled me toward the back because she feared that in a rear-end collision, we would be the first ones flying out through the glass, and she definitely did not want that. So we settled for seats toward the middle instead. The bus departed at 9 p.m. and arrived in Paris at 7 in the morning. We didn't get any sleep because we laughed throughout the entire journey. We had several moments where we cracked up just by looking at each other and laughed until our sides hurt. Undoubtedly, we were the loudest on the bus after the roaring snorer a few seats away from us, who contributed to our laughter. There's always someone snoring loudly on long travel journeys, and this guy was real entertainment with his unique, rhythmic, unearthly vocals. Initially, I mistook his snoring for someone watching something on a laptop. Understandably, all the passengers were trying to sleep through the trip. The man sitting in front of us became annoyed with Flora and me because we were giggling constantly. In the second half of the journey, he turned toward us and angrily exclaimed, "Shut up and sleep!" in his broken French English. However, we couldn't contain our laughter, even though we honestly tried because our stomachs and cheeks hurt from laughing so much.

While we were on the ferry, I felt like a kid again, eager to explore every nook and cranny of the boat. Although the shops were closed, we found the buffet open and checked out the food options. We sat in all the different types of chairs, explored various rooms and lobbies, and even ventured upstairs and outside. Along the way, we took plenty of photos to document our journey. My favourite moments were when we went out to the deck and posed in the wind, which turned our hair into punk, electric shock, and straight-out-of-the-shower styles. We also sneakily took photos of people sleeping on the ferry. The funniest ones were of a big, tall man who was lying under the stairs, looking like a dead whale washed up on the shore. Another amusing photo was of a guy whose head was hanging down from the edge of his chair with his mouth wide open, resembling Edvard Munch's "The Scream" painting but with closed eyes.

Paris reminded me a lot of Budapest, and it got me thinking about why people call Paris the City of Love instead of Budapest. Although I understand the reasons, it didn't feel as romantic as I expected. The locals seemed grumpy, the weather was rainy, and the overall atmosphere was dull. I was grateful that Flora accompanied me on this trip! We visited iconic landmarks like the Eiffel Tower and the Louvre, and strolled down the Champs-Élysées. We enjoyed cappuccinos at bustling sidewalk cafés and smoked Vogue cigarettes with style. Interestingly, every time we lit a cigarette, someone nearby would approach us and ask if they could have one too. It made me question the romantic aura of the city.

As soon as the office hours began, I sprang into action and started making phone calls to fashion people with a reputation for being difficult, using the numbers I found online. Flora, who knew the city well, took charge of the map, which was a huge help. I would have been lost without her guidance. We navigated from one address to another, speaking with different people along the way, until we finally found someone who knew someone who might help us. Our last hope was the Rick Owens store in Jardins du Palais Royal.

At the store, I approached the doorman who said he was not allowed to give information to customers such as the address of the atelier. I explained that I was not looking to visit but simply wanted to post a DVD to the designer's atelier. I showed him the envelope as proof of my intentions and begged for assistance. Initially hesitant, the doorman disappeared briefly, leaving me in uncertainty about whether he was calling the police or consulting the store manager. However, to my relief, he returned with a note containing the atelier's address, and he said, "You don't know it from me. Now go!". I thanked him in both French and English then scooted out of the shop. I promptly posted the DVD at the nearest post office and spent the remaining hours of the day wandering the streets of Paris, feeling a mix of exhaustion and drowsiness.

On the return journey, the same snoring man was aboard the bus, but this time we lacked the energy to find it amusing. We were simply too exhausted. As soon as the bus started moving, Flora fell asleep right away. I rested with my eyes closed during the entire trip but couldn't manage to sleep. We reached London early in the morning and bid each other goodbye with a wave before heading our separate ways on the tube. It had been the longest but also the most fun day ever.

And now, two and a half months later, Rick Owens replied in an email:

> "*.....THANKING YOU FOR YOUR VERY ATTRACTIVE CD- I DON'T HAVE ANY NEED FOR YOU RIGHT NOW BUT APPRECIATE THE INTEREST.....*
> *BEST TO YOU*
> *R*"

Dressmaking workshop

I secured a stall at Spitalfields Market to showcase and sell my home-made pins. The response was overwhelmingly positive, with customers praising the uniqueness of my creations and offering supportive words. A fashion blogger even took notice, snapping pictures and requesting my contact details to feature my work on her page. An online start-up also showed interest, and showcased selected pieces of my pins on their website, but after half a year they closed their business, retaining the pins I had deposited with them—a clear case of theft in my world.

The positive reviews, however, encouraged me to take the pins to the next level and I sketched ideas for a women's collection, but I had no tailoring or sewing skills except for sewing clothes for my Barbie doll as a kid. So, I signed up for a 10-week dressmaking workshop to learn from M. W., an acclaimed fashion designer and Central Saint Martin's graduate, who was once hired by Alexander McQueen to work on a lavishly detailed garment, or so I heard.

Eric

Lena and I urgently needed to find a new flatmate for the third room because Eric left suddenly. *Thank you, almighty.*

Living with Eric was a nightmare. He had a penchant for drugs, was unpredictable and withdrawn, and seemed to spend his days holed up in his room claiming to work as a translator. The incessant blaring of music from his room became a constant source of frustration, leading neighbours to complain and even involve the police. The music disrupted our peace at all hours—morning, afternoon, evening, and even late into the night. Sleep became a struggle, and tranquility was non-existent. I contacted our landlord multiple times, pleading for intervention as Eric remained unresponsive toward us. The landlord's optimistic approach failed to address the gravity of the situation. He seemed oblivious to the fact that Lena and I felt unsafe due to Eric's drug use and erratic behaviour.

Eric neglected basic responsibilities such as paying bills and cleaning up after himself. During one of his week-long absences, Lena resorted to leaving a stack of his unwashed dishes outside his room in protest. There were days when he shut himself in his room, and on others, he wandered around with glassy eyes, slamming doors behind him. On top of everything, there was one occasion when he had sex in our shared bathroom with the door wide open. Whether intentional or due to sheer negligence, this was unacceptable. Lena and I were shocked and angered by this event, feeling as if we were unwilling participants in an inappropriate scene. We could have watched live porn but decided to leave the flat instead, infuriated. Never had I imagined facing such disturbances and challenges simply because of a shitty flatmate.

Christmas alone

The landlord wants to evict us since we haven't found a replacement tenant for the third room, and Lena and I are hesitant to pay the share for that room. This is the second time it has happened since I moved in six months ago. I have explained to the landlord that no one is interested in moving in for the price he asks for if the window is cracked, the walls are mouldy, the bed is broken, and the door cannot be closed. That room needs to be fixed first before being rented out. Unfortunately, my landlord doesn't care about the flat or the tenants; he just wants his money. However, I offer to help him with the room. I clean it, and he has to replace the furniture.

I am handling the flat search without Lena's help again. She doesn't seem to care much about what is happening at home. She says she is travelling home for Christmas and then she wants to move out. She's fed up with this place. That saddens me because it's not just about the flat but also our friendship that she is moving away from. I don't know why, but I thought Lena and I would stay together to support each other and continue to experience the ups and downs of London. I've known her for three years, and she's like family to me. I thought we were going to be flatmates for much longer. I understand why she is fed up, as I am also tired of the situation, and I want to support her in moving on, but right now, I can only see my loss.

So I am spending Christmas alone and I am OK with that. *Am I really?* I don my socks and immerse myself in a lot of Regina Spektor songs, finding comfort in her voice. I deeply miss Lena's presence, and it takes time to adjust to the quietness of the flat, but I embrace it as a new experience to live and feel. This marks the first time in my life that I've spent the festive holiday alone. There isn't a soul nearby, not even our neighbours; everyone has gone to be with their families.

During this time, it snows a little and then it rains a little. Eric's room door, which is now lying outside on our terrace, gets replaced between the holidays. There's a vintage photo of an unknown little boy on the front of the door that Eric left behind. When it snowed, it looked rather melancholic, as if the little boy was left alone in the cold, abandoned. After the rain, with raindrops clinging to the door, it appeared as though the boy was shedding tears.

Despite the boiler breaking a month ago and the uncertain timeline for replacement, the landlord's brother managed to get it to work minimally. I don't feel too cold, so it's fine. Luckily, the boiler cupboard is in my room, which provides me with extra warmth. On Christmas Day, there's a serene and holy atmosphere outside, and I feel safe in this quietude. Although I am alone, there's a sense of relief and security that washes over me inexplicably.

In the first days of the holiday, I mainly stayed indoors, basking in the warmth of my heated room and gazing out of the large window overlooking the roof terrace. Dealing with the ongoing house problems and uncertainties surrounding my benefits had been stressful for a while, so it was time to relish the peace I finally had. I found myself sleeping a lot, partly due to the darkness of winter but also as a way to recover from mental exhaustion. Then after a few days of rest, I sprang into action. I started by cleaning my room meticulously and then proceeded to tackle the entire flat. I delved behind wardrobes, climbed above cupboards, and crouched under the sink, leaving no corner untouched. I painstakingly brushed the wooden floor, ensuring every crack was free from the dirt and grime that had likely accumulated over years. During this cleaning spree, I stumbled upon heaps of mouse droppings in the lower cupboard next to the stove, where we stored our few pans and dishes. The sight nearly made me throw up. I was left wondering why no one had ever cleaned this area before and how long it had been in such a state. Donning a dust mask over my nose and mouth and wearing yellow rubber gloves on my hands, I grabbed an old towel, took a deep breath, and swept the mess into the bin. Afterward, I thoroughly cleaned and aired out the cupboard before sealing any visible holes with large chunks of toffee tape.

This is the first time in my life that I've had to contend with mice. We first noticed one scurrying in front of us back in October when the weather turned cold. Initially, I brushed it off as a one-time occurrence, but Lena saw it again, and she rightly pointed out that where there's one mouse, there are likely more, given their rapid reproduction rate. Living above a Tandoori restaurant seems to provide the perfect conditions for them. On the bright side, where there are mice, there are supposedly no rats. *Supposedly.*

I tried not to dwell on the idea of being surrounded by mice, but Lena's complaints about a sewage smell in her room, which faces the back of the building, hinted at a larger problem. Then there were the sounds, faint but unmistakable, of mice scurrying in the walls. It sounded at times like a chain dragging across the floor, so much so that I wondered if our upstairs neighbours had acquired a dog and were keeping it on a leash indoors. But that theory didn't hold up—why would they keep a dog chained up like that? The odd noises made Lena and me speculate; perhaps it was a pet, or maybe it was something else entirely.

One particularly unsettling night, I awoke to the sharp, eerie sound of what seemed like two (or more) mice or rats engaged in a scuffle inside the wall. The noise was so vivid and loud it felt like they were right next to my ear. I never quite pinpointed the exact location of these noises; they seemed to reverberate from within the walls, a disconcerting reminder of our uninvited housemates.

I requested the landlord to arrange for an exterminator to inspect the flat, but he took no action regarding the situation, and neither did my flatmates. So, using my jobseeker's allowance, I purchased mouse traps, and by New Year's Eve, I had caught four mice. They tended to come out in the dark, and whenever I heard the trap snap, I approached the kitchen with a mixture of fear and disgust. Seeing a dead mouse in the trap was a grim and unpleasant sight, a harsh reminder of the ongoing ordeal. Dealing with these scenes alone was incredibly challenging for me. However, during these moments of difficulty, I often turned to my oracle cards for guidance, and one particular message resonated deeply: "The Universe doesn't put you in front of challenges that you can't handle. Through these challenges you learn and grow so don't be discouraged by them, embrace them!"

After the thorough cleaning, I found myself happier and more at ease in the flat. I decided to treat myself with tiramisu from the shop, along with ingredients to bake a simple fruit loaf. I lit an apple cinnamon scented candle to create a festive atmosphere, and listened to Christmas songs on my laptop while baking the cake.

Some days after Boxing Day, I took a bus to Oxford Street and purchased a pair of boots on sale. I had been using my old ones with taped-up cracked soles until they became nearly unusable. Despite the city's shops being open and the traffic returning to normal, there was still a noticeable tranquility in the air. Everything and everyone seemed more peaceful, and I took pleasure in leisurely browsing inside the shops.

Wednesday, 29th December

For some reason, I felt it was a good idea to register with a GP. I've been in London for nearly four years and haven't done it yet. I looked up the nearest practices online and chose the one in Broadway Market, my favourite street in the area! I walked there in the snowy, now silent, otherwise bustling street, between Christmas and New Year's Eve. They accepted new patients, and I carefully filled out the forms they provided, paying attention to the questions. I understood all the words and expressions on the medical history list except for "contraceptives." I assumed they were anti-baby pills. Just to be sure, I looked it up in the dictionary on my phone, but the screen froze after I'd typed in the word. I had to approach the receptionist, who happened to be a guy, and I felt awkward asking him about this. I wasn't even sure how to pronounce "contraceptive" properly, so I just showed him the word on the paper, and he confirmed "it's to prevent pregnancy". Got it, thank you.

And no, I didn't take contraceptives or any other pills, as a matter of fact. No way I deliberately used artificial methods to mess with my hormones and disrupt the natural flow of my body.

Next, I had to meet a nurse who conducted general examinations like blood pressure, weight, and height checks. She was very nice, and it felt good that somebody cared about me, a feeling I hadn't experienced for a long time. She asked me if I wanted to do additional check-ups and read from a list of options from which I could choose. Among the options was the AIDS test, which I was curious to try. No particular reason, just why not? The nurse took a little blood from my fingertip, and the result turned up in 5 minutes. It was negative, which didn't surprise me, but it was good to know nonetheless.

I also watched Sex and the City in the holidays. Lena had left the series for me in her DVD case to watch if I felt alone. I was in bed with Carrie, Miranda, Samantha, and Charlotte for almost a week, binge-watching one episode after the other, bang, bang, bang! I was so hooked that when I went to sleep at night after my movie marathon, I was super excited to get up in the morning and hit the play button again. I was in love with the characters! I laughed and cried with them every day. I could relate to a lot they went through. London was not much different from NY. I felt I was part of their lives, and I was not lost anymore. I started to feel strong, positive, and inspired again. I turned "*fresh and wild*" like Wholefoods!

Did you know?

- Long-term use of estrogen-containing birth control pills is associated with an increased risk of breast cancer and cervical cancer
- The hormones found in birth control pills are synthetic forms of hormones that naturally occur in your body. When taking these pills, the level of hormones in your body increase and can generate changes in your body, such as a temporary increase in breast size or weight gain
- According to Natasha Campbell, author of the book "GAPS Gut and Psychology Syndrome", "*Contraceptive pills, or The Pill, has a devastating effect on the gut flora. By the time a woman is ready to have children, she has been on these drugs for a long period of time and has an abnormal gut flora. A human baby is born with a sterile gut and acquires most of its gut flora from the mother. So if the mother has an abnormal gut flora, that is what she will pass to her child, predisposing this child to eczema, asthma, and other allergies, and in severe cases to learning disabilities.*"

January 2011

The landlord visited to inspect the third room previously occupied by Eric, marking Lena's first encounter with him as she had always been hiding from him previously. I don't know why she avoided meeting the landlord. She didn't know why either. During our discussion about the flat's future and improvements, the landlord displayed a cooperative and amiable attitude. Surprisingly, he no longer seemed inclined to evict us. While enjoying tea together, I took the opportunity to inquire about our neighbours and the layout of the flats above ours. To my delight, I discovered that the flat above us is actually a two-bedroom unit, contrary to my prior assumption of it being a single-bedroom space. This realisation dispelled my misconception that the music producer tenants, who had moved in after Sean declared the death of Shoreditch, were a gay couple.

I totally understand now, why the tall guy from upstairs has been eyeing me curiously. Not in a creepy, stalking way but more out of interest. This good-looking 23-year-old with a model-like appearance, reminiscent of a youthful David Bowie but with better hair, has been trying to interact with me and invited me to their housewarming party. However, I had assumed he was gay and didn't reciprocate his interest. It's all about to change now. With this new understanding, I am slowly beginning to engage with him, like recently, upon catching a big mama mouse in the trap, which made me squeamish, I promptly sought help from my attractive neighbour, who fearlessly helped me dispose of the rodent, and stayed for a little chat after that.

February 2011

SM. magazine editorial

The fashion contacts I discreetly saved for myself during Starworks Press Day back in November didn't contribute much to my career until this week. I had sent out emails to everyone whose name I jotted down on my pocket tissue and the back of a Tesco receipt, and only one person responded. His name is Lee. Hello.

> *"Hi Zsofi,*
> *How are you? I was just wondering what you're up to at the moment? I have a few menswear editorial shoots coming up over the next few weeks. There's no money involved I'm afraid, but if you wanted to do some assisting I'm sure I could use your help. Let me know if you're free."*

I consider it a positive sign that Lee was able to spell my name correctly, unlike many others I have worked with or befriended, who still can't arrange the five letters in the correct order. It seems that people in London just don't care. It's easier for them to create their own version of me: Zsophi, Szophie, Sofie, Zofie, etc. R.E.S.P.E.C.T. should start here, with the name. Aretha Franklin lectured us, yet many still haven't graduated.

The call time was 10:30 a.m. on Saturday. Everyone was late except for me. *Why am I such a nerd?* The location was an exciting top-floor flat on Whitechapel Road, where we climbed out to the roof to do the photoshoot. The best thing about this flat was the bathroom with a separate entrance from outside the balcony.

Unique. I noticed a collection of skulls around the living room and an industrial sewing machine with a huge pattern cutting table, along with various colours of leather and lace fabrics. The photographer informed me that we were in his friend's home, who was a corset maker.

We were a small team of six on the shoot, and I was the only girl. While helping the model with the buttons on the cuffs of the shirt he was trying on for the look, I commented that he could be a boxer, and it turned out I hit the nail on the head. He said that he used to do boxing when he was younger. How much younger, I wondered, as he didn't look older than 19 now. He appeared shy and uncomfortable with me around. I wasn't sure if it was because I was a girl or the reason was something else entirely. His body language suggested I should turn away when he unbuttoned his trousers. He didn't speak much, just like Lee's other assistant, Jack.

This was Jack's first shoot, and he didn't seem to find ways to share responsibilities with me. I initiated small talk with him to encourage him to help me hang out the outfits on the clothing rail, but he didn't show interest in that. *Was he just here for decoration?* He appeared more passionate about flattering Lee by expressing how much he adored the new Dries Van Noten collection that we were working with. Eventually, I asked him directly to come and help me on the job.

The shoot progressed at a much slower pace compared to what I experienced with Io. Lee spent a lot of time deciding on the looks, and he made the model try on many different variations of the design before he was camera-ready. I didn't mind the slower pace because it kept me busy, and we could spend more time inside the heated flat than out on the frosty roof, at least. We wrapped up sometime after 3 p.m. as it began to turn dark outside. This time, I didn't handle the returns; instead, I just assisted Lee in loading the cab, and he arranged for a pick-up.

"Thank you for your help, Zsofi!" said Lee before we headed home.

"Anytime! Thank you for the opportunity!" I smiled back at him.

"Are you around next month? Can I text you the dates of my upcoming shoots?" he asked.

"Absolutely. I'd love to help again!" I confirmed, jumping for joy inside.

I was actually happy that only one person replied to my assistant request emails; it made the choice easy. Lee turned out to be a menswear stylist, which surprised me on the day, but I tried not to show that I didn't know about it. I admit, I am not particularly interested in menswear. I just did my job responsibly, which was pretty much the same thing as it was on the previous shoots with Io: unpacking the outfits and shoes from the bags, steaming, helping with dressing the model, keeping the area organised and tidy, being around the stylist with a kit bag in case they need something on set, and helping with returns at the end.

For me, every experience is valuable. I want to take it all in, come what may! I love shooting in different locations and getting to know London better. I also love working in a creative team! I feel the endorphins rush through my body on each shoot. It just feels so right to do this. I love what I do! I am so inspired! I am so alive! I've found my true niche in life.

On the way home, I took a shortcut toward Brick Lane in the dark afternoon hours, feeling satisfied with a job well done. It was always exhilarating to stroll down eclectic Brick Lane, the hub of vintage shops, street art, curry restaurants, and eccentric characters. The air was filled with music, and the aroma of BBQ from Café 1001 tantalised my senses. Though I was slightly hungry, I satisfied my appetite by browsing through the records at Rough Trade East. I was drawn to the cover art of albums even though I didn't know most of the bands.

There is something uniquely captivating about vinyl records! I often wish we hadn't moved on from them in favour of music discs and MP3 players. While I appreciate modern technology and inventions, I also hold a deep admiration for classics like vinyls and coffee percolators. Brewing coffee in the kitchen with an old-fashioned metal percolator feels like a divine ceremony, wouldn't you agree? Some things should never go out of style.

London Fashion Week

I took the initiative to reach out to 84 designers offering my help and assistance just two weeks before London Fashion Week. I visited the British Fashion Council's website and meticulously went through each designer's profile to find their contact details. At the same time, I was reading their bio and ran through my eyes the previous collections to get familiar with their work. It was an all-day job to sit in front of my 13-inch MacBook and compose personalised emails, which mentally tired me out by the evening, but my enthusiasm for London Fashion Week kept me fired up. Guess how many replies I received? Four. Two designers responded in the first week and another two designers wrote back to me during the week after. I jumped into work ASAP without initial meetings or interviews.

The quickest response came from R.C., where I was hired as an all-rounder. The atmosphere at the atelier was rather unfriendly: frozen air, employees with poker face, silence. Nobody was engaging in conversation. I didn't have the chance to meet the designer herself, as she usually worked behind closed doors in the back of the studio. Pat (presumably short for Patrick), the skinny gay studio manager who hired me, sent me around the atelier on my first day and instructed me to pick up the pins from the floor with my fingers. He explained that the pins were small and often hard to see, so I should look around carefully and pick them up one by one, then drop them inside one of the pin boxes at the pattern-cutting station. I started looking for hidden cameras because I felt like I was being pranked. Eventually, I came up with the idea to find a broom and sweep the entire atelier instead. I separated the pins from other waste, threw them into the pin box as requested, and finished this task faster than Pat expected.

Next, he sent me to the cupboard to find a box of customised ribbons of a specific size, which I struggled to locate. The cupboard was very well organised, with all the ribbons neatly categorised on one of the wider shelves. Despite this, I checked all the shelves with boxes of different contents just to ensure that no ribbons were misplaced. After my thorough search, I reported back to Pat that I hadn't found those specific ribbons, but he sent me back to check again. *Are you serious?* I was incredulous. I told him that I had checked all the boxes on all the shelves and found no ribbons like the ones he described. I suggested that they might have run out of them. He gave me an I-know-best-and-you-should-do-what-I-say look, and I couldn't understand what his problem was. Being a start-out assistant, I didn't want to cause any conflict on my first day. I might want to work here in the future, after all; R.C. is a big name in the industry, and the studio is within walking distance from my home. I remained hopeful that I might get to do something more sensible and exciting than just picking up pins.

When I returned to the cupboard, I pretended to search for the ribbons again, but in reality, I just moved the boxes around, thinking it was a waste of time. A lovely pregnant woman with thick glasses came over and informed me that they had indeed run out of those ribbons, and Pat was already aware of it. *Why did he ask me to look for something he knew wouldn't be there?* She saved me from the BS and invited me over to her desk, where she was trimming the ends of lace strips with two of her colleagues. They showed me what they were doing, and I joined in the trimming process. They didn't really need an extra pair of hands, but I didn't know what else to do, and neither did the studio manager, so I stuck with this group and helped them out.

My honest personality opened up the three women, and we started chatting sotto voce, which did not go unnoticed in the atelier. Even the girl with earphones who was sitting hunched over at the pattern-cutting table and didn't bother to help me find a broom was now eyeing us, looking annoyed. I doubted she could hear anything if she was really listening to music. One of the trimming girls, a Jamaican second-year student at the London College of Fashion, was doing an internship here, just like me, and she mentioned that she had hated being here since the beginning but felt better now that she had met me.

"When did you start your internship?" I asked.

"Three weeks ago," she said.

"Why haven't you looked for another internship if you don't like it here?"

"I was thinking about it... but now it's too late."

"Why is it too late?"

"The fashion week is in two weeks. It's hard to find another internship at the last minute. Plus I have to write an essay of my experience and need the reference for the school."

"If you change, you'll be able to collect two references from two different designers under your belt," I encouraged her.

"I don't think they'll give me a reference if I leave now."

I, on the other hand, don't need to submit an essay, so I take advantage of my freedom and choose to leave R.C. for M.K., another prestigious designer whose work I am actually fond of.

M.K.'s staff was cramped in a small room of chaos with two narrow walls erected as separation to divide the space by three. In the space on the right, two women were sitting with headsets making phone calls in several different languages, which I figured might be the sales department. They spoke fast and robotic. There were all sorts of stuff from fabric to papers lying next to them on the table and an inflatable mattress on the floor which took up all the space on that side of the wall.

"Chris is sleeping here," said Poppy.

"Who is Chris?" I asked.

"The production manager. I'll introduce you to him if I see him."

At just that moment, Chris said hello from behind us.

"Hi!" I greeted him. "Speak of the devil."

"Are you looking for a place to sleep?" Chris asked.

"No, I ..."

"We can share the mattress. Don't worry, I'm gay."

"Thanks, but no. I live close by."

"Whereabout?"

"In Hackney Road."

"Good for you! How much is your rent?"

"£400 plus bills."

He nodded and went on his business.

Poppy, M.K.'s assistant, welcomed me by hanging my plain black winter coat on the rail alongside the colourful collection. *My coat is in designer heaven.* I interpreted this gesture as a sign of being treated equally within the team. Since I was not a fashion student and lacked training in garment construction or sewing, Poppy assigned me the task of researching hairstyle and makeup ideas for the runway. She seated me in front of a pile of magazines and pink paper strips to mark pages where I found something interesting. I finished this task in half an hour, relying on my personal taste and current trends. The hair trend ranged from ponytails, braids, and bobs to messy and sleek hairstyles, or so I thought. Unfortunately, I remained unaware of Poppy's thoughts on my selections. I received no feedback from her, leaving me uncertain about how well I did, especially since I hadn't been given a theme or seen the collection, which would have guided my choices.

The designer was very friendly. Although I didn't get a chance to talk to her directly, we exchanged greetings when she walked in late in the morning. She had a natural way of mingling with her employees, creating an organic and pleasant atmosphere in the studio. The team comprised individuals from various parts of the world, including many students completing unpaid internships. Everyone was friendly and willing to help. While I attempted to assist with general tasks, most of my time was spent sitting and waiting in the middle of the studio, where people moved swiftly in and out, exchanging a few words, calling out names, and sharing occasional laughs. As the day progressed, I started feeling slightly uncomfortable with the lack of tasks, so I began creating small jobs for myself. I swept the floor, collected the bins, and offered to make tea or coffee for others. At lunchtime, Poppy suggested I take a break, although I wondered from what exactly. I wandered around the building with my homemade sandwich, and that's when I stumbled upon a group of students heading upstairs. Turned out they did pattern cutting on the first floor. I made friends with them, and one of the girls taught me about the lines on the paper pattern and let me try my hand at cutting.

I discovered that many of the interns were final year students, and I couldn't help but be curious about their plans after graduation. Most of them responded with uncertainty, laughing off questions about their future plans, embodying the carefree spirit of youth.

In the following days, my tasks expanded to include assisting with fittings, taking Polaroids of the models, organising previous years' Polaroids and folders, and running errands like buying fabric and stationery. I even helped warm up lunch for the designer in the microwave. One day, Poppy asked me to pick up some ready samples and leave one outfit for correction at a faraway North London factory to where I arrived as an icicle after the two-hour-long bus journey and some hiking in the snow. We didn't have snow in the city, but in this suburb part of London, I could have gone Nordic skiing. Coming here and back to the centre, consumed a significant part of my day, and upon my return, I was allowed to head home soon after.

During my time at the studio, I noticed a guy working alone every day on graphic design for textile patterns on his laptop. Curious about his work, I approached him to learn more about the software he used and what he was creating. I thought I might be able to contribute in a similar way and make use of my art diploma, so I asked Poppy if there were any graphic or computer-related tasks I could help with. Unfortunately, she couldn't think of anything at the time.

Then, over the weekend, I received this message that caught me off guard:

"hi zsofi
I'm afraid to say but i think i've over estimated the number of interns that i need at the moment. i've had to let a couple of

people go and it's first in last out in order to be fair. so for the remainder of this season i'm afraid we don't need the extra help that you offered however thank you for offering.
regards
poppy x"

Bummer.

So, I contacted the third designer who responded to my email, and I ended up working as a backstage dresser for her catwalk show. Her team was very human-like and grateful, which made it a pleasure to work with people who appreciate help, especially when I was working for them for free.

I was super excited to be backstage at a fashion show and experience the whole scene from setup until the lights went off. I just couldn't believe I was there! Somebody should have pinched me. There were two other backstage assistants from Korea who were students at LCF. We shared responsibilities, but I felt a bit left out as they spoke Korean between each other, which I didn't understand. Despite this, I managed to help them with the model boards and match the outfits with the shoes, socks, and tights based on what I saw on the Polaroids. I also witnessed their panic when they realised we were short on black tights, so I was sent out to the nearest Debenhams to buy extra pairs. Some models arrived at the last minute after running from another show, while others couldn't make it on time because their previous show was running late. More panic ensued when the hairstylist discovered that the latecomers' hair was covered in oil, and there was no time to wash it off and style their hair according to the theme. Eventually, everyone calmed down, and they decided to simply tie back the latecomers' hair.

Then we squeezed the pale, bony girls into the sample sizes; still, some of the outfits just looked too big, hanging loose and unattractive on the girls' fragile bodies. I could tell which models were naturally skinny and who was starving to be skinny just by looking at their faces. The skin and the eyes told the truth. Also, by observing the way they moved, I could discover the ones who found it harder to carry their bones due to a lack of strength and agility; symptoms that can be the result of not eating well or enough. Then we had an issue with the model who had fallen down in the street a few days ago, and now a massive purple bruise decorated her left calf. According to the Polaroid, she was supposed to wear ankle-length socks with heels, but because of her mishap, she was given black tights instead, which looked wrinkly on her chopstick legs despite being size small. Eventually, she swapped her look with another model and got to wear a maxi skirt design.

There were small breaks when I didn't know what to do, so I sneaked off to watch the hairstylists and make-up artists at work. I watched and recorded a clip with my phone about how they tied the scarves in the hair of the models and listened to an interview with the designer in the background. I also peeked out from behind the stage to see what the catwalk looked like and took a photo of the bright runway with the shades of people sitting around it. The energy was indescribable! The music was on loud, and I could certainly feel the level of excitement reaching its peak at the event. It was showtime!

We shared ten models among the three of us to dress, and there were twenty-four looks. Due to the shortage of models, four girls needed to turn three times on the runway, and we had to change them really fast into the second and third looks. As assistants, we needed to ensure that this happened in time so the girls didn't break the flow of the show. In the flurry of chaos, some buttons were left open, some shoes were unchanged, and some accessories were not worn—things that hopefully only we noticed.

The show wrapped up in a split second, and we rushed to tidy and pack everything before the next designer took over the space. As I did a final check to ensure all our rubbish was collected in the back, I realised I was the only one there at the end. The emptiness of the space felt starkly different—it was quiet and uneventful. When I retrieved my backpack from the storage room table, I noticed two hand steamers on the shelf above, the same type that Lee used. With no one around, I allowed myself to be cheeky and slipped one into my bag as a reward for my unpaid work. *Yes, I stole it—don't judge me.* The allure of owning one, especially knowing I couldn't afford it, overrode any hesitation, and just like that, the deed was done. I understand it may not be a big deal to those who can spare £45, but for me, it's a valuable addition to my stylist kit essentials!

On my way out, I thanked and bade goodbye to the two Korean assistants, promising to connect with them on Facebook to stay in touch. One of them noticed water dripping from my bag. Panic set in—I'm terrible at committing crimes! Thinking quickly, I blurted out, "It's my water bottle!" and dashed to the bathroom to clean up my bag. The nerves of stealing the hand steamer had made me forget to check if it had water in it. The act nearly backfired, but luckily, I escaped without a hitch.

LFW Presentations

Fashion Week isn't over for me just yet. I reached out to a fashion blogger whose email I saved from the November Starworks Press Day, and we finally met for a chat during which she gave me a glimpse into her world: juggling between her hated part-time office job and her passion for fashion blogging.

After four days of back-and-forth scheduling, "Let's meet tomorrow", "Sorry I can't make it. I have to work.", "Can you meet me here?", "Maybe tomorrow.", etc. we finally connected, and she generously invited me to join her for various Fashion Week events including a presentation, two exhibitions, and the "Ones to Watch" men's show. In her, I found my first fashion friend—a spirited Brazilian brimming with confidence and sass.

At 'Ones to Watch,' there were so many people crowding at the entrance that I lost her for a minute when she went ahead with her phone-presented invitation. However, she came back and pressed her phone into my hands from behind the security guy, who was too busy trying to control the crowd. The plan was to reuse her pass to get in, although the crowd ended up helping me more when everyone started to come forward and literally pushed me in, whether I wanted it or not. The security didn't even get the chance to ask for my invitation. Everyone was rushing to grab the best seats, it was chaotic. The Brazilian and I remained more chilled amidst the frenzy. We chose seats in the third row but ended up watching the show standing. After the show, on our way out, we grabbed a free glass of champagne and some candy at the pop-up bar before leaving the venue.

A birthday party

The student I'd met at R.C. invited me to join her for birthday drinks at Hoxton Bar and Kitchen. I was thrilled—I loved the place and had been there many times for music gigs. Eager to celebrate her special day, I happily offered to buy us cheap drinks, but I couldn't afford to pay for food too, so I lied and said that I wasn't hungry.

As we settled in, I realised I'd stepped into a very different kind of gathering than I was used to. The table was full of her big, warm extended family—brothers, cousins, partners—chatting and laughing with an ease that spoke of years of closeness and shared history. Their energy was magnetic, but also a little intimidating; I suddenly felt like an outsider trying to enter a world that wasn't mine. The names flew by too quickly for me to catch, and conversations carried on easily without me. I smiled, nodded, and sipped my drink, but couldn't quite find my way into the flow.

After a few attempts to make small talk over the booming music, I accepted that this wasn't really my moment. I politely excused myself, slipped away, and decided to call Flora for comfort. She was my rock in London, along with Lena. Flora told me she'd be in East London the next day, and we made plans to catch up. Just what I needed.

MM look book

I assisted Lee on a look book shoot. The photo studio was located in the basement under a supermarket, with part of the ceiling made of glass through which we could see people walking above our heads. It was oddly amusing to me for some reason. Despite the spacious and brightly lit studio, it was freezing cold down there. I had to keep my winter coat on to stay warm. There were no heaters, and it felt like we were shooting outdoors.

Jack was here too, taping the soles of the shoes while I steamed the garments. There wasn't much to steam since the outfits arrived on the hangers and this type of fabric, they used for the collection, didn't crease easily. Although we encountered an issue with the MM tops, many of them needed to be unpicked and widened around the crew neck as the model couldn't fit his head through.

The atmosphere was friendly and laid-back. Once Jack finished taping, we explored the breakfast table and the human-sized wooden bungalows installed within the studio. Lee explained that these bungalows were rented by photographers who worked there, some using them for storage, others as makeshift homes. Though officially not allowed to sleep there, many did so anyway, finding it cheaper than paying separate rent.

Everyone on the shoot was friendly and chatty except for a man with a unicorn-bun-tied hair, presumably the creative director, who only conversed with the photographer. He sat through the shoot behind the camera, spinning in a wheeled IKEA chair, his neon socks flashing between his baggy jeans and oversized sneakers, one foot in orange and the other in green.

It was a long and tedious day. Jack and I were stuck at the stylist station, occasionally taking turns to walk back and forth between the racks and the set to warm up our limbs and see if Lee needed any additional help. However, the design assistant handled most of the work that we, stylist assistants, should have been doing, making it feel like a waste of time for us to be there. By midday, Jack and I had run out of things to talk about, and he resorted to sitting on the floor, playing games on his phone to pass the time.

I decided to leave the shoot earlier for two reasons: firstly, I felt useless, and secondly, my lips had turned purple from the cold. I told Lee that I needed to go home because some people were coming to look at our broken boiler, and I had to let them in. I was too cold to care whether he believed me or not.

March 2011

Changes on the home front

The moment has arrived: Lena is moving out. The mere thought of her absence brings tears to my eyes. She gives me a long loving hug, offering reassurance that I can visit her new place whenever I wish, even suggesting I move in with her since her new room is spacious. Her comforting words provided solace; she's been my pillar of support. For a second I considered to packing up and moving with her, however, deep down, I knew that fleeing wasn't the solution. I admit I'm scared to be alone, but I feel I need to stay where I am in order to find myself.

Easy doesn't make you grow.

These days I reminisce about the fun times we shared while living together:

- Playing Bingo with the elderly people down the road.
- Sneaking through the fence to play tennis next to the striptease bar.
- Delving into oracle cards and horoscopes.
- Trying our hand at origami (thanks to Lena's paper heart tutorial).
- Enjoying the scent of LUSH products wafting through the flat (courtesy of Lena's job).
- Attempting to make sushi, though our efforts fell short.
- Tuning in to the Elvis Presley night at the tandoori restaurant below us. Every other month, an Indian man decked

out as Elvis serenaded the diner with the King's hits, making the floor and walls vibrate with the beat.
- Enjoying movie nights with DVDs borrowed from the library. After watching "Into the Wild," we seriously contemplated what could be more challenging: (a) Surviving in the city, or (b) Surviving in the wild?

When Lena left, I decided to invest in the flat and turn that hole into a home. With my two new flatmates, we picked up used paint from a recycling yard and added colour to the walls. We changed the shower curtain and sealed all the holes in the kitchen through which we imagined mice could enter. One of my flatmates hung his paintings on the walls and brought home two wooden shelves, salvaged from the street, to provide extra storage space in the kitchen. I cleaned the mould from under my window with vinegar and antiseptic spray—I found this method online—and finally unpacked the rest of my belongings from the big cardboard box I hadn't touched since I moved in. I repainted my yellow walls, rearranged the furniture, and replaced the large sheet of paper over my desk with new pictures and goals for the future. It was a fresh start.

At the same time, my romance story with the handsome neighbour began. Lena used to keep her bike outside, on the terrace, leaning against the metal barricade, that was just left there with no purpose. The landlord stored a few things up here, or they might have been left behind by previous tenants, I didn't know. We still had a lot of free space and were not bothered by the stuff. One day, I looked out my window and saw the handsome neighbour's bike parked at the exact spot where Lena's bike used to be. This was the first sign that made me think that something was quietly evolving.

If we lose a loved one, someone new comes into our lives. We always have the same amount of love. Apparently.

Then I took up smoking. It wasn't the nicotine craving that drove me, but rather the desire to join the handsome neighbour in his daily ritual. He would often be seen smoking by his window, lost in thought or perhaps lost in the music he was so passionate about. One day, summoning up my courage, I decided to break the ice. "Do you want to join me on the terrace?" I called out. To my surprise, he accepted the invitation, descending from his flat to join me in the shared space. Despite his reserved nature, there was a certain charm about him. His eyes held a spark of passion whenever he spoke about his music career. Confidence seemed to radiate from him, adding to his appeal. It made me realise that confidence truly transcends mere physical appearance, and can be one of the most alluring traits a person possesses.

SM. magazine shoot

I was in the midst of a menswear editorial shoot with Lee, and he opted to have the outfits delivered directly to my address since he resided farther out in Zone 4, beyond the reach of the delivery service. Fortunately, my flat sat right on the cusp of zones one and two, which proved to be advantageous as I welcomed a parade of prestigious designers to my doorstep.

A couple of days before the shoot, I had spent the whole afternoon dashing out of the flat, up to the roof, and down the stairs to greet the deliveries from Dior, YSL, Burberry, Prada, Armani, Bottega Veneta, and others, all securely sealed in labelled carrier bags. It was an exhilarating but nerve-wracking experience—I couldn't help but wonder if my humble abode would collapse under the values of esteemed merchandise it was honoured to store. At the same time I was extremely excited to see the content of the bags, but I didn't open them until the shoot, of course. However, the sheer volume of deliveries left my room feeling overrun, prompting me to strategically relocate some of the luxury items. Dior and Bottega Veneta found themselves sharing space in the kitchen, where I hoped they'd keep each other company without attracting any unwanted attention from rodents. I was praying that no mice would prefer Italian fashion over the peanut butter in the mouse trap, and that everything would remain clean and untouched in the coming days.

I also lined up some bags along the corridor wall and to safeguard the precious cargo, I made my flatmates swear on their lives they would be careful not to trip over them or spill anything on them, and that they LOCK THE DOOR whenever they were out of the flat.

As March began, the weather was starting to warm up. However, despite the thaw, the nights remained bitterly cold. With the heating turned off, I found myself bundled up in winter socks, a cosy knitted jumper, and thermal leggings just to keep warm. The luxurious navy YSL coat I found in one of the garment bags, that I hung on the wing of my wardrobe until the shoot, became my unexpected nighttime companion. Intrigued, I unzipped the bag and slipped into the oversized coat finding unexpected comfort in its embrace. Eventually, I draped it over myself in bed to keep me warm under the lingering chill of the night.

On the day of the shoot, Lee lent a hand as we carried the bags to the location, which happened to be in the photographer's home just a few minutes away on the same street. Maneuvering fifteen bags of fashion, we made three trips on foot, working up a bit of morning sweat and giving our arms a good workout. Despite the physical exertion, I still felt a bit groggy, so I poured myself some hot instant coffee, a beverage I wouldn't normally drink. The photographer ensured that everyone was wide awake by cranking up the music in his rented two-bed apartment. His flatmate crawled out of his room, grumpy, and left for the day. We listened to everything from 90's rock (thank you for Bon Jovi!) to modern dance and R&B.

As I sipped my coffee from a Backstreet Boys mug, I witnessed a rather absurd scene unfold. The photographer tasked his new assistant with the mission of finding his lost USB stick. When the assistant inquired about where the stick was last used, the photographer responded with a nonchalant "I don't know," followed by a mischievous giggle, which was anything but apologetic. The assistant, clearly puzzled, embodied the familiar first-day-on-the-job eagerness to impress and dutifully took on the task. You know when you are on your first day at your new job and want to do everything right and you want people to be pleased with your work? And your employer may ask you to do something ridiculous or unusual and you feel fooled yet you do it? It was *that* situation. How was the assistant supposed to locate such a tiny item in a space that wasn't his own? And how could he feel comfortable rummaging through every private cupboard and drawer, moving items around in the home of two strangers? Why hadn't the photographer taken more responsibility for his own belongings to begin with? And these are the people we, rookies, are expected to learn from. Ugh.

What's wrong with these people? Do they not realise how fortunate they are to have young, talented individuals willing to work for free? What gives them the right to act more like assholes than professionals? Why is it fashionable in the fashion industry to be mean?

I'm happy with Lee. He doesn't have a bitchy side, or if he does, I'm unaware of it. And that's perfectly fine with me. He's polite but somewhat distant, and that's okay too.

Anyway, we were shooting the spring/summer issue on the rooftop in 10-degree Celsius weather. Everyone was dressed warmly except the model, who was styled in short-sleeved tops and shorts, visibly shaking from the cold. His complexion quickly changed from white to red, and his lips from pink to purple. Despite this, he remained silent and followed instructions professionally, not even complaining when asked to lie on the frosty ground.

Feeling sorry for him, I kept an IKEA blanket under my arm, which I had brought from home, and I tossed it over the model during brief breaks to help warm him up a bit. I even rubbed his arms to stimulate blood circulation, hoping to restore his original colour.

By now, I had grown more confident in my role as a stylist assistant. I quickly learned what was expected of me and even had my own kit bag that I brought to the shoots. What did I pack in my kit bag? Pins, clips, scissors, rubber bands, hair bands, needles and threads of various colours, toffee tape, sellotape, double-sided tape, wet wipes, tissues, a blanket, a small towel, and a hand steamer. The hand steamer had already proven useful as Lee's had started to malfunction.

After spending a few hours working outdoors, we moved inside to shoot some additional looks in front of a canvas taped to the wall. The model remained very quiet, and I wasn't sure if he was enjoying himself. I offered him a hot drink, but he declined. The shoot progressed slowly, with many pauses for thought and adjustments to the model's looks. We only ended up using a few of the sample outfits and two pairs of shoes out of the ten lined up on the DIY rail. As we wrapped up late in the afternoon, the sun emerged, and I couldn't wait to return home to enjoy the summery atmosphere in my yellow room. Sitting on my sofa bed, gazing out the window over the roof terrace, brought me a sense of comfort. The sun's warmth soothed my soul.

Over the next two days, the delivery men came to my address to collect the fashion bags. One of them arrived on a motorbike, and agreed to take me to the end of the street when I told him I was pressed for time. "Yeah, okay, but only till the end of the street because you don't have a helmet," he said in accented English. I nodded in acceptance, and eventually, he took me and the Armani suit a little further than the end of the street, dropping me off near the Old Street roundabout where I could catch the bus 55.

Arriving at the store on time, I was directed towards the elevator that would take me up to the top floor to drop off the sample. It was my first time inside the Armani flagship store, or any Armani store for that matter, and I was in awe. The in-store elevator was particularly impressive—it was a glass cubicle from which I could see everything below and above me as I ascended.

As much as I enjoyed having the fashion bags parting in my room, I am relieved to have space on the floor again. The "luxury store" in our flat is now officially closed... until next time.

H. magazine shoot

Two weeks later, Lee and I found ourselves back at the same photographer's apartment, which was conveniently close to my home. This time, the weather was bright and sunny, and we were delighted to be working outisde on the rooftop. I was amazed by the rooftop paradise I had just discovered! The various roofs in the neighbourhood were interconnected, allowing us to traverse them easily. It was a lot of fun!

Our model, Oscar, took full advantage of the sunny weather, indulging in some sunbathing while munching on croissants and serenading us with his singing. His lively and easy-going personality made him a joy to work with, even when he was tasked with weight lifting, smoking, and spitting water in front of the camera. He seemed to relish these playful antics, bringing laughter to the set.

To alleviate some of the struggles faced by the models when changing shoes between looks, I had purchased invisible socks. Lee generally preferred the look of models without socks in the photos and it was often challenging for them to slide their sweaty feet into the sample shoes. I had thought these socks might help ease the process. However, the invisible socks were only available in women's sizes and appeared a bit small for male models like Oscar. Nevertheless, Oscar, being the hero that he was, managed to squeeze his large feet into them, and wore them thankfully inside the D&G shoes.

Do you want a cookie?

Do you want a cookie?" my flatmate asked with a smile, and I couldn't help but giggle. The way he pronounced "cookie" with his South African accent sounded very similar to the Hungarian word "kuki," which translates to "penis." "Kuki" is a child-friendly term for little boys' private parts. So, if you ever find yourself in Hungary, be cautious of how you pronounce the word "cookie," as some may view you as a pervert or even worse, a pedophile.

April 2011

Adidas feature with an abrupt end

Following the H. magazine shoot, I handled some returns and encountered a man inside the elevator of the PR building. Standing next to me, towering at six feet tall, he carried a massive fluorescent green suitcase. Curious, I asked if he was a stylist or perhaps an assistant like me. He replied that he was a menswear stylist, primarily involved in editorials and commercials. I introduced myself and expressed my eagerness to gain more experience as a stylist assistant. In a gesture of goodwill, he swiftly retrieved his phone from his jacket pocket, saved my number, and assured me he would reach out if he needed an extra hand.

Honestly, I didn't anticipate him following through on his offer, as he didn't strike me as someone who meant what he said. Yet, I was proven wrong when he called me the following week, leading to an exciting opportunity to work on an Adidas feature for C. magazine. My spirits soared with excitement, only to plummet the next day when I encountered him once again.

I was tasked with picking up items from the Adidas store in Covent Garden and transporting them to the dodgy area of Hackney, where the stylist lived. I arrived at the store with my big, wheeled suitcase and a pair of IKEA bags that were not enough to carry all the Adidas, mostly shoes in boxes. I explained my predicament to the PR girl, stating that I couldn't carry more stuff in one trip. Her solution? Call a cab. I reached out to the stylist, asking if he was willing to cover the cab fare. His response was a firm no. Instead, he advised me to cram everything into the bags I had or ask for extra bags at the store. Frustrated, I explained that it was not just a matter of bags; I physically couldn't manage more with just two hands. Eventually, with the help of the sympathetic PR girl, we creatively rearranged the items to fit as much as possible into the bags I had with me.

I left much later than I planned, and the PR girl felt sorry for me when I wobbled out of the store. I was weighed down by a large and now heavy suitcase in one hand, a smaller plastic bag in the other, and two fully packed IKEA bags hanging from each shoulder. I felt like a fully loaded Christmas tree, minus the lights.

It hit the peak of the rush hour when I reached the tube station, perspiring and red from the huffing and puffing under the load. Covent Garden station is one of the few stations in Central London for which platform access is only by lift or an emergency spiral staircase with 193 steps. The lift was a great saver of my life and my time but there were still some stairs to reach the platform after descending. How was I going to carry the stuff down the stairs? I stopped for a moment in the rushing crowd and just stared at the stairs in front of me with a desperate look on my face when somebody from behind kindly offered to help me with the suitcase, for which I was ever so grateful. The next challenge was to squeeze onto the train amidst the crush of peak hour, where only paper-thin people seemed to have a chance to wiggle through the crowd. But with my bags in tow, I felt as large as a sumo wrestler. I had to wait for three trains to pass before I finally saw the crowd thin enough for me to get on. A transfer at Holborn only added to the stress, and by the time I reached Liverpool Street, I was a human wreck.

Before continuing my journey to hell, I decided to drop home first and re-pack the stuff from one of the IKEA bags into my travel backpack and tape the smaller bag to the suitcase, thus having a free hand to touch my Oyster card on the bus that I was taking to the final destination. From the bus stop, I still needed to walk for twenty minutes to the stylist's house. Late and exhausted I faced a daunting trek through unfamiliar streets. It was dark, I was three hours late, and Hackney's reputation for crime lingered in the back of my mind. However, I could cope with the darkness, the lateness, and the fact that Hackney was a popular borough for crimes like robbery—*brand new Adidas, anyone?* What truly weighed on me was the stylist's reaction to my tardiness. His disdain was palpable, his lack of assistance disheartening. Now that I was here—suitcase, backpack, little bag, and IKEA bag—he was pissed off instead of being happy that I made it. He did not help me carry the bags inside. I wasn't sure if it was because he was mad at me or because he was naturally unhelpful. *The key to success is support, not dominance.* He walked in front of me, opening the doors in the corridors we were going through to reach his base, but instead of holding the doors for me, he let them swing back at me. *Asshole.* Inside his flat, he made me unpack the bags and told me to come in the morning at 8 a.m. His curt instructions left me even more alienated. I repeated that I would be there by 8. Then he corrected me and said, "At eight." I didn't understand. So, if I happened to get there five minutes early, he wouldn't answer the door, or what?

He was not the person I wanted to assist, and so later that night I decided to end our collaboration. I might have reconsidered and tried to resolve the misunderstandings if I had been paid, but I wasn't. I believe if somebody expects you to work for free, the least they should do is appreciate your help. That should be the minimum compensation for your time and efforts, especially after lugging half the Adidas store across London. I informed him politely that I wouldn't be coming in the morning and spent the rest of the week trying to forget about this experience. However, Io's words echoed in my mind, "Everyone works differently, so I can't guarantee that the experience would meet your expectations." It begs the question: Is it too much to expect to treat your assistant the way you would want to be treated? Maybe it was just another lesson in the cutthroat world of fashion.

A press day and a book signing

The Brazilian invited me to accompany her to an invitation-only event, a Press Day hosted by a fashion PR representing collections from emerging designers. We saw some inspiring pieces and some absolutely revolting ones too. At the entrance, they asked for our business cards, which I didn't have, so I simply left my name and email instead. I hadn't earned the credit yet to justify having a business card, but both the Brazilian and Lee encouraged me to create one for myself. Lee had his made because he's a freelance fashion stylist, but who am I? Just a stylist assistant. Do stylist assistants even have business cards? Nevertheless, I went home and designed one for myself in Photoshop, which I printed and hand-cut in my bedroom. Under my name, I wrote "Fashion Assistant."

A week later, I invited the Brazilian to a book signing party hosted at the Fashion and Textile Museum. The author was celebrating the release of her fashion book with a lovely speech, drinks, and canapés. Guests were also welcome to explore the museum's current exhibition for free, which made me ecstatic as I had been planning to visit it. Among the guests, I spotted Matt Berry, whom I recognised from the comedy series, IT Crowd. I couldn't stop smiling. Although I was too shy to say 'hi' to him, he seemed very chilled, and dare I say, kind of bored.

Matt Berry, if you're reading this: You were terrific in the IT Crowd! Thank you for making me laugh.

S. M. magazine launch party

I was promised a copy of the magazine upon its release, but it never arrived. Instead, I found the images online and happily discovered that I had received credit. Additionally, I received an invitation to the magazine launch party, which I attended with Sargon, a hat designer friend from Germany.

First, Sargon and I met up in the afternoon for coffee at Oxford Circus. After that, we headed to a jazz event in Dalston, then took the bus back to the city centre to join the crowd at the magazine launch party in a posh, sweaty, airless club. Arriving late, we missed the free cocktails and goodie bags that Lee mentioned when I spotted him at the bar. He was cheerful, out of his shell, and I wondered how much he had drunk. Lee was nerdy, not the drinking buddy type. I could imagine one glass of alcohol would be enough to make him smile from ear to ear.

Sargon and I found a copy of the magazine on a coffee table and eagerly flipped through it, searching for my name. When I spotted it, I felt a surge of pride. It felt like I had achieved something incredible. Sargon was proud of me too, but his feelings were mixed with a hint of jealousy, which he hid beneath his gentlemanly gesture of inviting me for a glass of wine to celebrate. However, when he saw the prices at the bar, his jaw dropped open wide. We agreed to order just one glass of red to share, as we calculated that the price of a single glass was equivalent to the cost of three bottles of wine at the off-license. What can I say? My new world is evolving around expensive drinks and unaffordable clothes.

Before leaving the club, I returned to the coffee table to pick up the magazine and take it home with me, but it was gone. I regretted not holding onto it, realising that someone else had likely snatched it by now. What a bummer. I resolved to be more assertive next time.

Sargon

I met Sargon at a business mentorship program, where we quickly bonded over creative business ideas and a shared love for fashion. Specializing in millinery, Sargon is also passionate about garment construction and fine art. He's one of those guys who I just can't figure out if he's gay or not. Although he once commented on my "naturally beautiful" smile and attempted to kiss me on the lips when he leaned in for his usual goodbye x-es before catching his bus. Despite this, I still question his sexual orientation. Even more so, when I discovered that his name, Sargon, means 'Sun Prince'. Nevertheless, I prefer to maintain some distance from him. He's too eccentric for my taste, and besides, I'm more interested in my handsome neighbour.

I suspect Sargon might be a hoarder. He rents a room in a three-storey house in Notting Hill along with other artists. The building is old and currently under scaffolding, but the rent is surprisingly cheap. I'm not familiar with the building's history, but finding affordable rent in Notting Hill is as rare as a blue moon. During one of our Skype conversations, Sargon mentioned that he has no space in his room. He even gave me a glimpse of it when we discussed his outfit idea for an upcoming exhibition, but the room was so dimly lit that I couldn't make out any details.

When they threw a house party, I went over and playfully teased Sargon about his hoarder lifestyle, repeatedly asking him to show me his room. However, he firmly forbade me from entering. The heart of the party was in the living room, where one of his flatmates, Alex, performed with his rock band. Alex bore a striking resemblance to Eddie Vedder: short, charismatic, and wielding a guitar. (FYI, I used to have a thing for guitar players... and it was back.) As I observed Alex setting up the makeshift stage next to the kitchen, cracking open a beer can, engaging in conversation with others, leaving the room, and returning, I found myself captivated by him. I had completely forgotten about Sargon and his room, and I was even willing to set aside thoughts of my handsome neighbour. A sudden crush on Alex had made the party infinitely more thrilling.

Sargon introduced me to his other flatmate, a girl with an Italian accent. She smoked and danced to a rhythm only she could hear.

The gig had yet to start, but more and more people arrived. Sargon entertained some of us with a story from his time in New York. He could be quite the storyteller; some of his tales sounded so absurd that I questioned their authenticity. However, I kept my doubts to myself, finding his storytelling abilities highly amusing.

After the gig, I sat down on the only sofa in the room, and Alex dropped down next to me with a cheerful "Hi!" My heart raced in my throat as I fought back a blush. We exchanged a few words, and then just smiled at each other. But my excitement was quickly dampened when he flashed a smile, revealing his rotten teeth. *Seriously?!* I couldn't believe my eyes. I had to look away for a moment to process what I had just seen. When I glanced back at him, the flatmate-girl crawled onto his lap, and they began to kiss. Feeling awkward, I decided to vacate the sofa before things got too intimate. I sought out Sargon and asked him about the relationship between the flatmates.

"Are they together?" I gestured towards the dry-humping "lovers".

"I'd say they comfort each other... when they're bored," he replied nonchalantly.

"That's more than comfort," I remarked.

As Alex and the flatmate-girl stood up to head to the bathroom together, Sargon made a casual comment, "They're going to do cocaine in the bathroom."

"I think they'll do more than just drugs in there," I corrected him.

"Why do you care?" Sargon challenged me.

"I was sitting on the sofa, chatting with Alex, when the girl plopped herself in his lap, completely ignoring me...and um... Why does he let her do this? Where's his dignity?"

"We have penises. Not dignity. No man would brush off a woman who voluntarily sits in their lap," Sargon chuckled.

"Sad. Very sad," I replied with a sigh.

"Do you like him?" Sargon asked.

"Um, yeah... or actually, no, not anymore. Not after I saw his teeth! Did you know?"

"Yeah, he doesn't have good teeth. Alex is an artist, a rebel. He cares about writing music, smoking, drinking... He doesn't care about rules and societal expectations."

"Brushing your teeth is part of basic hygiene. It has nothing to do with societal rules," I retorted.

"Well, he doesn't care about cleaning his teeth... or cleaning in general," Sargon explained.

"Does he have the same opinion about showering?" I wondered aloud.

***

Sargon is brimming with creative ideas, but he rarely follows through on them. It seems he's waiting for someone else to take the lead, or he simply loses interest along the way. It's a shame because he's capable of so much. When I ask him why he struggles to see his ideas through, he confesses that he doubts his ability to bring them to life exactly as he envisions them. So it's not really about the process itself; it's more about his lack of self-belief. He gives up before even giving it a try.

Children whose creative passions aren't nurtured by their caregivers often grow up doubting their own talents. Flora and I grapple with this issue as well, but our approaches couldn't be more different. When faced with doubt, I'm fuelled with determination to prove others wrong—I thrive on the challenge. Flora, on the other hand, tends to believe that whatever she does is never good enough. She harbours insecurities beneath the confident facade she presents to the world. These beliefs extend beyond our creative pursuits and seep into our relationships as well. For instance, Sargon refrains from pursuing girls he's interested in because he already feels rejected by them, seeing the goal as unattainable. Flora, meanwhile, doubts her own worthiness, feeling she's not attractive or special enough. As for me, I chase after everything I desire. I know I'm capable and deserving, and I want others to recognise that too. Perhaps I'm seeking validation that my parents never provided.

Sargon is so entrenched in his habit of sitting on his ideas that breaking free from it would require more than just a conversation and he's reluctant to step out of his comfort zone. So he starts to work at [1]Le Book and becomes a selling agent instead of an artist. At least for now. One evening, he visited my place after work and lent me the latest publication of "The Book". We spent the evening browsing through the pages before heading out to grab take-out

---

[1] Le Book is a global network and resource that offers exposure to companies and members of the creative community

food. Upon returning, we settled in to watch Charlie Rose's interview with Karl Lagerfeld on my laptop. As the night progressed, we engaged in a lengthy discussion about our experiences with high street fashion in London. We lamented the lack of originality in the industry, with new releases often feeling like mere replicas of what was already on the market. Copies were welcome, innovation declined, creativity question mark. It seemed that the emphasis was placed squarely on selling and selling quickly. It was not about fashion anymore; it was about the business of fashion. And if you wanted to put a product on the market, you had to come up with new ideas fast because the trends were changing faster than the seasons. High-end brands typically release five to six collections per year, including fall, winter, spring, summer, and resort. Beyond these main and pre-seasons, there are numerous retail seasons, totalling 22 in all, including Health and Wellness Season, Christmas, Valentine's Day, St Patrick's Day, Earth Day, Halloween, Lawn and Garden Season, Allergy Season, Back-to-School, and more. What are YOUR thoughts on this?

May 2011

Thursday, 5th May

I went to Prince Charles Cinema to watch Swan Lake. Then had lunch with Serkan in Whole Foods where we bumped into Agyness Deyn.

Wednesday, 11th May

I'm gradually becoming a regular patron at Old Shoreditch Station, where I indulge in the most delightful hot latte served in a glass cup. I settle at one of the wooden tables and I immerse myself in the soothing rhythm of blues and jazz while I work on my laptop. A change of scenery infuses me with a fresh wave of inspiration and revitalised motivation. I've noticed a few other individuals, much like myself, scattered across the tables with their own laptops. It's reassuring to know I'm not alone in this routine.

I've developed a habit of pouring water from the free water jug next to my coffee, and I occasionally nibble on a few sugar cubes to boost my calorie intake. Back in November, I missed my period, and I attributed it to insufficient calorie consumption. I've learned that sudden weight loss or gain can disrupt the menstrual cycle, and the bowl of rice I used to eat likely didn't provide the full 2000 calories needed for a healthy woman's daily intake.

I usually spend a couple of hours at the café, sometimes indulging in two coffees back to back, and the bartender has already learned my name. Today, during a slow period, we stepped outside to smoke. I felt very relaxed despite the ongoing traffic we faced at the junction. The streets bathed in sunlight and vibrant colours emerged from the usual greyness. Shoreditch is just magical when the Sun is out. I love being here! I really do.

The bartender and I chatted away the time, and then he surprised me by asking if I liked wine. Before I could respond, he had already poured a glass of white wine from the end of the bottle, placing it next to my latte as a gift. Unsure if it was wise to drink white wine after two cups of coffee, I hesitated, but I didn't want to offend him. I did my best, taking slow sips with long pauses in between and plenty of water to accompany it. This prolonged my stay at the café more than I had initially planned.

Tuesday, 17th May

I was at the ATM outside Tesco when she appeared next to me, unexpectedly. A complete stranger with dirty clothes and a croaky voice. She stepped uncomfortably close to me while I was collecting the cash from the machine and asked, "Where can I sign up for benefits? Y' know, jobseeker's allowance or somethin'..." This was bizarre. First of all, she was standing too close while I was withdrawing money, an obvious sign of a lack of social decency. Secondly, why did she ask me? Was it written on my back that I lived on benefits? *I know it was not.* How did she know?? Did she see me at the job centre, or what? But if she had seen me there, she would know where to go... People, what on Earth is going on?

Friday, 27th May

One of the advantageous things about not having a job is that I can go wherever I want and whenever I want. I manage my own time. I am never too tired or too busy to miss a great opportunity like the

Yohji Yamamoto retrospective exhibition and the stylist battle late Friday at the V&A.

The Victoria and Albert Museum is definitely my favourite museum in London. It hosts the Friday Late, a free and drop-in event, every last Friday of the month. It celebrates all aspects of contemporary visual culture and design.

This time, there were installations where visitors could participate, putting on outfits to create the Yohji Yamamoto look, which was then photographed by a staff member. Additionally, there were plenty of other activities accompanied by DJ music, though I didn't check them out because my main interest was watching the stylist battle. A fashion stylist who had collaborated with a well-known Serbian designer, who highly inspired me, participated in this program, and I wanted to meet her. However, my friend insisted on leaving earlier than the battle ended, and I will never forgive myself for letting his bitterness bring my mood down and for being dragged out of the event. Nonetheless, I did contact the stylist later via email, expressing my request to become her assistant.

June 2011

Wednesday, 1st June

The weather was exceptionally pleasant, warm, and sunny. We found ourselves spending a lot of time outdoors on the roof. My flatmate took the initiative to hand-build a sitting area outside using wooden pallets, which he painted blue. Across the street, there was a peculiar incident unfolding. A crazy man atop the building opposite ours seemed determined to throw a carton of milk over to our terrace, across the road, as if testing his throwing skills. It was an impossible idea, especially if he was drunk as he seemingly was. Predictably, the carton landed with a resounding splash on the road below, startling a passing cabbie driver who responded with a rather expressive gesture, extending his arm out of the window to display his displeasure to the crazy man above.

Friday, 3rd June

Our money was stolen. Here's the situation: we have to pay our rent in cash and leave the total amount downstairs in the restaurant with the person at the welcome desk. Although we rent the rooms separately, we're required to pay the full amount for the flat at once. So, we place our share in an envelope, usually handled by me (the most reliable tenant), and take it down to the restaurant at the beginning of each month. This time, however, there was a new person at the welcome desk. I called my landlord first to confirm if it was okay to leave the cash with the new guy, and he gave the green light. I handed over the money and received a signed confirmation note stating that he had received £1350 from Flat 1. An hour later, the landlord called me with distress in his voice, informing me that the new person had absconded with the money. He came over to our flat to discuss the situation further, asking the same questions he had already asked over the phone. I listened sympathetically, but I also noted it was not my mess to clean up.

Later, the police reached out to me. The investigator was understanding and professional. I provided her with details, including the note with the person's signature, which I had photographed before handing it over, just in case. The landlord tried to persuade me to become a witness in case the culprit was caught and the case went to court, but I was hesitant to get involved. I mean, would I even recognise the guy if I bumped into him at the grocery store? Probably not! The police officer explained that I had a choice and I was not obligated to provide my personal details or testify in court if I preferred not to. She left her contact information with me, in case I changed my mind, but I never did.

Saturday, 11th June

I decided to take advantage of a free iMovie tutorial at the Apple centre in Covent Garden. After the session, while strolling towards the bus stop, I caught a glimpse of a tall, heavy man out of the corner of my eye. He sidled up next to me at the traffic lights, appearing somewhat sweaty and out of breath under his khaki trench coat. Sensing his presence, I instinctively took a step back, trying to distance myself. Suddenly, he started chatting me up, claiming he'd spotted me from a nearby coffee house and that I was the most beautiful girl he'd seen in London. He went on about how he couldn't let me pass by without asking me out or getting my number. The whole thing seemed utterly absurd to me. I mean, him running after me? Really? His gasping and homeless appearance only added to my skepticism. I muttered something about having a boyfriend, hoping he'd take the hint and leave me alone. But he persisted, trying to coax me into joining him for a cup of tea or coffee. I politely declined each time. As soon as the light turned green, I practically sprinted across the road and hopped onto the first bus that pulled up at the stop. From the safety of the bus, I kept glancing back with apprehension to see if he was following me or not, until I realised it was not about the stranger anymore, but rather my paranoia getting the best of me. Perhaps he was genuine, and to him, I was the freak acting strangely.

Sunday, 12th June

I embarked on a leisurely stroll through Brick Lane and Spitalfields Market, immersing myself in the lively crowds. The atmosphere here differed greatly from the bustling chaos of Oxford Street, in the best possible way. I explored the unique handmade designs and vintage treasures, satisfying my craving for artistic inspiration. Along the way, I picked up some bananas and avocados from the fruit stand and took advantage of a 2-for-1 deal on a bouquet of sunflowers at the flower market. Sunflowers have become my recent favourite among all the beautiful blooms and greenery at Columbia Road on Sundays. Simply gazing at them fills me with joy. Apparently, sunflowers were often associated with success in life and love, symbolising positivity and strength. In Chinese culture, they are believed to bring good luck and lasting happiness. Amen to that!

Thursday, 16th June

As I waited at the bus stop in Oxford Circus, a shocking scene unfolded in front of my eyes. A cyclist swiftly snatched a woman's wallet from her grasp as he zoomed past on the road. In the blink of an eye, he vanished into the traffic, leaving the woman frozen in shock at the bus stop.

Friday, 24th June

Upon returning home around 2 a.m. after a gig, I stumbled upon my flatmate sauntering on the roof in the darkness. Curious, I asked him what he was up to out there, but he just brushed past me saying "Went for a walk." *At this time on the roof?* Without further explanation, he retreated to his room, and we didn't discuss it further. I knew he had smoked a joint. Weed was his daily vitamin, and beer was his energy drink. He even relied on natural pills to combat his faltering memory. I'd witnessed his girlfriend's frustration countless times when he forgot their plans, like that one evening when he vanished shortly after promising to wait for her arrival from work to take her for dinner. She showed up at 6 p.m. to find he had already left, leaving her disappointed and annoyed.

Anyways, I try to refrain from passing judgment on my flatmate. I even felt a pang of sympathy when he ended up with a black eye after an altercation with a dealer. For the next three days, he remained holed up in his room, nursing his injury with a sullen demeanor. Wanting to lift his spirits, I bought him a get-well cookie. Despite his flaws, he's not a bad guy. In fact, he's quite amiable, and his circle of friends reflects that. They're a convivial bunch, all musicians and creative souls from diverse corners of the globe. I love the vibrant atmosphere they bring with them, whether they're lounging on our terrace, engaging in deep conversation about life, or strumming their guitars. Their presence infuses our home with positive vibes, reminding me of the unifying power of music.

Saturday, 25th June

"Bon Jovi!" I shouted, my voice lost in the lively atmosphere of Hyde Park as Flora and I danced on the grass outside the Bon Jovi concert.

We didn't have tickets, but the music was so loud that we could still enjoy the show from beyond the stage area. We both adored Bon Jovi! Unfortunately, we arrived towards the end of the concert, because we had been at an acoustic gig in Stoke Newington, enjoying Flora's latest crush—a guitarist from a local band. Despite missing most of the show, we were thrilled to be in the park, and we celebrated by singing and dancing along to the iconic tunes. It was the perfect end to a fantastic day.

July 2011

Saturday, 2nd July

As I strolled up to Dalston, I eagerly anticipated seeing the Richie Culver exhibition at a unique concept store that combined clothing, music, and books. The store boasted a curated selection of big-name designers like Issey Miyake, Preen, Yohji Yamamoto, Damir Doma, and Jil Sander, to name just a few. Stepping inside, I was greeted by a rush of excitement and a tingling sensation—a blend of admiration and awe washed over me. The interior was a masterpiece of natural decorations, with a wooden tunnel adding to its charm. The ambiance was serene and earthy, amplified by the soothing background music that filled the space. The staff exuded genuine kindness and warmth, no fake smiles. Their approach to customer service was refreshingly human. I could see myself living here.

After taking in the exhibition, I explored the fashion offerings. I couldn't wait to see the Rick Owens pieces. I had never held a Rick Owens design in my hands, so when I found them on the rail, I ran my fingers along the fabric to feel the details. I had always admired Rick Owens' designs from afar, so feeling the fabric against my fingertips was a thrill. My eyes lit up when I spotted a pair of platform wedge tall sandals that I had previously drooled over in runway photos. I wanted to try them on but they didn't have them in my size, so I just slipped my hand inside and took a sniff from the leather. I was surprised by how light the sandals felt, almost as if they were made from cardboard.

As I made my way back home along the sun-drenched street, I encountered a delightful scene—a little girl ahead of me, gleefully blowing bubbles while trying to keep pace with her mum. The wind carried the bubbles in my direction, and soon I was surrounded by a cascade of shimmering orbs. I shared a smile with the little girl, who attempted to blow even more bubbles in my direction before they came to a halt at the bus stop. With a warm feeling in my heart, I continued on my way, buoyed by the simple joy of the moment.

Thursday, 7th July

On the vibrant first Thursday of the month, over 150 museums and galleries in east London throw open their doors until 9 p.m., treating visitors to late viewings and free events. With this in mind, my flatmates and I ventured down to Redchurch Street, eager to immerse ourselves in the art scene. The surrounding streets buzzed with the energy of youth, hipsters, and artists, each clutching drinks and snacks, generously provided by many of the galleries.

There was one place we couldn't get in because our names were not on the list but my resourceful flatmate struck up a conversation with the door lady, and soon enough, we found ourselves granted entry! As we sipped our complimentary drinks inside the gallery, we were transported back in time through the evocative portrait and fashion photos of the legendary British photographer, Brian Duffy.

Later, our journey continued to Strongroom bar on Curtain Road. I indulged in a juicy burger, relishing each bite while the guys finished their beers and then I just smoked with satisfaction outside the garden listening to the hubbub of the crowd. After an hour of soaking in the atmosphere, we embarked on our next adventure, stepping into Paper Dress Vintage Bar. Here, we were treated to the spectacle of a band's gig in the display window; an intimate performance with a handsome crowd. It was one of those places where you had to check out the toilet. The tiny bathroom walls were covered in eclectic posters and graffiti.

Saturday, 9th July

Flora and I had breakfast at Hackney City Farm, then headed to my place to get ready for the shoot we were having with a new face model from Models 1 agency. It was a last-minute arrangement, so I hadn't had time to prepare the styling, but Flora brought along some of her accessories that complemented the clothes I had lined up perfectly. Despite the spontaneous nature of the shoot, we had a blast, just us girls. We captured some shots on the roof and ventured down to the farm, snapping photos against various rustic backdrops.

Our model's striking beauty and height attracted attention from visitors at the farm, but their curiosity was not intrusive. Two weeks later, when Flora submitted the images to the agent, she received a personal call from the agent expressing delight with the photos. Flora was thrilled by the gesture, believing it to be a significant acknowledgment. If true, it signified that we were heading in the right direction toward exciting opportunities that could potentially connect us with influential figures in the industry.

Thursday, 14th July

My flatmate playfully complained that I tend to laugh too loudly at night when chatting with my friends on Skype. In response, I couldn't help but wonder, isn't my laughter a lullaby?

Monday, 18th July

The summer is scorching hot. Once a week, I make a pilgrimage to the outdoor pool at London Fields Lido for a refreshing swim. I prefer to go early on weekday mornings to avoid the crowds and enjoy the tranquility of having the pool to myself. As a means of cooling down during the sweltering nights, I have developed a habit of sleeping naked, often with wet hair. However, I refrain from opening the window in my room while asleep, fearing that someone might climb in from the terrace. My caution isn't unfounded; recently, one of these roof-climbing pickpockets has stolen my flatmate's laptop, bag, and wallet. They sneaked in through an open window and made off with whatever they could grab. To protect my belongings, I keep my room door and window locked whenever I am away, ensuring that my laptop and other valuables are safely out of sight.

Friday, 29th July

For the past year, I've been enduring the discomfort of a broken tooth, tucked away in the back of my mouth where it's thankfully not visible. It's not the most pleasant situation, I know. Affording an implant to fix it has been out of reach for me financially, so I've resorted to a makeshift solution: I simply avoid chewing on the right side of my mouth. It's not ideal, but it's been my personal dental care routine. However, a stroke of luck recently changed the game. I discovered that I'm entitled to free dental treatment thanks to the state benefits I receive. Eager to remedy my dental dilemma, I set out to find a suitable clinic in my area. To my delight, I stumbled upon a charming little dental practice nestled in Shoreditch.

At the practice, I was greeted by the most caring and professional lady dentist, who seemed genuinely invested in my dental well-being to such an extent that I felt unworthy of her attention. She took the time to explain everything about proper tooth care, from mastering the art of toothbrushing and flossing to recommending the best toothpaste. She also explained her plan about how she was going to save my broken tooth. I had a feeling that she might have perceived me as very young, or perhaps from a troubled home, or both. I listened intently, nodding along with gratitude for her guidance. After two weeks, my new tooth was ready—a gleaming, well-fitted, white crown. It was a moment of triumph, akin to securing my very own crown in the United Kingdom.

August 2011

The speed of London life

I find myself grappling with doubt once again, questioning the choices I've made. Am I truly on the right path? And if so, why do I find myself constantly questioning it? Leaving behind the security of a traditional job for the unpredictable world of the fashion industry, even if it means working for free, isn't what I regret. However, the financial insecurity and feeling of being stuck weigh heavily on me. In an attempt to reassure myself, I've created a list of pros and cons to evaluate my situation.

Pros:

I have the freedom to invest ample time in building my portfolio, indulging in reading and self-education, attending events, and expanding my network. I can enjoy leisure activities like swimming and do my weekly shopping without the rush of crowded before- and after-work hours.

Cons:

Financial constraints limit my ability to properly nourish myself, often leaving me with the tough choice between basic necessities and investing in my design work. Living on benefits brings with it both financial and emotional insecurities, leading to a barrage of unnecessary thoughts and questions. Moreover, the abundance of free time has brought about a certain loneliness, which my handsome neighbour, now a fellow freelancer working from home, amusingly refers to as boredom. On my most vulnerable days, I remind myself of the words of Katy Eary: "If you are going to be an independent designer, you have to accept that you may not make money for a number of years, but you should still find joy in what you are doing."

So, I'm still without a paid job, but I'm grateful for the benefits that keep me going. Yet, what do I do when I grow weary of reaching out to potential employers, lack the funds to further develop my designs, and feel so alone that it prevents me from doing any creative activities that I normally enjoy?

I decided to venture into the city centre to immerse myself in the presence of others. I browsed through the sales and perused the new seasonal collections along Oxford Street. However, instead of alleviating my loneliness, the bustling crowds only seemed to magnify it. I felt small and vulnerable amidst the hustle and bustle, especially surrounded by the frantic, impatient shoppers inside the stores. They rushed through the aisles like hurricanes, discarding unwanted items onto the floor, where they were trampled and damaged until the shop assistants could retrieve them. It was so barbaric.

Back when I lived in Hungary, I rarely felt the need to visit the city without a specific purpose. But here in London, I find myself restless, always yearning to be amidst the action. I wanna go, I wanna see, I wanna be there. I don't know where this urge comes from. I fear I'm afflicted by FOMO, a developing form of social anxiety on the cusp of the dominant social media influence. The pace of life in this city is unfathomable to those who haven't experienced it firsthand, and I'm surprised by how quickly I've adapted to it—or perhaps, I should say, become accustomed to it. Yet, amidst the crowd on Oxford Street, I can't shake off a sense of tension and emptiness. Maybe it's the vibration I pick up on, or maybe I'm an empath. *Could I be?*

An empath is a person who is highly sensitive to the world around them and is able to receive information on an energetic and emotional level. They are able to easily pick up on the energies around them, especially when it comes to others' emotions.

In the end, I simply purchased a large sketchbook to compile the fashion contacts of stylists, designers, showrooms, management agencies, creative studios, magazines, etc., that I had gathered so far. It dawns on me just how many phone calls I've made and how many letters I've written, with no significant outcomes. They say London is the land of opportunity, but what happens when this land becomes overcrowded? There's a long line of people waiting outside this metaphorical house of opportunity. Some are patient, moving slowly, hoping their turn will come. Others are pushy, stepping over their peers. Some search for the back door, while others somehow manage to bypass the line altogether. And then there are those who have waited so long that they've forgotten why they came in the first place. While it's true that London offers more and better opportunities than many other EU capitals, the competition is fierce. You need good contacts, or better yet, that ONE contact that can catapult you to the front of the line.

Thursday, 11th August

The stylist I had contacted in May, following the stylist battle at the V&A, agreed to meet me for a chat over coffee near Holborn station. I felt that I had made a positive impression on her, and soon after our meeting, she reached out to me to assist her on an editorial for F. magazine.

We styled James Phelps from the Harry Potter movies, but since I hadn't watched the film series, I didn't recognise him. Nonetheless, I carried out my job on the shoot as usual.

There's a distinction between styling models and styling actors. Models essentially serve as clothing mannequins, wearing whatever is chosen for them without much say in the matter. Their role is to showcase the garments, enhancing the product's details and appeal. Actors, on the other hand, portray themselves, and their outfits must complement their personal image. Phelps, being an actor, was selective and declined many of the outfits presented to him. While this narrowed down our options, it also posed a challenge for the stylist, who had to adjust her ideas accordingly. Nonetheless, she was patient and respected the actor's choices, allowing him to select the coat, shirt, and trousers for the portrait photos accompanying the magazine interview.

The next day, I handled a couple of returns, and the stylist bombarded me with emails regarding a Burberry coat she had forgotten to give me and now urgently wanted returned. Unfortunately, I didn't check my emails until I returned home after completing the round of deliveries I had been entrusted with, nearly at the end of office hours. Since I didn't yet own a smartphone, I had informed the stylist about this limitation, expecting urgent matters to be communicated via phone call or sms. Despite this, she chose to use emails for the urgent request. Feeling uncertain, I braced myself for another day of bus fare in case she sent me back into town with the coat the following day. Early in the evening, I made the journey to her house in Stoke

Newington to collect the coat, the reimbursement for my travel expenses, as previously agreed, and to discuss the dates for her next projects.

Upon arrival, I knocked on the door, and when she answered, she mistook me for Annika, the other assistant on the shoot. She stood in the doorway as if she didn't recognise me, and I tentatively asked, "Do you want to discuss the dates for the next shoots?" Just as I opened my calendar, she interjected, "You're not going to do them." Despite her evident frustration, I still held onto hope for fairness regarding the travel reimbursement. As I reached into my wallet to retrieve the receipts, she abruptly shut the door in my face. I knocked again, but she didn't respond.

As I walked away, feeling baffled, I spotted Annika approaching from the bus stop, looking breathless and exhausted. She told me that she was fed up with the day. It was the second time she had to make this journey—first for the Burberry coat and now to collect her travel money. She had been running errands in town since morning too. I sympathised with her situation and asked how she managed to return the coat on time. "I had to run. I hate her!" she exclaimed with frustration. I told her that the stylist didn't give me the reimbursement she'd promised. Annika expressed shock and added, "The b$!ch better pay me!" We exchanged a hug and parted ways.

Around 8 p.m., I arrived home exhausted. I headed straight to the shower, to scrape off the confusion lingering from my encounter at the stylist's place. The sweet scent of my rose-pink soap helped soothe my frayed nerves, and later as I sipped chamomile tea in my sun-yellow room, I felt a sense of calm wash over me. I knew I was going to be fine. I was bonetired and I snoozed halfway through my tea without intention. As soon as my head hit the pillow, the Elvis night began in the tandoori restaurant, but I was just too knackered to care to be annoyed by the beat and the loud singing.

And then, at 11 p.m., Sargon called me. I answered the phone, my voice groggy with sleep, that I regretted after hearing why he was calling. He told me that he wanted to hook up with a woman but had a quirk: an aversion to feather-filled bedding. He couldn't spend the night due to his peculiar allergy, yet the woman, adorned in plumes and downs, refused to take him seriously. He said that he preferred just having sex with her on the sofa and going home afterward, and he needed a solution from me.

"Where are you now?" I inquired.

"Just grabbing some wine at the off-license." he responded.

"Heading back to her place then?"

"Well, I have to."

"You don't have to."

"She would be disappointed."

"Or because you want to have sex. This is ridiculous, you know."

"I feel bad."

"For yourself? Or for her?"

"I just feel guilty about the whole situation. She doesn't believe my allergy."

Why do I have to be part of this conversation? I couldn't care less about someone else's sex life. I just want to drift back into sleep.

"Well... if you want to have sex with her, you'd have to make her very drunk so that she wouldn't notice when you sneak out in the middle of the night," I suggested, half-jokingly.

"Not helping," he grumbled.

"I am not you, Sargon. I'm not sure what the right move is here. Sorry."

In the end, Sargon went home without sex and the woman slept alone in her bed.

Friday, 12th August

Sometimes, I feel, talent is the thing you need least in fashion. You need attitude! A lot of it.

Sunday, 14th August

My room became a battleground against an invading army of newly hatched brown ants (or perhaps termites?). They marched relentlessly from one corner of the wooden floor to the shelf unit. *Oh, why? Why is it happening to me?* In a frenzy, I wiped them out with a vinegar mix, only to find them resurfacing the next day. So I wiped them off again. And again. And it went on for six days in a row. I couldn't help but wonder: were they here last summer too? If so, how did I miss them?"

Monday, 22nd August

Last week, Lee texted me and asked if I was available to assist him on his next collaboration for SM magazine. It had been a long time since I had seen him, and I was excited to work with him again.

The shoot was held in a spacious studio at Waterloo. Our model hailed from Minnesota, staying in the city for four days before returning to the States. He stood out from all the models I'd encountered before. Naturally kind, polite, and down-to-earth, he exuded a sense of maturity despite his young age of only 20. His warmth and healthy confidence were palpable, making him a pleasure to work with. This was the first time I had felt embarrassed in front of a model. When the time came to assist him in changing between looks, I felt anxious and overwhelmed with emotions, freezing momentarily before regaining control and proceeding with the task. When I saw him in underpants I just lost it. I had to avert my gaze and reach out without looking at him, just to retrieve the McQueen leather pants he had been wearing. As I helped him with the buttons of his shirt cuffs, a spark of heat shot through me at the touch of his hand and the proximity of his body to mine. I couldn't help but visualise how nice it would be to hold hands and be in his arms. I felt totally embarrassed, smiling excessively around him and blushing like a fourteen-year-old. I was too scared to look up and catch his glance because I knew he was smiling too. Even Lee could sense that something was off with me. I had to look away many times just to cool myself down, breathe, and pretend to be a professional. It was bad. Really bad. I was eight years older than him and I really liked him. You know, when you meet somebody and you instantly know you've encountered someone special, and you want to learn everything about them. I even hunted him down on Facebook.

As for fashion, we worked with esteemed brands like YSL, Burberry, Dolce & Gabbana, Christopher Kane, just to name a few. Today, our studio overflowed with samples, resembling a miniature Selfridges. Gorgeous coats, shirts, hats, smart suits, and stunning shoes lined up, satisfying my hunger for beauty and quality alongside the model. The atmosphere among the team was delightful; from the set designer to the photographer, everyone was a joy to work with. We gathered around the coffee table for lunch, sharing food, stories, and laughter like a close-knit family. Even Lee appeared happier and more open. There was a palpable sense of positivity in the air, perhaps fuelled by the good weather. This summer has been exceptionally warm, blessing us with plenty of long, sunny days.

At the end of the shoot, our model was excited to grab a beer from the fridge, a drink he wouldn't legally be allowed to have in the U.S. yet. With enviable joy and enthusiasm, he dashed out the doors, eager to experience as much of London as possible during his short stay. I offered him tips on my favourite off-the-wall places, including some tourist spots he might enjoy, secretly hoping he would invite me along, but he didn't. *Wake up, Zsofi. This is London, not a fairy tale.*

Tuesday, 23rd August

As I made my way to Liverpool Street Station, I spotted John sitting at his usual spot on the pavement of Shoreditch High Street, sketching away. John, the homeless man, and his staffie, George, were familiar figures to everyone in the area. I dropped some coins from my purse into the cup in front of the dog. Then, on a whim, I asked John if he knew how many pictures he had ever drawn of George. He glanced up at me briefly, then returned his focus to his sketchpad, mumbling a response that I couldn't quite decipher. I wasn't even sure he responded to my question. It seemed like one of his many musings rather than a direct answer to my question.

The end of summer

It's been six months since I started smoking regularly, and I'm thoroughly enjoying it! I've developed a ritual of sorts where I wake up just before 6 a.m., go for a jog, then return to the flat. There, I have a cup of hot coffee and a cigarette on the roof before anyone else is awake. I cherish these solitary mornings before the city stirs awake;

it's a truly magical feeling. Watching the sun's first rays hit the roof and then basking in its glow throughout the day in my room is the best part.

Afterwards, I usually take a quick shower and retreat to my room. Sometimes, I do stretching exercises on the floor, or simply drift back to sleep, only to wake up again an hour later to the unintended noises—footsteps, door slams, key rattles—as my flatmates and neighbours head off to work. My room faces the terrace and is adjacent to the main entrance of our small block, so I hear everyone come and go.

I've been seeing my handsome neighbour more often over the summer, largely due to my initiative. He's clearly interested in me, but he hasn't made a move yet. My flatmate thinks he's shy, while Flora believes he's the type who doesn't know how to approach girls because he's always had them approach him due to his good looks. As for me, I wonder if perhaps he just doesn't have much going on in his mind. It could be that simple.

"Are you falling for '*A cock*?" asked Meian, Flora's flatmate, a neck-to-toe tattooed girl who was as open about her sexuality as Samantha in Sex and the City. Funnily, Acock was the family name of my handsome neighbour which stirred a joke between us girls.

"He's not *a cock*!" I protected him.

"His name is a great indication that he is..."

"He's my neighbour and he is not *a cock*. It's just his name."

"Is he the one in the top flat?"

"No, he lives on the second floor. A German girl rents the top flat."

"Are you saying that the cock is in a sandwich?"

Lol. Meian's dirty fantasy opens new, unwanted perspectives in front of me.

My handsome neighbour's living room is directly above my bedroom, and the sound of his footsteps on the creaky floor brings me a sense of comfort, knowing he's home. When I hear him leave the flat—the door slamming and locking—I hurry out of my room just to greet him on the terrace, though I pretend it's because I want to smoke. *I want him to take me in his arms and crush me with passion.* Even when he returns late at night from his part-time job at the pub, I find myself naturally waking up 5-10 minutes before he opens the door. I'm unsure of the origin of this connection, or if he feels it too, but it's palpable, and I can't ignore it.

Eventually, after one of our rooftop parties, he became drunk enough to sit beside me on the bench outside, attempting to hold my hand under the throw we used to keep warm. He bluntly asked, "When are you gonna kiss me?" In that moment, it was as if my rose-tinted glasses were stepped on. I reprimanded him sharply, "You're the man, act like one!" He tentatively moved closer and performed a lifeless kiss in my mouth which, instead of being the highlight of the night, turned out to be a profound disappointment. When he suggested I see his bedroom, I found myself unable to say yes. *If the kiss was this underwhelming, what could I expect from sex?* I gave him a hug, conceding that he did smell good, and went to my own bed to sleep.

Later, I mentioned that I'd like to grab coffee sometime and get to know him better before taking things further, hoping to salvage my feelings. However, he seemed to interpret my message differently, as he didn't ask me out again. Instead, he brought up a much younger girl from the pub the next day and effectively distanced himself from me. In fact, he and his flatmate moved out in September, leaving me with a broken heart.

Debenhams, Oxford Street

"Can I help?" A middle-aged shop assistant stepped next to me as I wandered the women's floor.

"I am not sure," I said hesitantly and released a sigh.

"What are you looking for?"

"Love," I quipped, my tone a mix of jest and sincerity.

"Well, you might have better luck finding it on the men's floor," she suggested, her gaze confident over the rim of her glasses.

"I just came from there," I responded cryptically.

"Ah, I see. In that case, this is for you, my dear!" With a flourish, she pulled out a Lindt bar from her pocket, offering it to me. "And be sure to check out our new arrivals for the next season," she added with a wink.

"Thank you," I said, accepting the chocolate.

September 2011

Sunday, 4th September

In the afternoon, I Skype-chatted for hours with one of my childhood friends in Hungary. It began in my stifling room, but the stagnant air urged me outside to the roof, where we embarked on an online gaming adventure. Meanwhile, my flatmate went out to take care of his energy supplies a.k.a beers, and locked me out. Accidentally or on purpose? I was glad he remembered to lock the door but not glad because I didn't have my keys with me on the terrace. As dusk settled and a chill crept in, I resorted to tossing small stones at my handsome neighbour's window to get his attention and ask him to call my flatmate because I couldn't get inside. Little did I know, this was to be my final encounter with him before they moved out. Eventually, another flatmate rescued me, granting access with his spare key. I scurried to put my laptop on a charger while I was still talking to my friend online. It was a warm, quiet night, and I slowly fell asleep while my friend read a chapter from his new favourite book, "The Art of Loving" by Erich Fromm.

Friday, 9th September

I had no clue how they got hold of my contact, but I received an invitation to the launch of Passenger at Home House. The invitation detailed the premise of Passenger: to cultivate a creative hub showcasing musicians, artists, fashion designers, and filmmakers, promising a rocking party filled with the beautiful, the bold, and the brilliant. There was a British fashion showcase, a music video showcase, a live DJ, and a girl in the bathroom gushing about a lipstick she bought just because Kate Moss advertised it. Flora accompanied me as my plus one. We sipped on some champagne and watched the music videos first. The screening was loud, and the visual content really grabbed my attention. My favourite was "The Greeks" by Is Tropical. I instantly became a fan of the band and downloaded their music as soon as I got home later that night.

Sunday, 18th September

Lee passed my number to his stylist friend, Anthony, who required an assistant for his upcoming shoot—an editorial for Nylon magazine. That's where I found myself today. We convened at Anthony's place in the morning, and after a hearty breakfast, we headed down to the Tower of London area to shoot in public spaces.

We outfitted the models, two cheeky 19-year-old lads, in a mix of brands like Adidas, Nike, Ralph Lauren, Christopher Kane, Alexander McQueen, Yohji Yamamoto, Katie Eary, and more. Our impromptu locations were chosen on a whim, with the models using the streets as their playground.

I trailed behind with a wheeled suitcase carrying our wardrobe, while Anthony made occasional adjustments to the boys' looks. Surprisingly, the models had no qualms about stripping down in public. The photographer captured the scenes using a traditional, now vintage, film camera—a nostalgic throwback to my cherished Smena camera I received on my seventh birthday. Experiencing professional work done on roll film was like a breath of fresh air. The finished product had a unique quality that stood out from the digital masses, and I absolutely loved it.

Thursday, 22nd September

Fashion week is in full swing, and you can practically taste the excitement in the air. The city has taken on a whole new vibe. This year, I scored an invitation to the Inbar Spector show, where I had the privilege of watching the collection from the front row, next to the photographers who were nestled at the end of the catwalk.

Also, on the last men's day, I assisted Lee backstage at the MM show where, surrounded by male models and male everything (an all-male crew)—designers, stylists, hair and makeup artists, event coordinators, security, and more—I dove headfirst into the chaos.

Upon my arrival, I spotted the boys lounging on the carpeted floor, some in makeup chairs, while one stood tall against the wall, engrossed in a book. Backstage buzzed with a mix of excitement and nervous energy, filled with music, laughter, and the frenetic pace of hard work.

As the show drew to a close, I witnessed the designer's apprehension about stepping out onto the stage. His assistant, with a quick adjustment of his hair and collar, shared a joke to ease his nerves before nudging him out. Backstage erupted in applause upon his return, signalling the end of another successful show.

On a personal note, I received my very first [2]family bracelet—a wristband for backstage workers, which I grew fond of. It felt like being part of a family working with Lee and MM again. I decided to keep the wristband on my hand for years to come, a cherished memento of these unforgettable memories.

---

[2] Family is the name of the event management company that is printed on the wristband

Do you want to hear the joke that the assistant said to the designer?

Q: Why do fashion designers never have any good ideas?

A: They're too clothes-minded.

October 2011

You know what they say about love—If you lose a loved one, someone new is coming into your life to replace it. After my handsome neighbour moved out, in sauntered Bluebelle and Lily. Not the flowers, but two little children named Bluebelle and Lily. As far as I know, the flower is correctly spelled Bluebell without the 'e' at the end. Bluebelle's mum once told me about how many people write her daughter's name incorrectly, forgetting that crucial 'e' at the end. So, if you ever meet a Bluebelle, mind that 'e' at the end.

I find the name Bluebelle rather charming! She can be called Blue and Belle for short. However, I often find myself using Blues and Bluesy when I look after her. She grows especially close to me and I have a feeling she chose me to be her nanny. The first time I picked her up from kindergarten, just a week after meeting her and her lovely mum in Hackney, I braced myself for tears and tantrums, thinking she wouldn't recognise me, but as soon as she spotted me, she threw her arms up, ready to be cuddled and taken home. We instantly bonded, and even her mum and the neighbours noticed our special bond. Bluebelle showers me with endless cuddles and cuteness, while the five-year-old Lily is a whirlwind of entertainment, singing and dancing around us when we get home after school. I simply adore spending afternoons looking after them. They bring bundles of joy and laughter to my daily grind.

I'm positively chuffed and inspired not just by the kids but also by their folks' way of life; full of fun, creativity, and love. For instance, they've got a flour pot labelled 'cocaine' and a sugar pot dubbed 'fairy dust' in the kitchen cupboard among the usual cooking essentials. I'm quite taken with the massive wooden table in the dining area, all rustic and earthy, along with the other wooden bits and bobs around the house. With its blemishes and quirks, this place feels like home. I love spotting Lily's giant art book and drawing pens strewn about, and she gets a kick out of my drawing challenges, which I often dish out to keep her busy while I fix up some tea. I've been to many English houses that didn't quite feel like homes, but this one? It's just right.

Writer's note

Many years later when I noticed that my general health worsened I turned to alternative medicine and tried homeopathy. The practitioner, who provided me a list of dos and don'ts relating to food and nutrition, immediately strapped me to the IV to transfuse a dose of minerals and vitamins into my vein that my system was apparently running critically low on. I heard of many expats whose immune systems weakened after living in the UK for a great number of years due to the limited sunlight and humidity. According to an article in the Guardian "The British weather prevents much of the population from receiving healthy amounts of the essential vitamin from sunlight, and natural food sources alone are not enough to boost levels." And I was convinced that the tons of imported veggies and fruits lacked just as many vitamins as flavours. Apart from the IV and the nutrition advice, I got a small tube of homeopathic remedy called *Campanula Rotundifolia*. I knew that homeopathy often utilised plants, so I looked up the common name for Campanula Rotundifolia. To my delightful surprise, I discovered that the remedy I was being treated with was actually called bluebell: Campanula rotundifolia, also known as the harebell, Scottish bluebell, or bluebell of Scotland, is a flowering plant species within the Campanulaceae family.

Thursday, 6th October

A blind man stopped me in the street and asked if I could see whether his guide dog had done a poo by the curb or not. Carefully, he showed me the area where he thought the dog might have left his mark. I assured him that there was no poop there or in close proximity. He was worried that if he didn't pick up after his dog, he could be fined. So, I checked the area a few steps further away as well, just to reassure him that it was safe to walk along. He couldn't have been more British, the good man. Do you think the police would really fine a blind man for not picking up after his dog? Maybe he should live in Paris for a change to loosen up about the poop rules. The French, on the other hand, could learn from his sense of responsibility.

Did you know?

There are people in French cities who think that because they pay taxes, the street cleaners should clean up after their dogs. A 2015 survey based on the amount of poop bags sold across the world by the company Beco Pets saw France come bottom: 3,600 bags, to the UK's 1.85m.

Sunday, 09th October

Lee and I shot for Zink magazine at the Playboy Club. The interior was stunning, with red lighting, a spacious lounge, and, of course, bunny decorations everywhere (even cute little bunny candies!). This is one of those places where I just had to see the bathroom! So, in the middle of the shoot, I excused myself and marched toward the back. And let me tell you, it didn't disappoint! If you ever visit the club, you definitely have to check out the bathroom.

The shoot was an absolute blast with just the four of us: Lee, the photographer, the model, and me. The photographer rolled in with this massive bag of props: toy guns, balloons, bubble blowers, animal masks, funky plastic sunglasses, western hats—you name it, he had it. Lee, on the other hand, was a minimalist, bringing just one suitcase of fashion that we jazzed up with the props. And our model? Well, he showed up with the most infectious smile you've ever seen, the kind that could brighten even the gloomiest day. He was a total joy to work with. As for me, I was buzzing with excitement, as always. I had never been to the Playboy Club, and I admit, it wasn't on my bucket list, but I was down for the adventure. We spent the day goofing off with the props, laughing freely like we were children again. It was work, sure, but it felt more like playtime.

Sunday, 16th October

Amidst juggling this and that, but rather flitting about aimlessly, I decided to buckle down and focus on the tasks at hand. I dove headfirst into a two-week whirlwind of prep for my upcoming weekend park shoot. Booking models through a model agency, scouting locations, creating mood boards, and embarking on a shopping spree that involved a fair bit of swapping and returning consumed most of my days during the week.

In the past, I relied on my own wardrobe and contributions from Flora to bring our ideas to life, resulting in a visually stunning portfolio. Flora was a talented photographer, and I often collaborated on post-production, adding a creative flair that elevated our images to an artistic level. This time, however, I was determined to focus solely on fashion and styling.

I scoured TK Maxx for current collections and made a pilgrimage to Oxford Street in search of inspiration. By the end of my shopping spree, I had parted ways with £300 across four different stores, leaving me with high blood pressure, but I kept reassuring myself that everything was returnable. After a year of living on benefits, £300 suddenly felt like a hefty sum.

We rendezvoused with our model at Clapham Park and ventured into a secluded clearing shielded by towering trees to avoid unwanted attention from passersby. It was a sunny Sunday, drawing crowds to the parks, but we preferred our privacy for the shoot. We spread a blanket on the ground beside a sturdy tree, draping clothes over the branches and fashioning a makeshift changing area with a white sheet. Flora wielded her DSLR while I captured shots with my Smena film camera. We had a long but lovely day. I set up a mini buffet on our blanket with some take-out food and snacks that we nibbled on between the looks. Instead of a Sunday roast, we had a Sunday picnic.

Thursday, 20th October

The wall next to the bath in the bathroom had swollen up and started peeling off, appearing quite odd and raising concerns among my flatmates and me. We promptly contacted our landlord, who in turn summoned "his people" to fix the issue. They scraped off the scaling and repainted the wall. We were informed that the problem stemmed from drainage issues and water pressure within the building, which also explained the occasional toilet flushing problems and slow-running shower water. Interestingly, a staff member from the restaurant below informed me that excessive toilet flushing from our flats (including the other two flats above us) could lead to blockages in the bedsit toilet beneath the restaurant. "Is there another flat under the restaurant?" I asked with wide-opened eyes. "Yes, there are actually three rooms downstairs," the guy confirmed. The revelation left me astounded. I thought I lived in a shitty place but he topped me.

I can't fathom what those residents must endure—cold, damp conditions, possibly with no windows. Despite our own challenges with temporary sewage odors and mice invasions from living above the restaurant, their situation seems dire in comparison.

November 2011

Meian, who works at a tattoo studio, needed a temporary replacement for the receptionist for one day, and I volunteered. For two months, I found myself in Camden Town every Wednesday, braving the early morning chill until the souvenir shop opened under the studio. Once inside, I swiftly located the hidden staircase, ascended to the studio, unlocked the gate, and climbed even more stairs—there were so many! I admired the customers who made it up without gasping for air. Then, before the studio officially opened, I mopped the floor and sanitised the needles. Once open, I spent the day behind the reception desk, nestled next to the ceramic heater amidst the tattoo artists' portfolios and colourful artwork on the walls.

During the two months, I met a lot of tattooed people from around the world who turned up in the shop, and I picked up a few insights about tattoos along the way. I thoroughly enjoyed the experience and even entertained the idea of becoming a tattoo artist myself. After all, I was a talented drawer, meticulous, and enjoyed meeting new people. However, I ultimately never pursued it further after learning that many artists practice on their own skin or on pig's skin before working on others.

By the way, we had some interesting new neighbours. A Greek guy and his blue-haired friend, a girl who enjoyed going topless, much to the delight of my male flatmates and their group of friends who frequently hung out on our roof. But then soon after they moved in, the girl disappeared, and we were introduced to a tall guy who replaced her.

They started to secretly sublet the flat on weekends and when they didn't sublet it, they threw massive parties that often lasted for three days, driving me crazy. The noise and the fear that their drunken friends might crash through my ceiling began to chase me out of the flat, and I often ended up sleeping over at Flora's place. Despite multiple conversations with the neighbours and requests to lower the noise levels, nothing changed. When I called the police, they informed me that they couldn't intervene and advised me to report the nuisance to the council. Unfortunately, the council office is closed from 1 a.m. on Saturdays until 2 p.m. on Sundays, leaving no one available to assess the noise during the peak of the party. A friend suggested that I join the party if I can't stop it, but that isn't what I want. I want quiet and peace at home. I often cry myself to sleep for short, four-hour rests at night due to the stress, and I often stagger through the rest of the weekend with panda eyes. It feels like going back to square one, to the time when Eric used to live here. Perhaps it is a sign that a cycle has ended in my life, and it is time to move on. Besides, I am craving a bigger room anyway.

***

"Why didn't you open the door last night?" my Dutch flatmate asked when he arrived home from work.

"What door?" I wondered.

"The door of your room. I was pounding on your door, calling your name to help me clean up the water."

"What water?" I asked, bewildered.

"There was water coming from the ceiling in the bathroom. The floor was flooded."

"Oh God, I had no idea."

"I was knocking on the ceiling with the end of the broom to get the Greeks' attention and went down to the street at 3 a.m. to ring their bell because they were the ones causing the flood. I have no idea what the hell they were doing!"

"I didn't hear a thing."

"You always wake up at the slightest sound. How could you sleep through that?"

"I'm just as surprised as you are," I admitted. "I must have been dead to the world."

He's got a point. I'm a light sleeper. How could I have missed all that noise? Maybe the countless sleepless nights finally caught up with me, plunging me into an unusually deep slumber. On the bright side, I'm relieved I didn't have to deal with the water disaster, and my flatmate deserved to clean up solo. He was rather condescending the other day when he learned about how much we were due to pay for the water bill, taking his frustration out on me. As a newcomer to London, he's still adjusting to the high cost of living in the Big Smoke. This is his first time living away from home, and he's constantly comparing everything to life under his mum's roof.

It's karma, my love.

December 2011

Thursday, 15th December

I have been selected to showcase my design at Alternative Fashion Week (AFW) in April 2012. As I only submitted sketches along with my application I will have an awful lot to do and will need skilled help, and moneeeeeey to materialise my collection.

Between Christmas and NYE

While immersed in the challenges of financing the dress-making process and preparing for my upcoming show in April, I took a brief respite from my thoughts and speculations to visit Wimbledon. My purpose? To photograph the guitarist from a psychedelic rock band, wearing one of my designs: the mask with eye pins. These very pins had captured the attention of the Vogue editor the previous year.

The guitarist lives in a squat nestled within a very cool building, enveloped by trees, that used to be a wellness hotel in its heyday. The building boasts an abandoned pool area (sans water, naturally) and a bar adjacent to the lobby downstairs, offering intriguing locations for our shoot. His room, along with those of his neighbours, is secured by a lock upstairs, and they rely on mutual trust to ensure their personal belongings remain untouched.

Inside his room, spacious and complete with an ensuite bathroom and kitchenette, we cooked a simple meal post-shoot. Then we sat on the carpeted floor and dined while watching Pulp Fiction projected onto the wall.

A week later, I attended the band's gig in Shoreditch and continued to hang out with the guitarist over the next couple of months. At some point, I introduced him to Sargon, and the three of us started to meet regularly at the weekends. The boys enjoyed discussing 70s psychedelic rock bands, and I enjoyed preparing random cocktails for us when they came over to our rooftop terrace. It was our meeting point before heading out to check out gigs in the area.

One Saturday, after a concert in Dalston, we walked home together, stopping at random places where we enjoyed the music, prolonging the night and having more fun. One of the pubs we stumbled upon was swimming in disco lights, and there was an overweight DJ in a fluorescent outfit and a Chicago Bulls baseball hat. His energy and passion for the music captivated us. We watched him silently from the bar as he played 80s pop and techno. Nobody danced except for the DJ. The pub was sparsely populated, filled with older East Londoners, who seemed to be my parents' generation, smoking and drinking beer. Their presence made us feel that we didn't belong there, so we decided to leave after having a cider.

Eventually, I slept with the guitar player. *I bet you've guessed!* He's six years younger than me and it didn't feel quite right but I had not been with anybody for over a year and at this stage, I just wanted to have fun. We only slept together twice, and then he slowly drifted away from physical connection towards a virtual friendship on Facebook.

P.S. I bought myself two jumpers for Christmas this year.

January 2012

Thursday, 12th January

I started working on my AFW collection with the assistance of a master's degree student from the London College of Fashion (LCF). Initially, Meian, from the tattoo studio, introduced me to a tailor who had previously worked for Kate Moss. When the tailor examined the dress I had created at the dressmaking workshop, her reaction mirrored my own astonishment when I held the finished dress in my hands upon completing the dress-making course. "You have to focus on this!" she exclaimed as she reviewed my sketches and admired the eye badges on the dress. "It's so edgy and amazing, you have to focus on this!" she reiterated. I asked her to help me sew the garments for the show but she said her services were too expensive for me. Instead, she provided me with the email of a collective workshop where I might access a sewing machine for free. As I was not familiar with the different sewing techniques, and there was not enough time to learn, I looked for another solution. I came up with the idea of walking into the fashion college on Mare Street, and with the permission of the receptionists, I left a note on the job board with the hope of finding someone interested in collaborating. This is how I met the Canadian student, who hopped on board with me and worked responsibly with admirable discipline and meticulous attention to detail on the side of her own collection for the end-of-year show. Over the next three months, we developed a respectful and dependable working relationship, gradually forming a friendship. She requested £10 per hour, while at that time I only earned £8 per hour from looking after Blue and Lily, resulting in me falling behind on payments. Eventually, I settled the outstanding balance in two instalments, concluding the payments owed in June. I was immensely grateful for her patience and trust in me. Reliable collaborators were hard to find in London, making it all the more remarkable that I found someone with such professionalism and integrity. I was blown away by the impeccable construction of the garments she produced!

Renée if you read this, I want you to know that I am forever grateful for your work!

February 2012

Wednesday, 1st February

Today I joined Lee on his styling job for ASOS. Unlike the creative freedom of editorial shoots, this gig was more about showcasing products on models. It felt repetitive and lacked the creative spark I'm used to. The stylist's task seemed simpler as we were limited to items on the rail and accessories from the side table. It was okay, but I found it rather dull. We had to churn out a certain number of looks per hour, all part of hitting targets.

Despite the promised pay, I ended up getting nothing for my efforts. Lee directed me to an employee who took my details, but I never heard back from them. Oddly, I didn't bother chasing it up. Perhaps I've become accustomed to assisting for free, seeing it as just another unpaid opportunity. It's not the end of the world.

During my lunch break, I popped down to the shops and bought a packet of click-on cigarettes along with a coffee at Pret. A typical lunch for the French, but a peculiar one for me. It marked my return to smoking after a four-month hiatus. What's more, I smoked alone in the street, something I'd never done before. Sure, I've smoked alone on our terrace and with others in public places, but never solo on the street.

Lee humorously suggested that I should date photographers because, according to him, they're the only ones who aren't gay. While the idea appeals to me, my past experiences with male photographers haven't been great. Every one I've collaborated with for test shoots has hit on me in one way or another. If it happens to me, who is behind the camera fully clothed with no make-up on, what must it be like for the models who are exposed in front of it?

These male photographers often assumed I contacted them because I was interested in them romantically. When they realised it was just about the project, they quickly exited my life, either offended or proud. One even turned to the model for her number after I refused to let him touch my hand. Then later, he submitted blurry, unusable photos, leaving me in a difficult position with the model agency.

When do male photographers become professionals and focus on work rather than the girls? While a handsome photographer may be attractive, the fashion-photographer-wannabes I've collaborated with seemed to lack the maturity and experience necessary for building a career in the profession they aspired to.

That's why I prefer shooting with Flora. Not only do we understand each other well as a photographer-stylist duo, but there's also no gender drama on set. Models have even told us they feel happier and safer shooting with female photographers like us, which speaks volumes about the environment we create.

Question:
Do you agree that new face models should be chaperoned on photo shoots?

I purposefully said new face because wisdom comes with experience, not with age. So you can be eighteen, an adult in the eyes of the law, yet have your first modelling shoot. Whereas someone who's been working in the industry since fifteen might handle an uncomfortable situation better at the age of eighteen than someone of the same age who's new to the scene. Eighteen is still very young and an innocent age just like the early twenties. This is the time when most of us take our first steps into the world of independence and work-life, and for many models, it's when they catapult to the peak of their careers.

Interesting fact:

Female models' careers are said to be over by their mid-20s. Male models, on the other hand, have more success well into their thirties and even forties.

Friday, 3rd February

On this rare snowy day in London, I don my lovely warm coat and boots and make my way to Victoria House to attend the London College of Fashion graduate show. The exhibition showcased new talents across various fields such as Digital Fashion, Fashion Photography, Fashion Media Production, Design Technology, Footwear, and Artefact. Among the students' work, I found the pieces from the Artefact and Footwear design departments particularly intriguing.

I quickly grew fond of a collection of platform shoes by a Chinese student and boldly approached her about borrowing her designs for my AFW show in April. Although she was interested in the opportunity, there was a significant hurdle: her shoes were only available in size 36, suitable for small feet, while most models had larger feet. She mentioned she could create new pairs for £600, and I wondered what made her think that I could afford that.

Nonetheless, after our conversation, I left with nothing but the memory of her naive personality.

Friday, 24th February

It's so bloody cold outside that I ran home from the bus stop.

March 2012

Saturday, 10th March

I joined Lee for another editorial shoot. While we waited to enter the photo studio in the morning, I noticed something different about him—his hair had started to turn grey, a change I hadn't noticed before. I mentioned it to him half-jokingly, and he attributed it to the stress he was facing at The Magazine, where he had recently started working as the fashion editor. I was taken aback by this revelation! The Magazine was one of my favourite publications and a major source of creative inspiration for fashion editorials. Secretly, I hoped Lee might bring me on board to work with him there, someday. It would truly be a dream come true!

Back to the current shoot. We were working with a very charismatic and flirty model from Norway, represented by Elite Model Management. Julia, the make-up artist, was completely swooned by his words, and she was even worried if it was okay to blush, given that she was married. Lol. We spent a solid 10 hours at the studio, but it was such a friendly team that the time flew by! We were a mixed, international bunch from Sweden, Ukraine, Norway, China, Hungary, and the UK. The mutual respect and interest in each other's talents made the cold studio feel warmer, and when we ordered pizza at midday, sharing it like a family around the coffee table, it tasted even better.

I snapped some background photos with my new smartphone, my very first one that I snagged on sale. As I wandered around exploring other parts of the underground studio, I stumbled upon a Triumph Bonneville motorcycle propped against the wall in one of the abandoned rooms. Lee asked me to give it a quick dusting so we could use it for the shoot. *Psst, don't tell Cinderella that I cleaned the bike! She might get jealous of me.* So, I gave it a wipe down, and the boys carried it to the set, where it gleamed in front of the wall-papered background. Then our model posed on it charmingly, decked out in a lot of Prada. Gosh, those Prada shoes were to die for! I would love a man with shoes like that!

Saturday, 17th March

The night bus was packed with young people, many of them drunk and weary. Among them, a girl nodded off a couple of times, eventually finding a stable position by resting her head against my arm. I didn't mind; it felt like a scene from Woodstock—peace and love. But when my stop came, I gently nudged her head onto another passenger's shoulder. She didn't seem to mind.

April 2012

Alternative Fashion Week (AFW)

I worked on the collection until the last minute. I needed a lot of eyes to cut out and pin on the outfits. During this process, I encountered an elderly lady willing to donate her 40-year collection of Vogue magazines to me. These magazines were a treasure trove, providing the perfect material for the eye badges I used to embellish the garments. I arranged to collect them from her house with the help of the guitarist. You know, the guy from Wimbledon. He had a car and offered to give me a ride. Over tea and cookies, we chatted amicably at the old lady's home before loading as many magazines as we could into the car boot and on the back seats. Despite our efforts, we had to leave many copies behind due to their weight and volume.

Throughout the final stages of preparation, I filled my workspace with the sounds of Beyoncé and Rihanna, finding motivation in their music as I meticulously pinned hundreds of badges onto the outfits that Renée had sewn for me. To alleviate the solitude of my bedroom-turned-workshop, I also played movies borrowed from the Hackney library in the background.

In the evening before the event, Flora and another friend bunked in my room to lend a hand for the show. They giggled and chatted through the night while I toiled away in the kitchen, racing against time to complete the outfits. As dawn broke, I found myself in a blend of excitement and nerves. Drawing on past connections, I enlisted the help of some acquaintances for makeup and modelling, plus I had done street and online casting, so I only needed two models from the organisers' pool for the day. Worries crept in, particularly concerning the strapless leather dress, which proved unsuitable for most models due to its tight, stiff quality. The model had to be the right size for this dress—neither thinner nor curvier, neither shorter nor wider. Unsure who would wear it, I spotted a girl on stage during the rehearsal who seemed to have the perfect figure for this dress, and I approached her. Enamoured with my design, she agreed to try it on. Flora stepped in to zip up the dress, joking about my fretting, but my concern lay in ensuring it was handled delicately. I explained the importance of a slow, careful approach, mindful of the delicate nature of the invisible zips on the heavy leather. This outfit was the most important piece in the collection, and I couldn't afford another mishap; I'd already broken the zip once before.

Anyway, the show went well, without complication. Thank God, no one tripped, no seams burst, and not a single pin flew into the audience. As the final model disappeared backstage and the applause began to fade, I felt a rush of relief, pride, and disbelief all at once. My first catwalk—a collection born from sketches on scraps of paper, from the hundreds of badges I pressed and pinned late into the night, from every penny of my income and more, and from the faith of street-cast girls who trusted me with their presence—had just unfolded in front of a real audience. For the first time, my work was not hidden in garment bags or tucked behind someone else's vision; it had walked the runway, alive and unapologetic. London is full of noise and endless competition, but in that moment, I knew I had carved out a space for myself. Small, maybe—but mine.

I met new people and saved their contacts in my phone. After the show, a man walked up to me, gushing over the outfits and the styling. He gave me his business card because he wanted to do an editorial of the collection for his online magazine. Some media coverage would be great, so I saved his card and promised to contact him. Then, the day after the show, I received an email with "Urgent request" in the subject line.

"Hello,
My congratulations on your fashion show yesterday.
My name is xxxx. I cover AFW for Russian Vogue and might be featuring you for some UK publications as well.
Also, I'm drafting new post for my blog now. Would you be able to share the photos (backstage/catwalk) with me? Please let me know what do you want me to mention in credits
I'll appreciate your prompt response.
Should you have any questions please contact me at ANY time.

Kind regards,
xxxx
Fashion Journalist & Personal Stylist"

I couldn't afford to pass up the opportunity, despite not having any photos of the outfits yet. After seconds of panic, excitement, and brainstorming, I convinced Flora and two models to do a photoshoot immediately after reading the email. In fashion, you have to act fast, or they'll find somebody else. I sent the images to the journalist a few days later, and she replied:

"Hi Zsofi,
I published a review about your collection.
Still waiting for Vogue's verdict.

Kind regards,
xxxx"

That marked the end of our correspondence, leaving me with a sense of resignation as I accepted the likelihood that Vogue had passed on featuring my design.

May 2012

I'm left with a profound emptiness, a void within me, a sort of black hole. It's the end. The past three months have been a whirlwind of activity, from building the collection to preparing for the show, and now... suddenly, everything is quiet. What comes next? I'm struggling to readjust to my slow-paced life and find satisfaction in the mundane activities of the day. The thrill and creative spark have vanished. All that's left is the collection, hanging on a broken rail in my bedroom, and a small debt to Renée. My friend in Hungary tells me I'm burned out and advises me not to worry, better days are ahead.

June 2012

Friday, 8th June

As I walked home from a gig at Hoxton Bar and Kitchen, I spotted a Jimi Hendrix-looking guy relieving himself against the wall of a narrow side street near Kingsland Road—a route I often took to cut my journey short. I quickly moved to the other side of the street to avoid getting too close to the scene. However, he wasn't content with just letting me pass. In his drunken state, he shouted something at me, “What's up baby? Haven't you seen da BBC?” At first, I didn't understand what he meant, and I wasn't even sure if I heard him correctly as I continued to walk away. Then, in a louder and more slurred tone, he clarified, “Big Black Cock,” before bursting into laughter at his own joke. Okie dokie. I got it now. BBC as Big Black Cock, not as the TV channel. Bless him! His joke was as golden as his piss.

Sunday, 17th June

It's raining cats and dogs outside and I'm sitting the day away in my room, lost in a deluge of thoughts. They say an average person has about 6200 thoughts a day, and today, every single one seems to echo the same question: “Why?” It could have been a delightful Sunday, strolling through the flower market, enjoying a coffee on the curb while listening to the street musicians serenade in Ezra Street. But no, it has to be another dreary, wet day, mirroring the rest of the week.

It's been raining a lot lately. Just the other day, I was heading to the British Library, armed with an umbrella. Despite its cover, I was drenched by the time I reached the tube station. Realising that spending hours in the library soaked to the bone might not have been the best idea, I decided to turn back home instead and change into dry clothes. With only a single pair of shoes—my trusty black sneakers—now sodden, I resigned myself to staying indoors until they dried. This incident prompted me to invest in wellies, so I bought a pair of black, knee-length horse riding rubber boots, which came in handy many times during the wet summer of 2012.

Saturday, 23rd June

I took a cab home late at night after babysitting, and upon settling into the car, the Pakistani driver turned to me from the driver's seat and said, "If you sick, tell me, I stop the car." A "hello" could have been enough but I appreciated his creative welcome words. In fact, I was very surprised by them.

"Pardon?" I asked, needing him to repeat his words.

"Before you throw up, tell me, I stop the car," he rephrased the same message.

"Why would I want to throw up?" I asked him kind of baffled because I didn't understand what his problem was.

"Are you not drunk?" he asked, continuing to glance at me in the rearview mirror while driving off.

"No!"

"Sorry! I assumed you coming from a party," he chuckled, relieved.

"No, I was babysitting."

"Sorry, sorry!" he apologised, raising his hands in a conciliatory gesture. "Many people throw up in my car, you know. I'm just trying to prevent another incident."

Friday, 29th June

I met up with the young Korean fashion photography student, Jeanette, whom I had befriended at Alternative Fashion Week. She purchased a handful of my badges and pinned them on her bag right in front of me. She was in awe of my design and she didn't hide it. I was flattered by her joyful reaction yet still wondered how something as simple as what I loved doing could make other people happy. Everyone I had met found it unique and asked how I came up with the idea. This prompted me to educate myself on copyrights and patents.

Since then, Jeanette and I had collaborated on a punk photo project, which eventually became her graduation piece. Now, the four of us—Jeanette, two models, and myself—gathered to view the large-scale prints exhibited on the walls at the graduation show. The models lined up to take a series of selfies in front of their photoshopped punk selves and posted the images on Facebook right away.

July 2012

Sunday, 15th July

The weather hasn't improved since June, and the forecast doesn't promise any better for the rest of the summer in London. They say this is the wettest summer in the UK in the last 100 years, but isn't that what they say every year? I often rub sunscreen on my arms to remind myself of the smell of summer, longing to feel even a hint of it. Flora, on the other hand, pays to use the solarium in a beauty salon just to experience the warmth that reminds her of the sun. According to the news, the highest and fastest-selling product in drug stores this summer is vitamin D. People are coping in various ways.

Last year, my flatmates and I spent most of our days outside on the roof terrace. It was so dry and hot that I had to escape to the nearby pool to cool off. Now, I can literally step out the door and swim on the terrace. Since there's no sun to dry the water up, the rain has accumulated here, forming jumbo puddles. If only we could use this water for bathing and cooking to save on the water bill! It's been grey and rainy since April. Finding the motivation to leave the flat is hard, so I spend long hours in front of the computer, re-editing many of my old images.

The crappy weather also encourages me to finally open those books on my shelf that I've never read. And I find myself increasingly drawn to the idea of moving to a new country. For some time now, I've been receiving repetitive signs pointing towards New York, accompanied by recurring dreams of travelling there. This pattern began about three years ago, yet I've struggled to decipher its significance. Perhaps I should remain vigilant and await the arrival of new puzzle pieces that may help me unravel the meaning behind these dreams. In the meantime, here are five things I'd love to do in New York:

1. Explore the city and capture moments with my Smena film camera.
2. Hail a yellow cab.
3. Arrange a meeting with Jae Choi at the Collective Shift and showcase my portfolio. (By the way, the other night I dreamt about working as Vinoodh and Matadin's assistant.)
4. Walk the High Line.
5. Visit family friends in New Jersey.

Saturday, 4th August

I've just had a one-night stand. The guy in question is a colleague of Flora's from Finland, coincidentally residing in my neighbourhood. Our encounter began unexpectedly when we crossed paths on the street. We spent the whole afternoon talking, and continued to stick together throughout the night. While the sex was forgettable, what resonated with me was the sense of security I felt when he pulled me closer and held me in his arms as we drifted off to sleep. It was a safe and warm place. For the first time in a long while, I felt I mattered, if only for a single night.

Saturday, 11th August

I visited the Ballgowns exhibition at the V&A. With most people preoccupied with the Olympic games, the museums were surprisingly tranquil. Amidst the grandeur and elegance of the exhibits, a dormant desire to become a fashion designer stirred within me. The gowns on display, ranging from the 1950s to the present day, were showcased on pristine white mannequins with giant white ball decoration around them. Of course, "ball-gowns"! My favourite pieces were from Hardy Amies, Tomasz Starzewski, Ossie Clark, Mark Fast, Roksanda Ilincic, Stella McCartney, and Vivienne Westwood.

Then I contacted the creative director of the online magazine I had met at AFW. They were still enthusiastic about shooting an editorial featuring my collection. So I left the outfits squeezed in a suitcase at their office-slash-photo studio for the entire month of August, shaking from the risk I was taking. No guarantee, only trust attached.

End of summer 2012

As the summer of 2012 draws to a close, changes sweep through the landscape of my life. I quit my apartment, moved my stuff to my friend's place, and am now homeless, starting a temporary position at The Room magazine in Budapest. I do not know which one is better: having a job but no home, or having a home but no job. Everything feels temporary, uncertain, yet somehow liberating. Perhaps The Room will provide room for me. Temporarily.

Then the tandoori restaurant transforms into a fancy wine bar. One of my flatmates moves back to his homeland, while the other moves in with his girlfriend. As for me, I'll be moving to West London upon my return from Hungary, whenever that may be. That's it, folks. The end of East London for me.

In the bittersweet moments before my departure, I find myself overwhelmed with sentimentality. Embracing the walls of my old room, I inhale deeply, imprinting the scent of the place into my memory. Tears well up as I reflect on the challenges and joys this humble abode has witnessed. Despite its imperfections, it provided me with a sense of security and belonging, marking it as the first place in London I called home.

September - December 2012

After basking in the sun for as long as possible, absorbing ample vitamin D, and indulging in juicy home-grown fruits, I flew back to the UK. Unfortunately, the temporary job I took at the Budapest magazine proved to be less than fulfilling. It was so not worth the experience.

I needed to be at the office only once and then I ended up doing the job—online correspondence—from my friend's sofa where I was crashing. The office was eerily quiet when I visited, with only two individuals present. One was either smoking or sneezing due to allergies while sharing personal anecdotes with me on the tiny balcony attached to the office.

He was friendly, but what did his life have to do with the job I came here to do? The other individual, a well-known fashion photographer signed with a New York agency, just didn't give a fuck.

Ah, fashion.

Tell me about it.

London Fashion Week

I hired three model wannabes, who had walked for me at AFW, and took them to London Fashion Week on Sunday. I paid each girl £50 and covered their travel expenses for the day as we visited several locations of the most popular shows. Since we didn't have invitations, our plan was to hang out in front of the big events, hoping to catch the attention of photographers and other important attendees. We also distributed flyers that I had made to promote my womenswear collection.

We were all dressed in my design, and together, we looked very cool as we had a lot of fun zigzagging from one location to another using public transport. Along the way, we played table tennis with some guys at King's Cross, swung on the swings at a playground, took selfies with a limo driver who was chauffeuring a celebrity to the shows (but he didn't tell us who it was), and with some random people in the streets who liked our outfits. Our day was filled with silly jokes and laughter.

After the Mary Katrantzou show, I thought I saw Anna Dello Russo, editor-at-large for Vogue Japan, across the road next to a car, where she appeared to be gazing at our outfits. Though I wasn't entirely certain if it was her, I decided to approach her. The closer I got, the more confident I became that it was indeed her. However, she didn't wait for me; she got into the car and drove off before I could greet her. I regretted not running after her; perhaps I could have at least given her a flyer. Now, it feels like a missed opportunity.

***

Until Christmas, I work for a very wealthy family. The father is a film producer, while the mother... well, let's just say she is a psycho. Despite my intuition warning me, I took the job because I hadn't found anything better at the time, and they offered to pay me £1000 per month in addition to providing free accommodation and food. Initially, I declined their offer, but the mother persisted, bombarding me with texts about how much they liked me and wanted me to care for their children. Originally, she had offered £800 per month but I threw in the £1000 salary expectation because I was sure she would not pay that much for a part-time live-in nanny position. But to my surprise, she got back to me saying that her husband agreed to pay £1000 and then I thought I had to do it, feeling somewhat obligated.

The children's mother is a stay-at-home mum—a bored, controlling, superficial, and often lonely woman, whose mood swings are as unpredictable as the weather. She exhibits behaviours that suggest she might be bipolar, at times slamming doors and breaking objects, only to later dismiss it as unintentional or urge everyone to forget about it. But I can't simply forget. It's evident she struggles with unexpressed anger, which permeates the atmosphere and affects the children's behaviour, serving as a reflection of her emotional instability.

Despite residing in a spacious house in Notting Hill, the place feels claustrophobic due to the suffocating atmosphere. During breakfast, the parents sit at opposite ends of the rectangular kitchen table—the father absorbed in the newspaper while the mother gazes out the window while sipping her coffee, her eyes shadowed by dark circles. The father is seldom present, seemingly always seeking escape from home. He departs each morning before the children awaken and returns late at night when they are already in bed. He's often away on work trips at the weekends. I've observed him loading bottles of wine into the car before these trips, and I get the feeling these are not exactly "work trips". When he stays at home at the weekend, he goes to church and takes the kids out for pizza.

The Filipino housekeeper, who visits twice a week, shares tales of previous nannies, most of whom departed after just six months, with some lasting only a couple of months. "The girls don't feel good. They look for another family," she confides in slightly broken English. Well, this girl is no different. Following suit, I terminate my contract after just four months.

Do you want to hear another nanny story?

While searching for positions, I interviewed with another family who lived in a massive 6-bedroom house with a large garden and two cars. They already had a live-in maid. They offered to pay £600 for 50 hours of daycare, which included covering Saturday mornings, plus up to 2 days of babysitting per week. The father of the children, a toddler and a baby, explained how generous they were and that I deserved this good salary. Half of it would be paid to me in cash, and the other half would be deposited directly into my bank account. They wanted to avoid paying taxes for my work, naturally. It infuriated me. They were trying to coerce me into working illegally in a country where I had every right to work legally. They would make significantly more money by hiring me than I would earn by accepting the job.

During our meeting, the song that played in my head was "Killing Me Softly" by Fugees. I felt tired just by listening to the father's attempts to butter me up. I played along, masking my resentment, thinking, "you're killing me softly..." I left, telling them I would inform them of my decision the following week, which I didn't do. Their house wasn't that impressive after all, lol.

He's strumming promises but he's not nice,
Killing me softly with his lies,
Killing me softly...with his lies...killing me softly
...with his lies...killing me softly

British Fashion Awards

I street-casted a girl with afro hair and took her to the London Coliseum, wearing my design, for the British Fashion Awards. I paid for our tickets, two cheap seats, and let her stay in my room for the night, giving her my bed to sleep in while I moved down to the floor. I bought a few tops, all returnable, for her to try on, which enhanced the look of the badge dress she was going to wear. Additionally, I purchased a couple of brightly coloured nail varnishes and lipsticks to complete her image, and we were ready to hit not the red carpet, but the entry for the guests who paid to be at the award ceremony.

Looking back now, I regret not pushing the model onto the red carpet. I might have been able to pay a small sum to the guard to let her walk in with the celebrities and be photographed. It could have been a great promotion! I wish I had thought of this on the day. Now, I have to wait for another year for this opportunity to come around.

Anyway, the night went well. We drank rosé and took a lot of photos. Some other guests also took photos of the model and asked where she got the dress from. I received compliments as a designer, such as "Clever idea!", "I have never seen anything like it!", "The dress is so dope!", and "You look stunning!" Not me, the model. I wore a white T-shirt and a black Maison Margiela skirt that I bought at Retro Woman, paired with flat sandals featuring white pearl details at the front.

Edie Campbell won the Model of the Year Award, Christopher Kane won the Womenswear Designer of the Year Award, Kate Moss won the Special Recognition Award and Sienna Miller has great hair colour! Strawberry blonde, innit? "Innit" is my new favourite expression. *It's cold today, innit?* Is "innit" a more primitive version of *ain't it*? Let me check in the vocabulary.

Vocabulary results:
innit = isn't it
ain't = am not; are not; is not; has not; have not

The next morning, I woke up early while the model was still asleep. As I got dressed in the semi-dark room, I noticed something odd on the bed through the mirror. Curious, I turned around to investigate and discovered that the model was bald, and the strange furry thing on the bed next to her was her afro hair. It was a wig! I hadn't known!

I attempted to take a sneaky photo of her sleeping next to the wig, as there was something very documentary about it that I wanted to capture with an artistic eye. However, it was too dark for my phone, so I simply kept the memory of it in my mind.

January 2013

From January, I start sleeping on the couch in Flora's flat. Soon after, I move into her flatmate's room—the girl with the many tattoos—because she's moving in with her boyfriend, and I can take over her room in March. I've always wanted to live in this room ever since I first saw it when I came over to hang out. It's a spacious, bright, wooden heaven with a double bed, a two-seater sofa, a desk, shelves, and plenty of under-bed storage for all my stuff. I'm going to be very comfortable here.

Despite being an ex-council flat, now privately owned by a landlord who lives overseas, it has a unique charm. This charm comes from the people who live here: Flora, my close friend and creative partner; a caring and shy Spanish girl who loves to imitate Beyoncé; an Italian girl who thinks her coworkers are idiots and has a contagious laugh; and now me. This is the first time I've lived in an all-girl flat and the first time I've had a TV—not in my room, it decorates the living room.

"Meian's room smells like sex," I started an unexpected conversation with the girls yesterday in the living room. The Big Bang Theory was on in the background on Comedy Central, but nobody was paying attention.

"Let me smell," Flora said, getting up from her usual spot on the floor where she sat on a cushion by her laptop. She made her way to Meian's room and the other flatmates trailed after her. They all started sniffing around, making sour faces.

"Yep, there's definitely something," Flora confirmed.

The Spanish girl left after a few seconds, and the Italian flatmate chimed in, "It smells like vagina."

"Ew, don't be cruel!" I said, turning to her.

"Meian loves sex," Flora reminded me.

"I know. You've told me all about her lovers and troubles... stuff I wish I didn't know."

"Her boyfriend lived here too, secretly. He moved his stuff in, and they pretended he just stayed over at night. And we pretended we didn't know because she never told us."

"That's healthy!" I said sarcastically. "And she's been your friend for how long? Six years?"

"Well, a London friend," she corrected me.

"And you don't confront London friends?" I asked.

She gave me a look, as if to say I didn't understand how indirect British people could be.

"Wait, where's the big wooden table?!" Flora exclaimed, her eyes wide with shock.

"Yeah, I remember that table in the room. I'd love to have it. Where did it go?"

"No clue. But the landlord will be mad if it's gone."

"Looks like they replaced it with that black office desk that's bolted to the wall."

"What? Oh my God, the landlord will be so mad! We can't leave holes in the walls; that's damage to the property. She knew that!"

"She also knew that the three of you gave her your shares for the electricity bill that she ended up spending on herself," I reminded Flora of what she'd told me about Meian a year ago.

"Oh shit."

I wrote an email to the landlord about the desks so he wouldn't take the damage fee out of my deposit, just in case. Then, I spent 3.5 hours thoroughly cleaning the room (yes, just one room!). I scrubbed filth off every surface and filled an entire bin bag with the rubbish Meian had left behind under the bed, behind the sofa, at the bottom of the wardrobe and drawers. When I was finally done, I sneezed and blew black stuff out of my nose—the dust was that bad. I aired the room out for a week, day and night, and used fabric freshener to change the smell.

Meian considered cleaning beneath her; it never even crossed her mind to tidy up the room after she moved out, which was a week later than we had agreed upon. I was already paying for the room, and she still hadn't packed a single thing. When she finally came over to do so, she ended up chatting with my flatmate all night. When I asked her when she intended to start packing, she got offended and made her boyfriend do the job for her. This was the same boyfriend she had moved in with, behind whose back she had been sleeping with other guys. Meian was always on the hunt for another man. She only stayed with a guy until she could manipulate him or until she found someone better—someone with more money, more influential friends, who took her to fancier restaurants, or lived in a nicer house. Money, not love, was her craving. Once she said she wanted a rich boyfriend so she'd never have to work again.

She did entice a well-known actor in the past, whom she loved for his fame. The man struggled with alcoholism and turned violent after drinking. He slapped Meian, and she thought she could endure the abuse as long as he was rich. She desperately wanted to keep him to live a comfortable life by his side, but they didn't date for long. After the breakup, Meian tried to get back with him through his mom, with whom she was often on the phone, working her charms, but it didn't help. Much to our relief.

Although Meian and I are not besties, I don't want to see a sister get hurt, even if I don't approve of the way she treats others.

Catalina

Catalina, my Spanish flatmate, often makes me laugh when she channels Beyoncé and dances to "Single Ladies." It's become her signature thing in the flat. Her parody is hilarious, just like her accented English. For example, she says "bitch" /bitʃ/ for "beach" /bi:tʃ/ and "iceland" /'aɪslənd/ for "island" /aɪlənd/.

"Have you been to the Canary Island?" Catalina asked wistfully not caring that the 's' is silent in island.

"To the Canaries or to Iceland?" I asked back.

"Canary iceland," she confirmed.

"It's 'island' with a silent 's'," I told her.

"Whatever. Have you been there?"

"No, I haven't."

"I miss the bitch," she said with a sigh.

"What do you mean? London is full of them," I chuckled.

"The beeach, Sofija. The beeach. What's so funny?"

"Nothing. Tell me more about the bitch," I encouraged her.

She squinted at me and said "They're black on the iceland..."

"Black bitches. Noted."

"Yes, bitch."

I wasn't sure if she meant that for me or if she was just being Spanish.

"They are black and hot. The black sand can burn your feet if you're not careful," she continued.

"Are you saying that black bitches are hot?"

"Sofija, come on! You are making fun of me."

"But YOU... just... said that black bitches are hot!" I laughed with tears.

"I am not talking to you anymore. You always laugh at me."

"I'm laughing with you, not at you."

"I am not laughing."

"Learn to!"

Eventually, she dropped a smile and continued the conversation.

"I am starting to resent talking to you."

"Aww, wow, you used a new word: resent. I haven't heard you use it before."

She hated me now.

"Can we get back to the bitches? I haven't tried the black bitches but I love white bitches," I said, trying my best to imitate her accent.

"The white bitch is not as hot as the black bitch."

I think she's found her sense of humour again.

"Do you have a bitch-dress? Do you play bitch-ball... and do you surf on the bitch?" I asked eagerly.

"Good night, Sofija!" she said, moving into her room.

London Collection: Men

I assisted Lee backstage at the men's show. Driven by curiosity, I asked one of the models how much they made to walk in the show. He said three hundred something. Not bad for a few hours of work. And if they did two shows, they could pocket £600 for the day, which was pretty good!

Wednesday, 23rd January

Last night, I went to see a band in Camden Town. The gig was so engaging that it made me forget about my unanswered emails with the fashion coordinator who, after confirming my position at the magazine I am interested in working at, has not given a sign yet. And it has been a month now.

In the meantime, I have started to look for other positions and came across a designer's post on Facebook who is looking for an intern. I got in touch with her, and a week later, I met her in Camden where her studio is based.

February 2013

I began working with the up-and-coming designer in Camden, a former employee of the London Ballet Company, who was preparing for her first LFW show in February. She worked in a collective studio where I shared a desk space with other creative individuals. Every day, I brought my laptop to handle the administrative tasks she entrusted to me, along with designing graphics and taking photos of outfits for her social media platforms, which granted me creative freedom.

Two weeks later, I assisted on the lookbook shoot, which was located in the suburbs of London. I took the tube to the end of zone 4, where I was picked up by a car. After an hour's drive, we arrived at an abandoned building serving as the photo studio. With no heating or running water in the partially scaffolded building, I spent the day working with my coat on (again!), either keeping my hands in my pockets or exhaling warm breaths into my palms.

During the short breaks, I listened to the sunny work experiences of the makeup artist from L.A. and vaguely smiled at the designer, who loudly gushed over the stylist's talent every time he changed the model's look. The stylist, a regular contributor to magazines like Harper's Bazaar, Schön, GQ, and Elle, played along with the designer, constantly exclaiming "Stop. Stop." with exaggerated hand gestures and fake giggles, acting he was undeserving of the compliments. Our model was a TV presenter, apparently, as I was told she worked at MTV.

To keep busy, I took photos and videos with my phone, later editing and sharing them with the designer who was very happy with me for doing extra work. On the day of the show at the ME hotel, where I was stationed at the door coordinating guests, I brought my friends in for free to enjoy the fashion, live music, champagne, and mini hamburgers amidst an underwater video installation with whale sounds and jellyfish projected on the walls around the room, along with a contemporary dance performance preceding the catwalk show.

After the show, as I walked back to the hotel room where we dressed the models, I encountered a long, dark silhouette resembling a creature unfamiliar to me. Unsure of where the lights were in the corridor, I used the flashlight on my phone to illuminate the figure.

"Hey," said the figure. "You have a light?"

As he approached, I realised he was a drag queen, drunk and lost but kind. He explained he was here to DJ but had no idea which floor the venue was on. He needed the restroom to adjust his outfit. I offered to let him use our room, where I had entered to tidy up. He stationed himself in front of the beauty mirror to adjust his wig and asked me to unzip the back of his latex suit. Then, he applied some baby powder to his chest and arms before I helped him back into the body-tight costume.

Before the show, my weekend was filled with various tasks. I was mindlessly busy as I had started a full-time work placement at Net-A-Porter earlier in the week. On Friday, I stayed late at the company to assist in preparing the editorial team for an upcoming shoot. On Saturday, I worked with the designer in Camden Town all day before leaving to babysit in Hackney in the evening. I stayed overnight at the kids' house and commuted to central London early the next morning to help with the show.

March 2013

New home. New job. New hair. I decided to change things up by cutting my long, thick, brown hair into a shorter style and dyeing it blonde. I absolutely love it!

Now, I work at the biggest online luxury fashion retailer, which is conveniently within walking distance from my new home. I'm one of three interns assisting the fashion editor and stylists at the company's weekly magazine, tailored for "women with great style and great stories." It's my first experience with a nine-to-five job in London, and initially, I'm unsure how to feel about it. Working in an office and waking up at the same time every day feels strange at first. However, I gradually find comfort in the predictability of the routine lifestyle, which ultimately provides me with a sense of security.

The office is located on the top floor of the nearby shopping centre. Every time I ascend the escalator, I feel a sense of pride. Only the "chosen ones" have access to the top floor, and I relish the opportunity to see the expressions on the faces of those I leave behind on the lower floors. I can't help but wonder if they're curious about where I'm heading further up.

I spend most of the day in the fashion wardrobe, which is an entire room protected by a security code; only those with the magnet card can enter. This is where the stylists prepare the luxury outfits and accessories for their fashion stories and editorial shoots. The room is very disorganised, with many shoes missing a pair, having been waiting in piles of boxes longer than I have worked here. Additionally, there are a few expensive pieces of jewellery among the bags thrown under the tables where the accessories are laid out. My intern buddy, who, by the way, is studying to become a pharmacist, thinks that the employees have hidden the small jewellery there to steal them later, and I wouldn't be surprised to hear if it was true.

The working hours are rigid, with punctuality expected, and any tardiness is promptly questioned by the editor. We're required to remain in the wardrobe until 5 pm, regardless of whether we have tasks to complete or not. There are days when we finish slightly earlier, yet still, we're compelled to linger in the wardrobe, counting down the minutes until the clock strikes five.

Meanwhile, I'm attempting to reapply for Jobseeker's Allowance now that I'm working full-time without pay. Consequently, I left early on Fridays to submit my paperwork at the Jobcentre. I informed the editor, a cold and unfriendly woman, that I had a doctor's appointment because something told me she'd rather hear this than the truth. In response, she wheeled her chair away from me, maintaining a considerable distance to avoid catching any potential illness from me. I couldn't help but wonder what her reaction would have been if I had disclosed that I was leaving early to sign up for the dole.

The other thing that strikes me is that all the employees have a cabinet where they can hang their coats and bags. We, interns, have to drop our coats and bags on the floor under the desks where the editorial team sits. Every time I finish my work, I have to crawl on my hands and knees to reach my belongings, which, for some reason, are always further behind under the desks than where I placed them in the morning. I don't understand why they don't provide a spare rack or give us some chairs where we can keep our stuff.

During the internship, I pick up a new lunchtime routine—it's all about the Pret run! Smoked salmon ciabatta, green juice, and a high-fibre muffin (yum!) are my go-to picks. I've turned the handicapped toilet cubicle into my secret lunch haven, where there's plenty of space and privacy. Plus, I get to sit up on the counter next to the wash basin, keeping my coat and bag right by my side instead of dumped on the floor like usual.

Lunchtime in the mall is always a chaotic affair—never any space to sit down at the coffee shops, and the crowds can be a bit overwhelming. I don't want to go back up to the office to eat either because I'm just happy not being there. So, I hold my nose and consume my lunch in the restroom.

Do you believe in God?

An African woman on the bus grabbed Flora's arm just before we made our way down from the top deck to get off, and she asked her with despair, "Do you believe in God?" I immediately cracked up, but Flora didn't find it funny. The lady probably worried about Flora's rock chic look—leather jacket, Dr. Martens, dyed red hair, and black cat-eye make-up—and wanted to "save" her. Flora, insulted to the bones, simply retorted, "Don't touch me!" while I tried to navigate the stairs without tripping.

Panic attack

Catalina, my flatmate from Spain, nearly had a panic attack when she realised she had left her phone at home. The two of us were strolling down Uxbridge Road toward the shops when, after about ten minutes, she began frantically searching her bag.

"What are you looking for?" I asked.

"My phone," she said.

We stopped so she could carefully search her bag. She started handing me items to hold while she dug deeper. I could hear her breathing quicken and her voice sounded panicked.

"What's wrong?" I inquired.

"I have to find my phone," she replied, on the verge of tears.

I was taken aback. "We're just going to the shops. We'll turn around in an hour. Why is your phone so important right now?"

"You don't understand..." she trailed off.

"You're right. I don't," I conceded.

"Something bad can happen," she insisted.

"Like what?" I asked.

"What if my parents or my brother call from Spain?"

"You can ring them back as soon as we get home," I suggested calmly.

"And if something happens to them, and they can't reach me on the phone?"

"Or maybe I just shoot myself right now," I thought. I didn't say this out loud, but if I had, it would have been just as surprising as Catalina's reaction to her missing phone.

"We have to turn back home," she ordered.

"Hey, I'm right here. Have we met?" I reminded her that she wasn't alone, in case she forgot.

"You're not funny, Sofia!"

Yes, I am!

"I am your friend and flatmate. I have my phone with me. I know your full name, your birthday, your address. I've seen your thongs in the laundry several times and I know about your disgusting habit of eating peanut butter toast with cucumber for breakfast. You can call your parents from my phone anytime," I reassured her.

"Stop making fun of me!" she raised her voice, still stressed.

"I wasn't joking. You can send your family a message from my phone and let them know that they can reach you on this number, in case 'something bad happens'," I suggested another solution to help her calm down, but she insisted on finding *her* phone.

"Ahh, it's here, I've found it!" she said, relieved but still nervous.

She then put everything back in her bag and looked at me like nothing had happened.

"What was that all about? Are you really that dependent on your phone?" I asked.

"You never know. Something can happen..." she replied.

I'd heard that before. And I still didn't understand.

"I think someone is going a little nutsy," I said, half-friendly, half-judgmental.

"I know it's weird, but that's how I feel," she admitted, and we continued our way to the shops."

I'm happy to socialize; it's so good to be surrounded by people I can share myself with. However, my flatmates mostly sit together in the living room, staring at the screens of their phones, laptops, or sometimes both. The TV is on in the background, usually tuned to the Food Channel or Comedy Central, and at first, it feels like no one is present. It takes me some time to adapt to this norm, but at least I have friends around me to hang out with, even if their attention is flaky at times. I can share my feelings, thoughts, ideas, bad days, and good days, which I couldn't do much with my previous guy flatmates.

What happens to those who don't keep up with social media and don't want to vegetate in front of photos of other people's travels, parties, and babies? What if I want real human connections? What if I want the truth about people and not the fake smiling selfies? What if I don't care whether I fit in or not? The sad truth is, if you aren't surrounded by people who also seek real human connections, you're just as alone as those who prioritise relationships through digital devices. How come some people are so empty and bored that they're more interested in other people's lives than their own? If you're one of these people, get out there and live!

May 2013

Went to Thorpe Park with my flatmates—*whoever designed the Stealth ride, I hate you!* Made margaritas at home, partied in Camden Town, partied in Notting Hill, fooled around in the polaroid booth at Rough Trade, watched girls strutting in front of 1001 Café, ate many toasted falafel wraps, made hamburgers with peanut butter and coleslaw at home, drank lots of green tea, put up red fairy lights above my bed, wrote a short script, watched some KUWTK, and sent out applications for fashion assistant positions.

June 2013

LCM SS14

I hadn't seen Lee since January. He looked older and more exhausted than I remembered. We were doing two men's shows at LCM. The "family" was back, and we had new kids on the block—Lee had recruited four extra hands, interns he borrowed from The Magazine where he now worked full-time. Meeting the competition—other stylist assistants who were much younger than me—was a bit unnerving. It hit me that I could be replaced in an instant, from first assistant to thin air... or maybe I have already been replaced. Who knows?

I got to know J., the super funny and earnest—*Gosh, how much I miss honesty and wit in London!*—gay Italian assistant who helped me steam the outfits. J. had been in London for six months and was on his twelfth internship. I congratulated him on the vast experience he had amassed in such a short time, and on having to ask his parents for more money each month to survive.

Many of the models were exceptionally good-looking, with profiles that made me blush and made J. exclaim, "I'm in heaven!" I overheard snippets of a conversation between two models about a guy who had cut his wrist backstage at one of the shows. I couldn't fathom why anyone would do such a thing. What could drive someone to cut their wrist at a fashion show? Write your ideas below.

The next day at the second show, J. told me he had met a Hungarian model, and I didn't let him go until he showed me who. I got very excited because I had never met a Hungarian model before, and it would be fun to say "szia". "Szia" means "hi" in Hungarian. He pointed to a boy standing right next to me who turned out to be Belgian, but he joined us on the mission to find the Hungarian model. We soon realised these boys looked a lot alike, making it difficult to remember who was who.

The boys went back to work but I kept searching for the Hungarian model, sneaking away from the team for a short while. Soon, I spotted "Bence," a Hungarian name, written on a board among the models walking for Craig Green. I went closer to the model board and saw a faceless blue figure in the photo next to the name. Then I walked to the line-up and looked for the blue outfit. It was pure chaos! So many people and loud backstage music. I found three models in blue, but ironically, all the Craig Green models' faces were hidden behind scarves and hats that matched the abstract costumes. I left it at that. It seemed I was not going to say "szia" to Bence. At least not here, not today.

Saturday, 29th June

I moseyed down to central London to celebrate the launch of the first issue of Exalt magazine. Inese, the talented makeup artist I met at LCM, joined me for a glass of wine—orange juice for her—and a McDonald's hamburger afterward.

July 2013

I reached out to a stylist (E.F.) whose ad I found on the LCF Fashion Network, one of the Facebook groups I'm part of. She was looking for assistants, so I inquired about the details. It turned out she was shooting a kids' wear lookbook for a designer in Notting Hill. Seriously, how could she leave out the fact that it was for kids' wear? Fashion people are usually not the biggest fans of working with children. Except for me, since my side job involves babysitting, though even I find shooting fashion on kids less inspiring. Despite my reservations, I agreed to help because I wanted to stay busy. After all, gaining some more experience couldn't hurt.

The shoot was planned to last four days, but I left after the second day, even though I had assisted the stylist with a week-long preparation beforehand. On the first two days, we worked on location in an old house on a charming little street near Old Spitalfields Market. Everything inside was wooden and vintage: the floors, the doors, the furniture, the staircase, and the attic. It was a very cool building!

A steep, creaky staircase led up to the attic, which connected to the roof terrace and the smaller top rooms. I trekked up and down those narrow stairs many times, as we were setting up one of the attic rooms as the wardrobe and dressing room for the children. The stylist mentioned she was pregnant and couldn't carry anything heavy, so I was the one lugging the bags up and down.

As we were still setting up the wardrobe and the background, many of the parents had already arrived with their kids and were waiting downstairs in the dark lobby area. Without a coordinator, I became the go-to person for their questions since they saw me frequently moving about. They asked, "When does the shoot begin?" "How long do we have to wait?" "Can we get some light here?" "Where's the toilet?" "Can we go out and come back later?" "Where's the nearest café?", etc. I didn't know any of the information for these questions.

One time, as I was descending the stairs, something heavy landed on my head with a resounding bang, and I thought I might faint from the pain. Reaching up to touch my head, I felt a second painful hit on my hand, which I was using to steady myself on the timber. Initially, I thought a piece of the roof had fallen on me. Looking back at my hand, I realized the attic door had fallen down, trapping my hand against the timber. The door was so heavy I couldn't lift it with one arm, so I screamed for help. Through the slit between my stuck hand and the fallen door, I saw E.F. standing by the racks just a few steps away. She glanced at me and then walked away in the opposite direction. *Bitch!* Then, I saw the second assistant rushing toward me from the other end of the room. "Sofia, you okay? Sofia, I'm coming!" She lifted the attic door and leaned it against the stone wall, muttering to herself about pinning a "Don't touch!" sign on it later.

She guided me, my dizzy head, and my shaking, bleeding hand down the stairs to the bathroom. I kept touching the top of my head to check for bleeding while she pulled a chair under me and ran cold water over my hand.

"Your system is in shock!" she said.

"What makes you think that?" I asked.

"Because your entire body is shaking, and you're so white."

If I was in shock, it was because of what the stylist did—walking away and letting me suffer—not because of the accident. She asked me a couple of questions to ensure I was coherent while I tested my eyesight. My hand was still under the running water, and now I was just cold, so I turned off the tap and checked if I could move my wrist and fingers properly. The fingers were fine; my wrist was not. I didn't think it was broken, though. After sitting for a bit longer, I headed back to the wardrobe.

I decided to stay on the shoot after the accident because I felt guilty and wanted to prove that I could keep going. *Why did I feel guilty? I shouldn't have felt like I had to prove anything to anybody!* Anyway, I did as much as I could with my injured hand. As the day went on, I started noticing details that made me realise how disorganised and unprofessional this shoot was.

E.F. hadn't talked to me since the accident and was avoiding my glance. Was she afraid of sending me to the emergency room for a check-up because I would have to give out information to the nurse, and she didn't want to be held responsible? Or was she really that insensitive and thoughtless? Should I feel bad about badmouthing her? Because I don't. She was avoiding me, and I didn't understand why. And by the way, how come we had no first aid kit on the shoot? We were working with kids, and there was no medical support of any kind on location. Flora, whose day job was a production assistant at a film company, told me that there had to be a first aid kit on location shoots, or a paramedic on bigger productions, and the call sheet should always list the nearest hospital's address and phone number.

That night, I went to bed with my wrist swollen and decorated in rainbow colours: yellow, green, violet, and blue bruises, sprinkled with red streaks of dried blood on top. My head was fine, thank you, and my flatmate filled it with kind, supportive thoughts at home. Close to midnight, my shaking hand rocked me into a dream to the tunes of some gentle, repetitive knocking sound coming from the neighbours. I think they were having sex.

The next day, I got up and went to the shoot as if nothing had happened. I only refused to do the ironing, as I was right-handed and couldn't lift the iron with my injured hand. I was surprised, and actually slightly pissed off, that there was no lunch for me. I saw a few sandwiches on a tray, but by the time I was free to eat, all of them were gone. I had to go to Tesco to buy my own lunch with the stylist's tenner. It felt good to be away from the set, even for that short period while I was returning from the shop. I felt freer in the streets. In fact, my gut was telling me to quit this work. This position wasn't serving me, and I didn't want to waste my time working for an unprofessional stylist. So, at the end of the day, I spoke to her.

She didn't take the news well at all. She swelled with indignation when I tactfully explained that this position wasn't right for my experience—*it was beneath me!*—and that I needed to see a doctor about my hand. I expected some sympathy and understanding, but she showed neither. Instead, she blamed everything on me. We stood outside by her car, which contained my biggest suitcase that I had lent her to carry props. She refused to give it back now, insisting that I'd have to go to her house to pick it up after the shoot. Her house was two hours away from where I lived. *Thank you, bitch!* She made me feel guilty for speaking up and then punished me by making me go the extra mile with a bruised hand. What was wrong with this woman?

I didn't hear from E.F. until I emailed her the following week to arrange a time to collect my suitcase and get reimbursed. She replied, saying, "I am afraid I will never agree that you made the right decision, as dropping out of a shoot halfway through is unacceptable behaviour under almost any circumstances. Your attitude was incredibly unprofessional and frankly insulting, not only to me but to everyone on the shoot. It did not go unnoticed by the rest of the team, the parents, and the clients."

Let's break the message down.

"...I will never agree that you made the right decision as dropping out of a shoot halfway through is unacceptable behaviour under almost any circumstances."

My wrist could have been broken, and I might have had a concussion. Shouldn't I be more responsible for my health, which is crucial for performing well at work?

"Your attitude was incredibly unprofessional and frankly insulting, not only to me but to everyone on the shoot."

This confused me. I spoke to her privately at the end of the day, outside, where nobody else was around. "Unprofessional"? Quite the opposite! I acted professionally by recognising that I needed to step away. It seems E.F. believes that honesty is unprofessional and insulting.

Honesty is only insulting to the ego, our conscious mind, the part of our identity that we consider our "self". The ego is an inflated feeling of pride in one's superiority to others.

And who does she mean by "everyone"? She was just too scared to face me alone. She needed to put the crew behind her to feel better about her insecurities. I stood in front of her by myself, and in return, she attacked me with a herd of angry words, attempting to make me feel small and guilty. Maybe such behaviour made her feel powerful. I, on the other hand, didn't allow myself to identify with her derogative comments. *Way to go, Zsofi, thicken up!*

"It didn't go unnoticed..."

Of course, my absence didn't escape notice. I played a significant role on the shoot. I took on additional responsibilities beyond the typical duties of a stylist assistant because I found it instinctive to lend a hand. With ample experience, I was capable of working independently and confidently, knowing what tasks required attention. I responded promptly and was always prepared to assist whenever necessary. On top of that, I managed the arrivals of parents and children, attended to their needs such as snacks, drinks, and directions, and addressed their inquiries as they impatiently waited in the dimly lit lobby due to poor organisation. My natural kindness and helpfulness resonated with everyone, and the parents appreciated my genuine concern. Naturally, they observed my absence.

"I am in tomorrow before 11 a.m. if you would like to collect your cash and suitcase," she added at the end of the email. I just replied that I'd be there before 11. There was no point in writing anything else. She didn't see me.

I had a peculiar sensation as I traveled to her house, though I couldn't quite pinpoint its origin. I ran through various scenarios in my mind, preparing for both an apologetic "I'm sorry blah blah blah..." and a more blunt "Take your stuff and leave my house!" comments. When I arrived and knocked on the door, a man greeted me with a cheerful smile. He invited me in, handed over the money, and retrieved the suitcase. I inquired about E.F., and he informed me that she had taken their son to kindergarten and wouldn't return until 11. *The coward!* I nearly chuckled to myself as I walked away. It was pathetic that an "established stylist," as she called herself, felt the need to hide from a rookie.

This marks a significant turning point in my life. I'm starting to grow a thick skin and toughen up for the game. Over the past three years, I've faced challenges that have toughened me: from dealing with mice and unreliable flatmates to enduring heartbreaks, loneliness, financial struggles, shaming and other BS at work. Now, I'm stepping into my own strength and integrity.

What is integrity?

According to Brené Brown, "*Integrity is choosing courage over comfort; choosing what is right over what is fun, fast, or easy; and choosing to practice our values rather than simply professing them. This means that integrity involves making difficult choices that align with our principles, even when it's inconvenient or challenging. It's about living out our values consistently, not just talking about them.*"

August 2013

Sunday, 4th August

Out of curiosity, I searched my name online and found myself on The Fashion Spot (TFS) website—a hub for fashion enthusiasts covering runway reviews, celebrity styles, fashion trends, and more. I stumbled upon my work with the Belgian model who Flora and I collaborated with three years ago for a portfolio update. It was one of our standout shoots, and our photos are still featured on the model's online portfolio. Since then, she has gone on to sign with major agencies in Paris and Barcelona, and has begun to build an impressive resume with appearances at top shows like Chanel, Dior, Celine, A.F. Vandevorst, and Nicole Miller, as well as being featured on Fashion TV. I am proud of her accomplishments. However, I can't help but feel a bit disheartened as my own life hasn't seen much change since then. I'm still waiting for that breakthrough, recognition, and the financial reward for my creative services.

Tuesday, 6th August

Today, I met Jessie J's stylist, who was looking for two assistants and invited me for a chat. While she seemed very nice, I wasn't feeling enthusiastic about this interview. She was seeking one assistant skilled in sewing and altering outfits, which wasn't my forte, and another assistant who was flexible with tasks. When I considered my strengths, I wasn't sure I'd be the right fit. Additionally, I realised I wasn't keen on being a full-time runner for minimal pay.

I am tired of living on the edge and running around for others without fair compensation. I have to figure out what it is exactly that's holding me back from wanting this. Rejecting an offer from Jessie J's stylist would either be a big mistake or a big problem with me.

Right now, I long to return home. Not to Shepherd's Bush, but to Hungary. I crave a break from the pressure and chaos of the city.

Friday, 23rd August

This marked the third email I had sent to A. T., formerly the assistant to Lady Gaga's stylist, now an established stylist herself whom I greatly admired. Our initial contact was in 2011 when I congratulated her on her portfolio. Then in 2012, I invited her to Alternative Fashion Week to see my show. Although she didn't turn up, she responded to my invitation which gave me some hope. And now, in 2013, I had sent her photos of the badges I created in response to her public message seeking a designer for collaborative work for Rollacoaster magazine. She emailed me back the same day.

> "*YEs i LOVE YOUR badge stuff!! i'd love you to do something - I think you'd be perfect for this - email me and I'll send you the details x x x.*"

Today, on Friday, I discovered that she'd need the badges by tomorrow, and I am currently in Hungary. If I wanted to see the badges on Azealia Banks on the cover of Rollacoaster, I'd have to fly back today. I couldn't wrap my head around it. I was in London all year, and it has to occur during the only week I am out of the country. I immediately check for available flights and find one for the evening, landing at 21:35 in Stansted. This means I could be back at my flat around midnight or 1 a.m. If I work through the night, I might manage to make enough badges for the project. Then next day morning, I could meet Anna to pick up the outfits that need customisation, then work a few more hours from home, and hopefully deliver the outfits by the evening, though it might be too late for her. The idea of dropping everything, flying back within hours, spending extra money on the ticket, not sleeping all night, and delivering designs for which I wouldn't even get paid sounds insane! Yet, it is A. T., AZEALIA BANKS, and ROLLACOASTER magazine! Even if I didn't get paid, Azealia might like my work and want to hire me to design a stage outfit for her, or perhaps my badges would get discovered in the magazine. I am painting possibilities on the canvas of my future. The pressure of these thoughts brings me to tears, though. I am so close to a dream opportunity, yet the amount of work still required to reach it feels overwhelming.

Why does it have to be so hard? Does it have to be hard at all? Or is it simply a toxic pattern, a false belief waiting to be broken?

Saturday, 24th August

I didn't go.

September 2013

Monday, 2nd September

I've had a revelation—I want to be a personal assistant. That's my calling! I envision myself as a PA to an accomplished artist or a visionary designer whose work inspires me, and perhaps even jet-setting alongside them on travel adventures.

Exhibition: The Photography of Punk

Attending a ShowStudio opening always guarantees an unexpected experience. Once, real people adorned the walls, seamlessly blending into the exhibition's interior—a sight both eerie and fascinating. Another time, I found myself at the wrong address, missing out on the spectacle entirely. And now, I've been immersed in a collection of graphic gay sex illustrations and provocative photos from the late '70s and early '80s punk era. To cap it all off, there was the punk ale, with a kick that left me seated on the curb outside, beside a guy who was the spitting image of Kurt Cobain.

To be frank, the exhibition was rife with penises, S&M imagery, and explicit gay content—a voyeuristic journey into someone's clandestine pornography stash. I teased Catalina, my reluctant companion, asking her which item she'd choose to buy from the collection. "Oh, I'd buy several!" she slurred with a touch of sarcasm, her hand gestures failing to align as she accidentally knocked over a beer. I could feel she wanted to kill me because I had begged her to come with me, and she hated to be here. We had expected punk fashion and music, but instead, we got a dose of gay porn.

Upon returning home, we examined the eclectic offerings available at the ShowStudio online shop, uncovering a trove of bizarre items from avant-garde designers. Let me share some of my "favourites" below.

- "F**k Me Dress"—*£6000 plus VAT!*
- "DIY 'After Anarchy' Hood"—*if you are too lazy to cut one for yourself at home, you can buy it for "only" £200. Let's hope the original hoodie was not from Primark.*
- "DIY Fruit Stained Slip"—*and if you don't feel dirty enough you can watch the video about how to make fruit-stained clothes in a fetishistic way.*
- "Anorexia Nervosa Cuff"—*who doesn't want one?*
- "Brand New Smile"—*I know people who would benefit from it.*
- "Illustration by Jowy Maasdamme"—*I genuinely like this one.*
- "Pheasant pieces in a pickle jar"—*£400... no comment.*

Saturday, 7th September

Past midnight. After some gig. The fish and chips guy drew a heart with ketchup next to the chips I bought to munch on my way home.

Dash magazine launch party, East London

Accompanied by Inese, my new makeup artist friend, I waited for her for twenty minutes under the overground bridge in Hoxton in the rain. When she arrived, she was carrying a massive box of chips. We spent another 15 minutes under the bridge while she finished eating, and then she dropped the bombshell: she was traveling back to Latvia at the end of the month. *No! You can't leave!* A pang hit my stomach, and for a moment, I struggled to breathe, my eyes threatening to well up from the sad news. Another friend departing London. In an instant, I steeled myself, forcing the feelings and tears back to where they belonged: inside. Inese's departure brought forth a flood of emotions, reminding me of the loss of other friends with whom I once shared experiences, adventures, and challenges in London, away from our home countries. In the bustling and often superficial city of London, forming meaningful friendships is as challenging as landing a paid role in fashion. As one of my friends once remarked, "London is like a big, international airport where people arrive and soon depart." Friendships forged in such a fast-paced environment are hard to maintain; just as you get to know someone, they are out of your life. I think I have developed abandonment issues.

P.S. I barely remembered the party, except for the DJ's striking blue hair!

Friday, 13th September

Friday the 13th wasn't an unlucky day for me. I had the opportunity to work with Nolan Funk! I want to celebrate!

So, I was on set with Lee, working on an editorial, and the model looked oddly familiar, but I couldn't quite place him. He struck up a conversation with me while I was kneeling in front of him, tying his shoes. He was nice. American nice. He asked me where I was from and why I arrived late. I told him that I was originally from Hungary and that I worked as a part-time nanny next to my fashion job and today I had to drop off the kids at school. It was a casual chat, and I was enjoying it. It was a human gesture, something I am not used to from models. They don't normally ask any questions or talk to me at all. But never mind. I mentioned to him that he looked familiar. "We've done a shoot before, haven't we?" I asked. He responded, "I don't think so. I'm not a model." Turned out, he was an actor from California. Ah, that explained his American nicety! He was very confident, somewhat cocky, as he strutted around in his underwear between looks, showing off his gymnast's body. But why did he seem so familiar? I still couldn't figure it out.

We were halfway through the day when I stood behind the photographer, watching our actor pose in front of the camera. Suddenly, it clicked! He was the guy from "The Canyons," the movie written by Bret Easton Ellis (my favourite author, whose books I've read in both English and Hungarian), which I had just watched a few weeks ago. He played opposite Lindsay Lohan in the movie! I couldn't believe it. Best day ever! I had to text Flora.

At the end of the shoot, when Nolan was led to another room for an interview, Lee and I stayed alone in the studio. I told him I had recognised the actor and asked if he had watched "The Canyons" or knew the books by Bret Easton Ellis, but nothing rang a bell for him—not even "American Psycho," "The Rules of Attraction," or "Less Than Zero." So, I continued to keep my excitement to myself. While we were waiting for the cab to load the bags of fashion, Nolan came back to say goodbye—nice manners! Honestly, I was impressed. I couldn't help but smile at him. He shook hands with Lee, and then turned to me. I reached out my hand, and he grabbed it, leaned closer, and kissed both of my cheeks. I was officially melting. He wasn't even my type, but his confidence was so charming that I could barely contain myself in front of him.

Sunday, 29th September

Today an old lady on the bus told me, "You've got so beautiful teeth and a nice sound of voice."

November 2013

Meeting The Fashion Director

"Gosh, what is she doing here with the Sainsbury's bag?" a well-dressed woman exclaimed to her equally well-dressed teenage daughter, both appalled as they saw me in Selfridges.

I waddled noiselessly across the jewellery floor in my muddy rain boots and messy hair, carrying a big orange Sainsbury's plastic bag. I looked exhausted on the outside, but I felt glorious on the inside. I had just finished an editorial shoot for The Magazine with The Fashion Director and was in Selfridges to do returns at the end of this important day.

In late November, Lee asked if I was available to assist him on a shoot for The Magazine. I eagerly said, "Of course!" and soon after, I received the call sheet. I was thrilled to see The Fashion Director's name—let's just call him The Fashion Director—and his contact number on the sheet. I had been wanting to work with him ever since I arrived in London, and now his number had practically fallen into my lap! Additionally, I loved, loved, loved that the production company listed my name third on the top of the page, below The Fashion Director and the Fashion Editor, who was Lee. It made me feel special.

We all gathered at the trailers near an abandoned grassy field in a valley in Walthamstow at 8 a.m., except for Lee, who arrived more than an hour late due to traffic. Ironically, he lived the closest to this end-of-the-world place yet managed to arrive the latest. The problem was that he had all the outfits and accessories for the shoot, so I couldn't do anything until he showed up. I knew that when he finally did get here, we would have to unload the taxi and lay everything out from the suitcases at record speed. So, I drank another coffee and waited.

I introduced myself to everyone in and around the trailer: the two photographer assistants, the producer, the production assistants, and the four models, one of whom was the then 16-year-old Jean Campbell. Soon, the photographer assistants followed the Very Famous Photographer out to the field to scout the location. The models sat quietly inside the trailer. Carla, one of the production assistants from Switzerland, was setting up a breakfast table outside in the cold wind. I offered to help and we started chatting. She seemed a bit stressed, so I told her I was happy to assist with anything until the stylist arrived. She said it wouldn't be necessary since she was almost done but appreciated if I could pass her the hammer from the toolbox.

As I lifted the lid of the metal box, the wind snapped it back aggressively, catching my thumb in the lock. It hurt like hell. My thumb started to bleed, and my nail slowly turned purple. Carla ran for the first-aid kit and put a thick plaster on the cut. I thanked her and withdrew inside the trailer, sitting next to the models. Sandra, the makeup assistant with whom I had worked before, joined me with a cup of tea and we discussed what we had been up to since the last shoot where we met. Then out of nowhere a very tall, charismatic man stepped inside the trailer. It was him, The Fashion Director. I had never seen him before but the way he carried himself, he exuded dignity and respect, told me that was Him. He greeted everyone and asked where Lee was.

"Lee isn't here yet. He texted me that he's running late because he's stuck in traffic," I informed him from behind the table where I was sitting then added, "I'm Sophie, Lee's assistant."

"When did he text you?" he asked.

"About 20 minutes ago."

He went out to talk to other people, and I texted Lee to let him know that The Fashion Director was already here and asked how far away he was. Lee replied, "I don't know. The traffic is not moving. I'll text you when I'm at the gate." Next, I heard The Fashion Director on the phone with him.

Then he came back inside the trailer and sat down. Even while sitting, he was still taller than me. He asked me where I was from and how long I'd been in London. We ended up having a grown-up conversation about work and goals in fashion until I suddenly realised that here I was, talking to The Fashion Director, a man of compelling integrity. I started to feel nervous and stopped talking. This was when I noticed he was looking at me differently than most people did. He was actually interested in my thoughts and paid attention to what I was saying. He looked right into my eyes and deeper within. It felt as if he recognised my worth, if that makes sense. It was difficult to contain myself; he had such a powerful presence! I began to feel hot, my heart was racing, the blood rushed to my cheeks, and I didn't want him to see me blushing, so I excused myself and went outside to the cold. *I am such an idiot!*

Lee arrived shortly after I regained my composure, and the chaotic unpacking process began. We had to find space for six suitcases filled with luxury brands like Louis Vuitton, Prada, Versace, Lanvin, McQueen, Karen Millen, Jason Wu, J Brand, and more, along with the shoes, the kit bags, and the steamer. We managed to cram everything into the back of the trailer in disarray next to the makeup artist station, utilising every available inch of space. Shoes were scattered on the floor, chair, sofa, and even balanced precariously atop towers of shoeboxes I hastily assembled. Most of the bags found their place on the sofa, sharing space with jewellery collections. I hung as many clothes as possible on the built-in rail and draped the rest wherever I could, including on the handles of storage units. The room resembled a poorly organised closet, leaving little room for movement. When Lee and the model were inside, I found myself pressed against the wall, barely able to move.

One of the models struggled with English, so when Lee asked her if it was okay to remove her bra because the colour was showing through the McQueen top, she didn't respond. Lee appeared stressed, a side of him I hadn't seen before. He was usually decisive and well-prepared for shoots, exuding calm confidence. But not this time. Knowing that these girls were very young, I turned to the model and patiently explained that we needed her bras off. I took off my coat and pulled up my jumper to reveal my bra strap, gesturing and asking, "No bra, okay?" With a shake of my head and additional hand gestures, she finally understood and had no issue removing her bra.

"Chuck on more rings! Loads of them," demanded The Fashion Director hurriedly as he checked the models' looks before they headed out to the field. Then, the Very Famous Photographer chimed in, mentioning that it was wet and muddy outside and suggesting that the models should wear their own shoes and change into the designer footwear on the spot. Despite the production company's clear instruction to "wrap up warm and be prepared with waterproof boots/wellies and clothes" in the call sheet, nobody else came prepared with appropriate clothing and waterproof boots except for me (parka coat & knee-length rubber boots) and The Fashion Director (wool coat, Hunter wellies). It seemed like we were a perfectly matched pair. I also gave credit to the Very Famous Photographer, who sported a leather jacket and Dr. Martens, although that might have just been his everyday look.

Some Londoners are incredibly trend-focused, prioritising style over practicality in their clothing choices. This trendiness extends even to photo shoots, where individuals are more concerned with looking stylish than being comfortable. I once heard of a makeup artist who went to great lengths for fashion's sake. When called for a magazine shoot, she sent a courier to fetch her Vivienne Westwood cardigan from her home, just so she could wear it on set.

"Sophie, what size are your wellies?" Lee inquired, casting his gaze towards my black, knee-length horse riding boots. I sensed trouble brewing.

"Size 6.5," I replied.

"Would you mind lending them to the models? You can pick any other shoes from the room," Lee proposed.

Glancing at the array of designer shoes on the sofa, I smirked and replied, "Deal!"

The models took turns donning my boots, relegating me to the confines of the trailer for the remainder of the shoot. With the sun dipping below the horizon at 15:52, the crew found themselves in a race against time. They barely paused for lunch, hastily grabbing a few bites in between model changes. Meanwhile, I cozied up inside the trailer, enjoying a thick, hot veggie soup with Prada on my feet. Those shoes made me feel fantastic. However, disaster struck when I accidentally spilled soup on the Prada. Frantically, I scrambled for napkins to clean the mess. Feeling guilty, I stashed them away in the closet and opted for a pair of loafers by a lesser-known designer for the rest of the day, which in the end turned out to be more comfortable.

Apart from the Prada mishap, my day unfolded relatively calmly as I tackled the usual tasks on set, assisting Lee with the models and ensuring our area remained organised. Despite not darting between the field and the trailer, I found myself just as fatigued as the rest of the crew. The day consisted of a lot of tedious sitting and waiting, punctuated by sudden rushes to change the models. Battling the November cold only added to my weariness. With no heating inside the trailer, our only source of warmth, aside from the soup, came from hot beverages like teas and coffees, and the occasional blast of warm air from the hairdryer that the hair stylist kindly activated for us. Bless him for that.

As we wrapped up around half past three, amidst the chaotic rush of packing, I overheard the Very Famous Photographer asking if anyone had tape. One of his boot soles had decided to part ways with the top, and he needed to tape it back together.

"I have tape!" I shouted, prompting a proud look from Lee.

"My assistant!" he exclaimed. I dug out the duct tape from my backpack and offered it to the photographer, who graciously accepted.

He thanked me profusely as he tore the tape with his teeth and patched up his boot. Meanwhile, Lee cried up, "Some footwear samples are in horrendous condition. Look at this stain!" pointing at the Prada shoe before tossing it into the shoe-case, a suitcase we used for the shoes only. I shrugged and continued removing outfits from the hangers.

Lee called a taxi to take us to The Magazine's office. With one massive bag in my lap and another behind my head, we miraculously managed to squeeze in all the suitcases and bags, plus the two of us, into one car. I was insanely excited, yet didn't show it, to be heading to The Magazine's office for the first time.

Upon arrival, Lee enlisted the help of Quinn, the receptionist, to assist us with the suitcases. Then I found myself in the midst of the office, armed with checklists from showrooms, and began sorting the outfits by brand for the returns. Clothes were strewn across the floor and on the two available desks, presenting an overwhelming task. Quinn came to my rescue, taking over the jewellery sorting. He bore a striking resemblance to Pieter van den Hoogenband, the Olympic swimmer I had a crush on in high school.

"Hey!" I heard it from somewhere behind me while I had been kneeling on the floor for an hour, searching for the Karla Otto designers. Though I had a feeling the "Hey!" was for me, I initially ignored it. Then I heard it again, "Hey!" I paused for a moment and glanced over, noticing Quinn approaching. Now I turned toward him.

"Hey, everything okay?" he asked.

I nodded.

"What's your name again?"

"Sophie."

"What's ready?"

"Bottega Veneta, Fendi, Hugo Boss, McQueen..." I gestured toward the designer piles as I responded.

"I'll take them to my desk so you'll have more space around here." Quinn scribbled the designer names on post-it notes and placed one on top of each pile, then he started scanning the check-list.

About half an hour later, when almost everyone had left the office, I heard "Hey!" again, but I didn't turn in that direction because my name wasn't Hey. When Quinn approached me, I pretended I hadn't noticed he was calling me.

"Hey, do you want something to eat or drink?" he asked.

"I've got water, thanks."

"And food? There's a Tesco Express across the road."

"Maybe later, I'm good for now."

His attempt to check on me was unusual. Normally, nobody cared. Or perhaps it was just that the pressure was off him now, as only four of us remained in the office, allowing for a bit of kindness. By 7 p.m., it was just the two of us still working, and I was so absorbed in searching, organising, ticking things off the list, and packing them into courier bags that I didn't even notice when others had left the office. Lee said goodbye and checked on me before heading home, but I couldn't recall the rest of the staff bidding farewell. And this is a small office, with approximately 12 people, including the interns.

Meanwhile, Quinn had popped down to Tesco, though I hadn't noticed. Now he was kneeling next to me with a packet of biscuits.

"Do you want some?" he asked without the "hey".

"Sure, thanks." I took two pieces.

"Don't worry if you can't finish it all. I'll take care of the rest tomorrow," he referred to the piles of fashion still strewn across the floor.

"I'm afraid you'll have to, because I can't be here tomorrow. But I'll do my best to leave it uncluttered behind me."

"I'm so used to it," he sighed and took a bite of the biscuit.

"How long have you been working here?" I asked him, sparking a conversation that lasted a little while. Quinn saved my number too, as he often needed an extra hand, and I told him I had some free time. I'd do anything to work here. This is The Magazine!

Before I headed home, he asked me to return some jewellery at Selfridges. Since I was going in that direction anyway, I didn't mind, but I had to admit, I couldn't wait to finally get home, take a shower, and just lie in my bed. I had gotten up at 5:30 a.m. to be on time for the shoot, and now it was 8 p.m.

Quinn wrapped the velvet bag of rings in paper and placed it in a small carrier bag with the brand's name on it. Then he disappeared into the storage room and emerged with a large Sainsbury's bag, dropping the tiny jewellery carrier bag inside. I heard it land almost 4 seconds later.

"What's with the Sainsbury's bag?" I asked, raising my eyebrows.

"It's a disguise," he explained. "These are very expensive rings. I don't want anybody to recognise the label and risk them being stolen out of your hands."

"That makes sense," I agreed, then let a hint of sarcasm creep in. "Couldn't you find a bigger bag?"

"Just go. They're closing at 9. Will you make it?"

"Yes, there's enough time to get there."

"Keep the bag close to your chest."

"I will have to! It's raining."

"Text me when you're done."

"I will. Bye!"

I dug out my umbrella from my backpack and walked out the door.

"Guard the bag with your life!" Quinn shouted after me as I descended the stairs.

I waved back to signal that I had heard him.

As I stepped inside Selfridges, the brightness of the jewellery floor blinded me momentarily. Fatigue washed over me, and I entertained the idea of keeping my eyes shut until the next morning. It might spare me the curious glances from customers, who probably wondered why a homeless-looking person like me was wandering around. I didn't blame them. I must have resembled a less charming swamp fairy. Carrying the Sainsbury's bag didn't help matters; it attracted attention wherever I went. Despite this, I mustered the courage to approach one of the Cartier sales associates after helplessly circling the floor. The staff directed me to the back on the left, which required a few more laps before I finally located the booth.

"Hi, I'm here from The Magazine to return the rings from today's editorial shoot," I announced to the saleswoman, who greeted me with a smile. She gestured for me to take a seat and began to check her checklist. She didn't seem to have a problem with the way I looked, or she was just great at hiding it.

"Do you know which ones will be featured in the magazine?" she inquired.

"No, sorry," I replied.

She started to check the rings and I shyly sat down on the leather couch. My gaze often drifted to the clock on the wall. Time seemed to crawl by, and I found myself on the verge of nodding off. Glancing at the clock again, I realised 25 minutes had passed.

"Are you ready?" I asked, hoping to speed things along as I saw the sales associate tapping her pen at her chin.

"One is missing," she announced, scanning the paper list.

"It can't be. We had them all in the office," I protested.

"Let me check one more time," she responded. I couldn't help but feel impatient.

"Do you want me to help? Four eyes see more than two," I offered.

"Uh, no, thanks. I'll be fast," she assured me.

She meticulously went through the list again, matching each description to the rings, while I sank back into the stiff leather sofa. More waiting. Sigh. The tiredness began to feel painful. Fifteen minutes later, she exclaimed that she had found it. Finally. I requested her to sign a piece of paper confirming the receipt of all the pieces, and then I quickly texted Quinn to inform him that the rings had been returned.

As I made my way to the bus stop, I found myself squeezed between two very large women in the back of the bus. If I hadn't been so exhausted, I would have made an effort to escape the tight discomfort by moving to the top deck.

Guess what time I arrived home? At 11 p.m. I stopped at a kebab place to buy potato wedges for dinner. And guess what time I went to bed? At 2 a.m. My flatmate and I had a fit of hysterical laughter over a movie we ended up watching. And guess what time I woke up? At 7 a.m. Quinn called me. And guess why? Because a ring was missing. It was a different ring, that had nothing to do with the ones I returned yesterday, but he was panicking. I tried to calm him down by discussing the possibilities of where the ring could be. Then later in the afternoon, he texted me to say they had found the ring. One of the models had it.

Quinn

You meet a lot of interesting people in fashion. Most of them are bitches and none of them are your friends. Yet somehow, against the odds, I manage to form a friendship with Quinn. Despite his icy exterior, he possesses numerous admirable qualities, though he rarely displays them in front of others in the office. He's compassionate and generous, with a soft spot for animals, cartoons, and girls. Stop! Girls? Indeed. Despite his genuine interest in women, he lets the office staff believe otherwise because, as rumour has it, the Editor in Chief (boss bitch) prefers not to hire straight employees. His acting skills are remarkably convincing—I bought into the ruse for a good three months until he finally set the record straight.

Quinn plays a pivotal role in the office, far beyond just manning the reception desk. He's a coordinator, a personal assistant, and the editors' right-hand man. In fact, his official title is Senior Fashion Assistant in print. He's the one everyone turns to when something goes awry or if an extra hand is needed. He seamlessly juggles all the tasks required to prepare the biannual issues. And then there's this:

"Zofi, can you say *wurst*?"

"How about *fick dich*?"

"Come on, say it."

"Why?"

"Nothing, just say it."

"No."

Just like that. Quinn has a knack for throwing out random, peculiar tidbits without warning or explanation. He insists on calling me Zofi. I have to give him credit for attempting to pronounce Zsofi, even though I've reassured him that I'm perfectly fine with Sophie.

It happens all the time. I've heard my name butchered in all sorts of ways. But there are a few stubborn souls who are determined to get it right. They'd repeat my name three to five times, practicing until they nail the pronunciation. Yet, two hours later, they're back to calling me Sophie, and I never bother to correct them. The Hungarian "zs" sound is a challenge for those whose first language is English. If they inquire, I'll kindly explain that the "zs" sound is similar to the English 'ʒ' sound in words like "pleasure" (/pleʒər/), for example. Quinn's "Zofi" makes me cringe, to be honest, but he says it in a cute way, so I decide to live with it.

December 2013

Christmas

My room is just five steps away from the kitchen-living room (it's a two-in-one), where my flatmates and I spend most of our time. Yet, despite the short distance, the two spaces feel like different climates altogether. Honestly, there's not much difference between the temperature in my room and the inside of the fridge. Sometimes, I can even see my breath. Flora, who's been in this flat the longest, swears by running the heating on minimum without interruption, rather than switching it on and off at certain times of the day, is the best way to keep the flat warm in a cost-effective way. Our radiator system, situated under the unsealed windows, seems to let warm air escape easily. My room, being the largest in the flat, struggles to warm up evenly, if it warms up at all. So, when my flatmates are away during the Christmas holidays, I seize the opportunity to turn up the heating and relish the cozy atmosphere of our charming flat. For once, I quite enjoy having it all to myself. I switch on the fairy lights, light a candle, paint my nails gold, listen to Christmas songs on YouTube, and bask in the warmth. I am in a good place.

My Spanish flatmate also stays in the city for the holidays, but she's working the night shift, leaving me alone in the flat on Christmas Eve. I prepare a simple meal, put on my favourite white dress, red lipstick, and mascara to add a festive touch, and dine in front of the TV. Then, I curl up on the sofa in the living room. It's the warmest room in the flat and has the best vibe, even in the absence of my flatmates. This room holds many cherished memories, friendships, and moments of laughter that bind us together.

And my tradition of treating myself to a Christmas gift continued. This year, I decided on two indulgent delights: a ticket to see the American Psycho musical at Almeida Theatre and a raw chocolate raspberry cake from Borough Market. Ever since I first sampled a slice a year ago, I had been dreaming about this cake. This time, I opted for the whole cake instead of just a slice. I shared it with my flatmate, who, like me, had an insatiable craving for chocolate. She found it dangerously delicious but restrained herself to just a slice. Secretly, I was delighted—I got to savour most of this heavenly treat all to myself. It became my breakfast, lunch, and dinner, and before I knew it, I had polished off the entire cake in just two days. Merry Christmas to me!

New Years Eve

I spent NYE in Kensington with Isabella (Isa for short) and her roommate, Anna. Isa and I had met almost a year ago in a pop-up shop in Notting Hill, where we clicked instantly over our shared interests and bohemian lifestyles. We both brewed our design dreams from our bedrooms, held part-time jobs, and embraced the adventures and challenges London threw our way on a shoestring budget. It wasn't that we wanted our lives this way, but we couldn't afford to live any other way.

Isa, originally from Bulgaria, first landed in Milan to study fashion at the Instituto Marangoni before making her way to London. She initially changed her name from Izabella Levkov to Isa Lettiere because it had a certain flair for her fashion label. But then, she discovered that "lettiera" translated to "litter" in English, so she changed her last name again, and now it's Boni. "Boni" means beautiful, wonderful, talented girl.

She was building her clothing label from home while juggling a part-time gig as front-of-house staff at a West End theatre. To get to work, she rode a sleek black Dutch bike. After it got stolen once, she nonchalantly took someone else's unlocked bike from the rack to get home, guilt-free. She didn't like the stolen bike—it clashed with her style—so she returned to public transport until she could save up for a new Dutch bike.

Isa loved red wine and she didn't eat anything with dead animals in, or food that contained parts of living animals. She looked unhealthily thin, which worried me, although I didn't mention it to her.

I never quite understood women who shaved their entire bodies but left their upper lip hair untouched. Isa is one of these women. She wears her lady moustache with pride—it is part of her unique charm. It doesn't deter admirers of any gender, who often turn their heads as she passes by, effortlessly chic in her Parisian-inspired style. She knows how to live with passion and flair.

Though we don't see each other frequently, we've managed to stay in touch by inviting each other to art exhibitions, magazine launch parties, film screenings, cafés, and various celebrations.

Isabella lives in a dodgy basement room beneath a three-star hotel. Let me paint the picture for you: overused second-hand furnishings, including two single beds, a commode overflowing with books, gadgets, small ornaments, and cosmetics. There is an open kitchenette with a sink, a fridge, a microwave perched atop an electric hot plate cooker, and a female dress mannequin serving as a coat hanger. The dark carpet bears even darker stains, and paint canvases are leaned against the walls. Mouse traps are scattered around the room's perimeter, and boxes of all sizes and luggage clutter the floor, some doubling as desks for more gadgets, coffee mugs, and handbags. The ensuite bathroom is a tiny, shabby space with a toilet, a tap, and a shower, all desperately in need of refurbishment. In fact, the entire place cries out for a complete makeover. Isa often talks about moving, but it is never the right time.

A small round table was currently laden with popcorn, lentil chips, and champagne. Despite the burning incense, I could smell the dampness that was typical of many London houses. I had encountered this odour, along with mould on the walls, in every room I'd moved into—except for my current council flat room.

I've recently read an article comparing London to New York, suggesting that the standard of living and quality of life in London now rival those of New York. I've always lived in shared houses because affording my own place has been out of the question. My first rent was £220 a month. Two years later, I was paying double for a similar-sized room in a different area. Now, I'm paying three times my initial rent. I've witnessed a rapid increase in housing prices, yet I'm still below the average of £700 a month for a room in Zone 2. London ranks as the third most expensive city in Europe, after Zurich and Geneva. Many of us who come here sacrifice comfort for the chance to chase our aspirations and dreams in this bustling metropolis.

We literally chatted the time away until midnight. We reminisced about the Copenhagen trip we almost took together back in November, thwarted at the last minute when Isa realised both her passport and national ID card had expired. She called me the day before our flight to tell me she couldn't leave the country until her documents were renewed. So, I ended up flying to Copenhagen alone. We had planned a spontaneous, two-day escape from the miserable weather for a change of scenery. It turned out to be the worst and most unnecessary trip of my life. It rained cats and dogs non-stop the entire time I was there. I ventured out once to find a supermarket because I was starving. What was supposed to be a 20-minute walk to the main street and back turned into an hour-long ordeal after I got lost on Sofia Street. Soaked to the bone, I spent the rest of my trip indoors, drying my coat, jeans, and boots on the heater. The next day, I stayed in bed with a bucket of gingerbread biscuits and a book until it was time to head to the airport. In the end, it was a darker, colder, and more depressing experience than if I had just stayed in London.

As soon as the clock struck twelve, Isa and Anna launched into a Kim Kardashian-style selfie session, bombarding their friends and family with pictures. They went through a series of happy, sexy, cheeky, and genuine looks, each an entire ritual in itself. First separately, then together, they posed on the bed, standing and sitting, by the table holding the champagne bottle, next to the mannequin, and then next to me—*Help!*—with tongues stuck out, wide smiles, no smiles, hair in the face, hair out of the face, heads tilted back, heads tilted to the side, and so on. I couldn't believe this show. After they had WhatsApp-ed everyone they could think of, they turned to me with a new idea: writing positive wishes for the new year on post-it notes. We would fold them in half and draw them out of a hat, each of us pulling three wishes. These were mine: 1. success, 2. love, 3. travel around the world. Super!

Then, out of the blue, came the second idea: to smoke weed. Isa, spinning with high speed from alcohol, and Anna, not far behind, jumped up and down on the bed laughing like teenage girls at the notion of smoking for the first time. I didn't know what to say but ask, “Have you ever smoked?”

“No,” they replied in unison.

“Why do you want to start now?” I expect to hear a reasonable answer. Turned out, there was no such thing.

“We know the girl at the reception has stuff. Let’s go upstairs!” Isa said.

I have no idea what she was talking about, but I didn’t want to stay alone in the stinky basement, so I followed them upstairs to the hotel reception. There was a woman and her two male friends in the hotel lobby. They didn't look particularly reliable, but they seemed to know Isa and Anna, so I acted polite. Isa gave the woman some money, and she rolled a joint for them. When the woman found out that the girls hadn't smoked before, she explained how to do it in her croaky voice. I was sinking with embarrassment as the girls got hyped about being “bad” and excitedly anticipated experiencing an amazing feeling they had never felt before.

Back in the room, they realised they didn’t have a lighter. Anna ran back upstairs and returned with matches. She managed to light the joint after the third try and tried to take a few deep drags, but it was clear she didn’t inhale. Isa did the same and by the time they realised it, the joint had burnt into smoke. They started to complain that it didn't work and thought they needed to buy more. At that moment, I decided it was time for me to go home.

Shoreditch House with Isa

Last summer, Isa and I went to Shoreditch House for a dip. It was one of those rare sunny summer weeks when the city was burning hot (25 degrees Celsius), and everyone wished for an air conditioner at home. Personally, I adored these days. Finally, the summer collections in the display windows matched the current season, and I didn't feel wretched going window shopping in my raincoat.

When you see the blue sky without clouds for more than two days in a row, you know it won't last long, so you try to get the most out of it. When the heatwave hits, Londoners swarm the parks, outdoor pools, and roof terraces, finding any excuse to be outside. They throw BBQ parties all around the city, enticing appetites for the foxes and street cats that visit the gardens of semi-detached houses after the gatherings are over. On sunny days, everybody seems friendlier and happier, whether at work or in traffic. Enemies become friends, friends become lovers, and Isa becomes tanned. Life is great.

No one in London achieves a tan as dark as Isa does under the city's sun. I ran into her unexpectedly at Whole Foods, where I had stopped briefly for a restroom break before changing buses. Initially, I assumed she must have gone away for a mini-holiday. Isabella adores escaping to exotic locations, showcasing her adventures with selfies on Facebook. She often poses solo in bikinis or beach dresses—or as my Spanish flatmate would say "*bitch*" dresses—

against picturesque backdrops like sandy shores and pools. However, this time, I was mistaken. Isa had actually acquired her tan right here in London. As a member of Shoreditch House, a private club for hipsters and A-listers, she spent most of her free time mingling with the "*jetsetters, celebs, affluent artists, fashionistas, and musicians.*" She insisted I join her for a chill session by the rooftop pool; she could bring me in as her guest. I agreed, and I met her the following week, pool-ready.

Dipping my legs into the cool water felt incredible. We were sitting somewhat squeezed together at the edge of the pool due to the limited available space. A girl with long blonde hair, and with possible facial fillers, joined us. Isa introduced her as Bella, a music DJ. Bella recounted her recent trip to Berlin, and since we had all been there before, we shared our experiences. Our conversation then drifted to other places we wanted to travel to. Soon, a guy with an overdeveloped chest, blindingly white teeth, and high confidence squatted down beside Bella and invited her to a party. I was not sure if he wanted her as a guest or as a DJ because I paid attention to Isa, who wiggled on her laid towel to create more space around us, taking care of the towels left behind by a couple who had vacated their sun chairs.

As our conversation dwindled, we entered a state of daydreaming under the sun. Isa lay on her back in her burgundy bikini, eyes closed, while I scanned the other club members by the pool. Some sat with their MacBook Pros in the sun chairs, pretending to work while catching some rays. Others clung to the side of the pool in their Ray-Bans. Two tall, model-like men were sitting over a laptop at a table discussing something in their Speedos. Only one guy was swimming. Everyone exuded confidence and detachment, wearing their magazine-worthy looks without a smile in sight. It felt like people were simply trying to be around other cool people. These were certainly not the starving artist types I was accustomed to. I started to feel a bit intimidated. I didn't even fully peel off my summer dress, just tucking up the bottom to rest my legs in the water. It had a low back cut anyway. Though I longed to dive into the water and have fun, I suspected that showing joy would be a mistake here.

You have to look good, very good, in order to be taken seriously.

After a couple of hours soaking up the sun by the pool, we decided to head down to Brick Lane. I suggested grabbing a bagel, but Isa was still munching on the green apple she snagged from the club's reception upon our departure. Nevertheless, I bought two bagels anyway—one veggie for Isa and one smoked salmon for me. She'd surely appreciate it later.

We stepped inside the Laden Showroom to browse the latest collections from independent clothing designers. Then, we made our way to the juice bar. Isa knew the guy who worked there, so we decided to pop in.

We were greeted with warm hugs and kisses on the cheeks by the two guys working behind the bar. As they exchanged pleasantries with Isa—"Long time no see! How have you been?"—I stood back, observing their lively banter. It didn't take long for me to notice that these guys were completely taken with Isa's model-like appearance: her slender, fragile, sun-kissed figure in a silk slip dress (her own design), her mesmerising blue eyes... and her distinctive dark moustache. Meanwhile, my blonde hair, blue eyes, and lack of facial hair seemed to go unnoticed.

Isa is like a character out of a science fiction novel to me. Her demeanour shifts instantly when she's around guys, transforming from my sensible conversation partner into a flirty yet seemingly unapproachable silly, young woman who, under other circumstances, I might find irritating. I'm kind of a chicken to ask whether she intentionally plays games with guys, a skill she's perhaps honed in order to survive in the city, or if her behaviour is simply unconscious. Is this her way of entertaining herself? Isa, if you're reading this, give me a call!

She seemed more than willing to cater to their desires with giggles, whereas I wasn't as inclined. They clustered around her, their eyes wide and smiles broad, while Isa expertly played the part of the innocent, girlish charmer. It made me wonder if she had giggled her way into Shoreditch House, or if she had actually paid for the annual membership. But, like so many other things, I didn't ask. There was so much mystery surrounding her. Fair enough, she was a Cancerian. In any case, we ended up with free drinks and an invitation to the next reggae juice bar party, which we both knew we wouldn't attend, but we feigned interest nonetheless.

Isa's always been kind to me, and I'm torn between admiring and despising her ability to wield feminine charm to her advantage with men. It's a skill I lack. Well, at least the juice was refreshing!

January - February 2014

Helping Quinn at the office

I regularly turned up at The Magazine in January and February to help Quinn with his PA duties leading up to fashion week. We had to create the schedule for the editors and confirm their passes for the shows. Quinn handled New York and Milan, while I was responsible for Paris and London. It sounded simple enough—just sitting in front of an Excel sheet to plan the itinerary and load the information about shows, presentations, dinners, and parties the editors had chosen to attend. But the hard part was dealing with incomplete information, which often arrived at the last minute, causing us unwanted stress. Another challenge was when we hadn't received an invitation yet, necessitating relentless chasing of PR representatives to request attendance. This meant repetitively calling them until I got on their nerves, hoping they'd finally dignify me with an email that, more often than not, lacked the answer to my question. This was especially common with contacts from the "cradle of culture" (Paris). The Parisian attitude, generally described as indifferent, contemptuous, and rude, didn't help. You can imagine the rest.

The Fashion Director remembered me and walked up to me when he saw me in the office after Christmas. He asked how my holiday was with genuine interest, which made me nervous again, but I managed to speak clearly—until I started to feel Quinn's and Lee's unwanted attention on me. I picked up on their vibe, which carried the message of their disapproval as if I had no right to speak to The Fashion Director. This shook my confidence, and I began to babble. I even forgot to be polite and ask him about his holiday in return. I hated myself for it. I hated that my sense of loyalty to Lee stopped me from connecting with The Fashion Director, even though Lee's loyalty to me had evaporated since he became the fashion editor at The Magazine. The truth is, Lee has a weakness for cute gay guys, and his powerful title now allows him to hire anybody whose butt he's happy to stare at—a.k.a. young guys with an interest in gloss.

In fashion, vanity prevails and human qualities are suppressed.

I had an opportunity to impress The Fashion Director, and I blew it. I couldn't be my usual, mature self in front of him. After that, it felt like a gate had closed, and I quietly sank into nothingness inside. Yet, from this insecure place, I tried to salvage what I knew was already lost. The next day, I sent him an email expressing what I couldn't manage in person—how wonderful it was to meet him and how I'd love to work for him. I didn't mention that I found his unpretentious and grounded demeanor deeply inspiring, or that his air of confidence and charisma drew me in. I'd love him as a mentor! He responded, thanking me and saying he'd contact me if he needed help. But I knew it was a polite brush-off, a door that would remain closed.

Saturday, 15th February

London Fashion Week (LFW) began yesterday, and everyone at The Magazine is out and about, cruising between shows and parties—except for Quinn and I. We're holding the fort at the office. I came in voluntarily on this Saturday for a few hours, not just to support Quinn but because I relish the quiet of an empty office. It's easier to focus and be productive without the usual hustle and bustle.

Quinn slept in the office again. It's the fourth night in a row, but he says he'll finally go home tonight to shower and change his underwear. Cheers to that! He lives far away, in Zone 4, and doesn't like his housemates, so he prefers the office's comfort over a lengthy commute and an unpleasant home environment. He sleeps cozily on the giant floor cushions. When I arrived today, I dropped myself onto the cushions too until I waited for the Nespresso machine to brew my coffee.

"Do you want some breakfast?" I asked, stifling a yawn. "I've got croissants."

"I've already eaten," Quinn replied.

"What did you have?"

"I bought one of those expensive sandwiches from Pret," he said with a hint of satisfaction.

"The £3.75 sandwich?" I asked, slightly incredulous. I think that's the priciest sandwich at Pret.

"Something like that," he confirmed.

How poor can someone be with a full-time job in a multibillion-dollar industry to consider a £3.75 sandwich expensive in London? The Magazine is one of the most popular international fashion publications, its content stuffed with celebrities, the highest-paid models, and luxury fashion advertisements. Yet, they can't pay their employees fairly? Quinn works beyond humanly acceptable hours, shouldering significant responsibilities, yet his salary borders on the breadline. WTF??

Monday, 17th February

Quinn and I cherry-picked from the leftover invitations (the less important designers' invites). Unfortunately, we had to be in the office all day, so we could only attend events held in the evenings. By the end of the day, I usually lost my enthusiasm to go anywhere that wasn't home, especially if it was cold and rainy outside. However, I dragged myself to a "presentation & drinks" event today, hoping they wouldn't check IDs since the invitation I was waving was addressed to one of the contributing editors—a man named Dio Papr...something...s, with a last name full of unpronounceable vowels and consonants.

Eventually, I got in without any issues. I arrived for the last half hour, and the flight attendant-lookalike receptionist just glanced at my hard copy invitation and showed me the way in. Once inside, I saw everyone holding flute glasses, but I couldn't find the source of the drinks in the semi-dark room. I might have arrived too late, and they had stopped serving champagne. I walked around, snapping pictures of the GQ models showcasing the elegant suit collection. The suits were boring formal wear, but the models were handsome. They all stood on separate pedestals under the spotlights, like sculptures in a museum.

Tuesday, 18th February

I carefully removed an A1 poster from a lamp post outside Somerset House. It advertised the new "GIRLS RULE THE WORLD" issue of Dazed & Confused magazine. I wanted to remind myself of that message every single day for the rest of my life. Plus, I liked the cover photo so much that it deserved a spot on the wall in my bedroom.

Friday, 28th February

I found whiskey-filled chocolates in my bag. I think my flatmate wanted to surprise me by hiding them there. We often hide things in each other's bags, shoes, or coat pockets to steal smiles during difficult times—or just for fun, even without difficult times. I was hungry, having not eaten all day, and stuffed all five pieces of alcoholic chocolate into my mouth on the bus. I arrived home slightly dizzy and drunk. ...Just kidding. I didn't get drunk.

March 2014

A night at The Magazine

I was on my way home after a long day out in Hackney when I noticed from the bus that the lights were still on at The Magazine's office. It was after office hours, and I suspected Quinn was the only one in there, so I got off at the next stop. As I walked back toward the building, I WhatsApped Quinn to ask if he was sleeping in tonight and whether he wanted to grab a drink before he lay his head down on the floor cushions. He texted back, "Come up, it's OK. Press the buzzer."

I still get a thrill every time I see the name of The Magazine written on the buzzer. It fills me with pride that I have a reason to press it and access the building. I consider it one of my greatest accomplishments to work there, even if it is just temporary. When I share my joy with my flatmates, they don't get it. They think I am nuts for working for free.

Questions to ask yourself:

Do you value achievement over fulfilment? Or do you value fulfilment over achievement?

Do you live to work? Or do you work to live?

As I entered the office, the cleaning lady was mopping the floor, and Quinn hurried over to greet me, trotting across the wet surface. He ushered me to sit in front of one of the iMacs, eager to show me the portfolio of a photographer he had in mind to collaborate with. Then, in a sudden and uncoordinated motion, he spun my chair to face him and exclaimed, "Do you know what we need?" My mind pondered over the possible answer, perhaps "explanation", but before I could respond, Quinn pulled out a pack of dental floss from the pocket of his jeans and tossed a piece into my hand. I inspected the white string and couldn't help but quip sarcastically, "That's too small to strangle me with," and he broke out into laughter. Something about his behaviour was odd; he seemed either drunk or under the influence of drugs. As he began flossing his teeth mere inches from my face, he encouraged me to do the same. I couldn't help but wonder what the cleaning lady thought of all this. She'd just finished collecting the rubbish from around the room, then said goodbye with a smile, and left.

"Don't you have some work to do?" I asked Quinn.

"I always have work to do but I don't care. I'll get back to it later," he replied nonchalantly.

"Are you planning on sleeping in the office again?"

"The hamster died," he sighed.

"Is that some sort of English slang, or are you speaking in code?" I pondered aloud.

"You're so funny, Zofi," he chuckled before elaborating, "It's my housemate's hamster."

I couldn't fathom why he felt compelled to share this with me. Quinn was certainly acting weird tonight.

"Do you want to be bad?" he queried, his voice taking on a sly tone.

"Aren't I?" I responded playfully, attempting to mimic a sultry tone and adding a tongue pop for good measure.

"Interested in some cocaine?" he whispered into my ear.

"What?!" I exclaimed.

"Why not? Have you never tried it before?" he asked, almost looking down on me as he posed the question.

"Nope."

Quinn pulled me into the bathroom, lowered the toilet lid, and locked the door, despite the empty office providing ample privacy, and we surreptitiously did cocaine. He was not forcing me, it was my choice. I was curious. We exchanged furtive glances as we indulged in cocaine. "You swear this isn't washing powder?" I questioned. Quinn chuckled, assuming it was another jest, but I was genuinely concerned. After he gave me a brief rundown of the "user's manual", I cautiously rubbed a small amount of the substance against my gum, observing as he snorted a larger dose. It felt like a scene straight out of a movie as he prepared the powder with a rolled banknote and divided it with his bank card.

"How can you snort it through your nose? It's disgusting!" I expressed my dismay.

"It goes straight to your brain," Quinn explained.

"Is that true?"

"Yes. It hits you faster."

"We're not in a hurry," I reassured him. "Plus, you seemed pretty high when I arrived."

"Well, I had a little... so what?" He shrugged. "How are you feeling?"

"Uh, I feel strange doing something like this in the restroom," I admitted. "But I'm relieved that the toilet has just been cleaned." Then we delved into a lengthy conversation about our lives, though it was mostly me doing the talking, and I didn't even notice.

Shortly after, we returned to the computer and continued discussing photographers and models we'd worked with, as well as those featured in the current issue of The Magazine. After a couple of hours, I prepared to head home. Quinn accompanied me, as he wanted to go to Tesco for a midnight snack. However, when we reached the street entry, the door didn't open. We tried multiple times, with and without the key, but it was definitely locked.

"How come you can't turn the lock with the key you have?" I inquired, puzzled.

"You can, but only from the street side," Quinn explained. He started to panic, blaming the cleaning lady for locking the door with the key when she left. And I couldn't help but chuckle at Quinn's distress over being stuck inside.

"Are you stressed out because you can't go out to grab a midnight snack?" I tease.

"No!" he fired back.

"Well, you were going to sleep in tonight anyway, and if worst comes to worst, I can sleep on the floor too and sneak out in the early morning."

"No, no, no. We have to open the door!"

"I don't snore," I pretended to be offended.

Then, noticing Quinn's body language, I asked, "Do they know that you tend to sleep in?" However, I didn't get an answer because Quinn was preoccupied typing on his phone with sweaty fingers. Through the glass door, I spotted a truck pulling over in front of the building, and I began to wave at the driver, asking him to come closer. Quickly, I typed on my phone: "WE ARE STUCK INSIDE. CAN YOU HELP US OPEN THE DOOR FROM OUTSIDE?"

Quinn approved the message, and I pressed my phone against the glass door to show it to the driver. He signalled with his arms, "Ok, but how?" Quinn pointed at the letterbox, which had two openings: one in the back that we could reach from inside and one at the street front. He showed the driver the key and then put his arm through the shoebox-sized letterbox, flipped the flap that opened directly to the street, and instructed the driver to take the key from his hand. The driver did so without difficulty, slipped the key into the lock, and the door swung open. We thanked him for his help, and the panic was over.

"Wow, that's lucky to have a mailbox like this!" I exclaimed, totally in awe, praising our teamwork.

Weekend shoot for iPad Air

I found myself as the third assistant on a weekend shoot, joining forces with the creative director whom I met through the father of the kids I currently look after. Our mission: shooting an advertisement for Apple iPad featuring a world-famous music composer.

The first day on the shoot was rather uneventful. We were indoors in a theater-like building where the American crew was filming an orchestra. My tasks included some taping and straightening the curtain behind the orchestra before the shoot began. After that, my job was to sit next to the kit bag with a walkie-talkie, which I could barely handle. At midday, the orchestra members stood up and left the room. I tried calling the creative director to see if we were going on a lunch break too, but I couldn't reach her or the other assistants on their phones. After waiting alone in the spacious room for a while, I decided to follow the orchestra and ended up eating with them in the canteen. I kept an eye on the walkie-talkie and my phone, but I didn't hear from anyone on the British production team for a good while.

To kill time, I took a walk around the building and had a short chat with an angry and weary lady who turned out to be one of the American producers. Then, I had coffee with the photographers next to the coffee truck, who were much friendlier and more talkative than the British team (no offence!). After an hour of wandering, I headed back to the stairs next to the kit bag to sit through the second half of the day. The creative director's first assistant finally showed up, and I asked him where they had been. He said they went for lunch and wondered where I was. I replied, "If you really wondered, why didn't you call me?" He looked away, unable to handle the confrontation. "I went down to the canteen to eat lunch too," I added. His eyes widened, and he told me that the canteen was for the client and we weren't allowed to eat there. Well, that's what happens when they forget about the third assistant. I ended up with *the* good lunch of salmon, roast potatoes, and a fruit plate instead of the BLT sandwiches or whatever they had.

Apart from the lunch drama, nothing else really happened. The orchestra played continuously until we wrapped up. At the very end of the day, the famous composer posed for the photographers. We moved the chairs from the background for the shoot, and then we called it a day.

The shoot continued on Sunday outside the Tate Modern. I wore sneakers and light layers under my coat, thinking we'd be working indoors again. It was freaking cold, and my feet quickly turned to ice. I shivered throughout the day on set, and my hands weren't spared either when I was sent to clean the glass on the Millennium Bridge with a bucket of water and a cloth. For two hours, I dipped my bare hands in the cold water, attempting the impossible task of removing frozen gums and other stubborn stains from the entrance of the bridge. I felt miserable washing the glass in front of the public. The bridge was jam-packed with tourists, neatly dressed for their visit to one of the largest museums of modern and contemporary art in the world. Being assigned to this task felt like an undeserved punishment. My hands turned red and stiff, hurting from the cold. Whenever a wave of pain hit me, I reminded myself of the £400 I'd earn for the day.

Sometime later, I was asked to switch tasks and rake the fallen branches on the frozen soil between the bald trees in front of the museum. The creative director believed the ground would look nicer on the footage if it appeared freshly hoed rather than dry and frozen. I agreed, but it was quite a challenge to hoe the hard soil with freezing hands. Nonetheless, I did my best. This activity somewhat warmed me up, and eventually, I was grateful for it. The irony? Neither the soil nor the bridge made it into the final cut of the video, which I watched months after we finished the project. On the bright side, I earned nearly double my rent in just two days—by far the highest-paid job I've done so far.

April 2014

Miami Fashion Film Festival

I wrote, produced, directed, and edited a fashion video that premiered at the Miami Fashion Film Festival in September 2014. Quinn was with me on this project. He styled our Net-A-Porter girl, Amanda, in high-end fashion from head to toe. Amanda was supermodel quality with a doll-like face, long thick brown hair, buttermilk skin, a statuesque figure, and OMG, those legs! Her long, lithe legs were like an art piece that made me feel bad about my short, shapeless stems.

I managed to bring three friends to help with the camera work and acting, and I found a talented makeup artist through an online casting. Unfortunately, neither my assistant nor Quinn's showed up in the morning, and they didn't even inform us that they wouldn't be coming. Despite this setback, we had enough people to proceed. We shot on the street outside an upscale hotel in the West End. The hotel manager tried to chase us away several times, but we managed to complete the shoot without any major complications or police intervention.

A huge thank you to my friend who bravely donned a bellboy costume and acted in public—he was brilliant! I also rented a better camera with a tripod to shoot from two different angles, but we didn't end up using it because the cameraman was unfamiliar with this model, making it money down the drain.

I spent two weeks editing the video, and my ex-flatmate's mate, a sound designer in Australia, completed it by adding the sounds and voices. He is a legend!

Altogether, I spent about £500 on this project, which means I'll have to cut back on expenses next month to be able to pay the rent and bills.

Also, I have to tell you this because it's just uncanny. Our cab driver to the hotel location was the late Alexander McQueen's cousin.

We all gathered in my flat for breakfast, getting the model and the actor ready in their outfits. When I called a taxi to take us to the hotel, the driver noticed our beautiful model and the camera equipment. He struck up a conversation with me, sitting in the front seat, asking what we were up to. I told him we were shooting a fashion video, and then he said, "Ya may kna me cousin, the late Alexander McQueen." My jaw dropped. At first, I thought he was kidding, but then he shared family stories in a Cockney accent, half of which I could barely understand. He even showed me his niece's drawings on his phone, mentioning she wanted to be an artist and asking for advice on her career path. It was tough to respond since I'm still figuring out my own path, but I managed to give some nice comments. I took this meeting as a sign that this project was meant to be. Wow, what a day!

May 2014

I strolled down to Gate Picturehouse cinema in Notting Hill to watch the fashion documentary "Advanced Style". It was a Monday, my day off, and I love taking advantage of the half-price tickets. There's something delightfully odd about hitting the cinema at 2 p.m. on a weekday. Before the movie started, I couldn't resist popping into the comic book store across the road for a dose of inspiration. Tucked away in the back, they had a treasure trove of old fashion magazines like Vogue, i-D, and Dazed & Confused. Flipping through those glossy pages always sparks my imagination. And of course, no trip to the neighbourhood is complete without a browse through Retro Woman, where I've scored some incredible deals on second-hand designer labels. From Marc Jacobs to Chanel, there's always a gem waiting to be discovered. It's become a little tradition of mine to treat myself to something nice with my babysitting money whenever I'm in the area.

The movie was absolutely charming! Observing these wonderfully stylish elderly women in New York and immersing myself in their lives for an hour was truly the highlight of my recent experiences. Emotions surged within me, from joy to vulnerability, as they evoked memories of my grandmothers and the feelings I cherished around them as a child. My heart overflowed with love. Additionally, the film provided me with insights, highlighting how far I've traveled from my birth country and the disconnect I've experienced from my past.

As the movie drew to a close, the rain outside stopped, and sunlight filtered through the clouds, casting golden sparkles over the streets and buildings. It was a breathtaking sight! Stepping out of the theatre, I pushed the door open, and the sun's rays enveloped my face, lending me a luminous glow. It felt like ages since I last basked in sunlight, with most days being cloaked in clouds recently.

May 2014 - October 2014

Personal Assistant for an A-list designer

In this role, I often feel like I'm living out scenes from "The Devil Wears Prada." Much like Andy, I find myself juggling cups of coffee in one hand while walking the dog with the other, for example. I've noticed that I'm not encouraged to ask questions, but rather expected to anticipate my boss's needs without being told. If something goes awry or if I can't find something that's out of place, the blame falls on me. I have to act quickly and promptly at all times without knowing what exactly I am supposed to do.

I stumbled upon an online job ad for a Personal Assistant Intern position to a fashion designer, and my eyes lit up with excitement. This job felt like the perfect fit for me. I was detail-oriented, a self-starter, respectful, reliable, and I had excellent organizational skills. That night, I stayed up late updating my CV and crafting a candid, ambitious cover letter. The next day, I was invited for an interview with Moses, and two days later, I received an email from Laoise—a name I couldn't pronounce and wondered if it belonged to a boy or a girl?—with exciting news.

"Hi Zsofi,

Thank you for your email, Moses said it was an absolute pleasure to meet you and that he feels you would suit the role of personal assistant intern very well.

Therefore, I would love to offer you the position!"

I immediately quit my nanny job and submitted my application for housing benefit to help me get through the summer. Before starting the new job, which was a week after the interview, I googled the designer, let's call him Jim "Jimmy" Kendal, and checked out his previous collections online.

From that point on, I've found myself back in East London every day, in a spacious and chaotic amalgamation of three spaces: an office, a fashion studio, and a storeroom, all rolled into one. On one side of the room is the office team, including designers, PR personnel, sales staff, and accountants. On the opposite side is the production team, with wide pattern cutting tables, sewing machines, and metal storage units filled with fabric rolls, paper rolls, dummies, and various other tools scattered about. Portable clothes rails loaded with JK designs, hangers, boxes, and plastic containers dot the space haphazardly.

The design intern table, where I am seated, is positioned at the back of the room, next to an open storage area filled with a chaotic jumble of items, along with more boxes and plastic bags whose contents remain a mystery to me. From my vantage point, I have a clear view of Jim Kendal's desk, which is separated from the rest of the team by clothing rails. He often calls out my name from there: "Soophie!"

I was also handed a two-page manual containing various guidelines and information, including:

- Key email addresses and passwords.
- Specifications regarding the desired font type and size for electronic communications.
- A warning regarding spam emails.

- Jim's address and the nearest bus stops to his house.
- A list of key employees, some of whom were no longer with the company.
- Details about Jim Kendal's private and confidential second job with a prominent designer that must not be mentioned to anyone outside the office; I am going to refer to it as M.E.
- Specific coffee orders for Jim Kendal (large flat white with an extra shot), Kirstie (the Managing Director, who preferred a regular skinny latte with a spoon of sugar), and Alba (the dog), along with Alba's daily routine and feeding guidelines.
- Information about petty cash.

During my first week, I took the time to get acquainted with the new email system, fulfill tasks like fetching coffee for the designer and the Managing Director, purchasing stationery supplies, attempting to feed the dog (who wasn't keen on following me to the kitchen where his bowl was), and getting to know the other interns. I also made a habit of jotting down notes on my hand and wrist until I remembered to carry a piece of paper with me whenever Jim called me to his desk. When I asked the designer about signing a confidentiality agreement, he simply laughed. I guess it meant a "no".

I couldn't contain my excitement when I spotted the sleek new iMacs everyone was using. However, I was given a vintage iMac instead, which I had to unearth from the cluttered storage area myself. As I began working on it, I quickly discovered technical issues—the software didn't run smoothly, and it seemed to struggle. It only lasted for two weeks before crashing suddenly. It went to sleep one night and never woke up again. I took it to a repair service near Paddington, where they deemed it beyond repair due to its poor condition. From then on, I continued to use my own computer, a 13-inch sticker-covered MacBook, which I brought with me to the office every day until the end of my internship.

I was promised a monthly travel expense allowance of £150, along with an additional £100. However, in reality, I only received reimbursement for £120, the actual cost of my travel card. This discrepancy was just the beginning of many frustrations that would plague me over the next few months, causing headaches, insecurities, and anxieties about my financial situation. To make ends meet, I took on a one-day nanny job and continued babysitting on weekends. However, this additional work left me feeling exhausted and drained, to the point where I began to care less about my manners, which surprisingly turned out to be an asset at the company.

Oh, and I have no idea about my working hours. While some interns and coworkers begin to leave around six, others stay until much later, sometimes as late as eight or nine. Unsure of the expected departure time, I settle on leaving around 7:00 or 7:30, aiming for a middle ground.

Jim Kendal (JK)

Jim is a good-looking, enigmatic man in his late thirties, who is addicted to cigarettes and coffee and is a workaholic—a trait common in the fashion industry. Fashion is not just our passion; it is our lifestyle—a silent force that we live and breathe.

He wears black jeans, creased T-shirts, and white sneakers most of the time. His speech, often rapid and laced with dialect, poses a challenge for me to comprehend at times. To make sense of the clutter of sounds that I heard, I try to catch the keywords and build the meaning around them. If I am not certain about what he said, I ask back, which annoys him. Generally, when people turn to him with questions, it annoys him. Period.

Jim has a staffie, called Alba, who shadows him wherever he goes. If he is at his table, then Alba is sure to be found at his feet or occasionally resting in the chair next to him. If Jimmy leaves the studio or just pops out to the restroom, Alba is right behind him. However, this allegiance occasionally results in comical mishaps, such as Alba getting inadvertently trapped on one side of the closed door when she doesn't pick her legs fast enough to keep up with Jim. She is a quiet and well-behaved dog. It takes some time for her to adjust to my presence and recognise me as her caretaker, a process that requires patience and trust-building, particularly given my initial apprehension around pit bulls.

My new boss often sends me to buy painkillers for him. God knows what he is up to outside the office that makes him want to start the day with coffee and painkillers.

I was still a rookie at the company when he sent me to buy Solpadeine for the first time. I checked the product online and snapped a photo with my phone to ensure I got the right one. He insisted on the soluble version, so I jotted down a reminder on a post-it and stuck it to my phone screen. I was meticulous. I believed it was a straightforward task: go to the nearest pharmacy, buy the product, and return. But things got complicated when the checkout girl asked,

"Solpadeine Plus or Max?" I tried to decide on my own to avoid bothering Jimmy, who never answered my calls. It was like he was testing me, making it difficult to do my job well.

"What's the difference between the two?" I asked.

"Solpadeine Max is stronger," the checkout girl explained, reading off the key contents from the packages. I only caught the word "caffeine"; the rest was medical gibberish to me.

Unable to reach Jimmy after two failed calls and a text message, I stepped out of the line to figure out my next move. Buying the wrong product would only make him hate me more. Then I came up with the idea of hiding my caller ID and try again. And guess what? It worked! He picked up the phone and tersely instructed me to get the stronger one before hanging up without a "thanks" or "bye." Mission solved, for now.

Kirstie

Kirstie, the Managing Director (MD), exudes a power-woman persona. She is the big boss who manages everything in the office, including Jimmy. She is vocal, cunning, and dominant. If she was a fairy tale character, she would be the Evil Godmother. She commands the head of a long rectangular desk, flanked by Moses, the sales guy, and Laoise, the PR girl. Whenever she is in, you can find her typing away at her laptop and sipping the coffee I fetched for her from her favourite artisan shop on Broadway Market. It is just a ten-minute walk from the office, and I am practically a regular there, sometimes making the trip three times a day for Kirstie and Jimmy's caffeine fix. Kirstie loves her latte with a spoonful of sugar and frequently requests an extra shot in the mix.

She has a giant schnauzer, a young and disobedient dog that nobody likes much. She doesn't bring him to the office often, likely because he barks a lot, but when she does, she usually asks me to walk him.

One time, during a coffee run, I decided to bring the dog along to kill two birds with one stone: walk the dog and get coffee. The dog pulled me hard on the leash, hurting my wrist, and jumped around, barking all the way to the coffee shop. I figured he wanted to stop at the park instead of just walking by it, which had been my original plan too. I intended to stop at the park for a bit before hitting the coffee shop, but after just two minutes of walking him, I was already exhausted and changed my mind. I just wanted to bring him back to Kirstie ASAP. If this dog were a man, he would be one of those good-looking guys who are empty inside, self-centred, and arrogant, with no respect for women's needs. An attention seeker. A narcissist. A taker. A dog bitch!

The coffee shop was dog-friendly, so I brought him inside, and a very embarrassing thing happened. The dog stood on two legs to reach the food placed in front of the counter, knocking down the entire shelf with delicious homemade cakes, muffins, and sandwiches. I managed to pull him away with only a chocolate muffin and a tuna sandwich in his mouth. Luckily, many of the items landed on the lower, empty shelf without being touched by the dog. I was ready to pay for the loss from the petty cash, but the girl just said, "Don't worry about it." I guess because I came there so often, she had mercy on me. I couldn't stop saying sorry for days after that whenever I came in to pick up the morning coffees.

Soon after I started to work here, I sent her an email, cc-ing Moses, who was responsible for the petty cash, to ask about the reimbursement for my monthly travel card and the additional £100 they had offered along with my travel expenses. They didn't reply. After waiting for a week, I walked to their desk to politely ask Kirstie face to face. As soon as I brought up the money, she looked back down at her screen and waved me away with a set of matte black fingernails, saying in a discouraging manner, "I am in the middle of something." She had a way of blanking people out when they said something she didn't care to hear. I looked at Moses for help, but he started click-clacking on the keyboard as soon as our eyes met. Acknowledging how "busy" Kirstie was, I sent her another email asking when would be a good time to discuss the offer, but she never responded. Reading her body language, I realised this wasn't about her being busy; it was about her not wanting to pay. During my time here, I also observed that she only talked to me if she wanted something from me. If I wanted something from her, she was always unavailable.

At the end of the second week, I took some time to think. I scanned the studio and my co-workers with mixed feelings, and asked myself, "Is it worth staying?" I could have just finished the day or, better yet, stood up then and walked away from those non-transparent people. I bet they wouldn't even have noticed. If I had left, I would have relieved myself of the mental and emotional stress that came with a toxic work environment.

If you were in my shoes, what would you do? What would motivate you to stay?

According to Stephen R. Covey, author of The 7 Habits of Highly Effective People "*Trust is the highest form of human motivation. But it takes time and patience, and it doesn't preclude the necessity to train and develop people so that their competency can rise to the level of that trust.*"

I am genuinely excited to work for an A-list designer, to be part of the creative atmosphere, and to build professional contacts. I want to soak it all up. So, I'll swallow my pride and stay. I promise myself that I will try not to be carried away by the bullshit I may experience here and stay loyal to who I am. I am wise and bold, and I'll figure things out.

P.S. I will take them as seriously as they take me. For the sake of balance.

Cecile and Victor

Cecile and Victor, the senior designers at Jim Kendal, have been at the company for two months. Both hailed from France, speaking with charming French accents.

Victor, a habitual smoker, has a knack for flicking his cigarette butts carelessly on the street. In the office, he often teams up with Jimmy for smoke breaks at the window. The large window behind Jimmy's desk opens onto a tiny roof between our office and the neighbouring building. They love climbing out to enjoy a cigarette or two under the open sky.

When I started my internship, there was another young intern at our table, but I only saw her once. I wondered what happened to her until Laura told me that Victor had stolen the intern's iPhone charger. She didn't come back to work after that.

There isn't much to say about Cecile. She loves wearing her Céline fur-trimmed slide sandals in the office. And perhaps I tell you that once, she organised a party at her apartment and even printed out the flyers in the office, so all of us knew about it. However, she only invited a selected few, and I wasn't one of them. Later that day, we were sitting next to each other on the bus—Cecile, Victor, and me—heading home after work. She opened up about how drained she was and mentioned wanting to cancel the party. I pretended not to know about it and told her I couldn't wait to drop onto my bed and be horizontal. Cecile then asked if I was coming to her party (so now I was invited?), and I just said I would think about it. I lived in West London and knew that once I got home, I wouldn't want to commute back to East London again. It was simply too far. Cecile understood, but Victor tried to persuade me, saying, "You can meet other people who work in fashion. It's a good opportunity to network and maybe find your next job at the party!" I knew these parties were mostly about drinking and drugs, not meeting sensible people who could offer me a paid job. Besides, I wasn't looking for a new job just yet. I really just wanted to get comfy at home, sink into the sofa with some hot soup, and hang out with my flatmates. So that's exactly what I did.

Liberty

Liberty, Libby, or L for short, plays a crucial role between design and production. Jim relies on her heavily, and it seems she has been working there for a long time, knowing her way around. However, she can be very superficial and phony, secretly bullying anyone who doesn't pay attention to her perceived dramas. She is always spinning, twirling, rushing, and just loud all the time, constantly calling attention to herself. She is quite the performer.

Over the summer, she made sure the entire office knew she was on a liquid diet for ten days and forbade anyone from eating near her. Victor enjoyed teasing L and often cheered along with her performances. It was unclear whether he did it for entertainment or to channel his annoyance, but they seemed to get along well. Victor would tease Libby with chocolates and curry when he ate next to her, and she wouldn't say a word to him. However, she made everyone else feel guilty for bringing food near her.

During one of our collective meetings at Jim's desk to discuss upcoming events and calendar dates, Alison, the digital designer with her long face and baby-smooth skin, softly raised concerns about certain dates. This sparked the opportunity in L to slide a post-it note over to Victor, dubbing Alison "Madame!" while stifling sniggers. Perhaps she did this because Alison had previously indulged in a pesto grilled cheese sandwich in front of her computer screen, just two seats away from Libby. Alternatively, it could be that Libby was just naturally mean.

During my internship, I witnessed her tears on several occasions. Once, she was upset because Jim denied her request for holiday during the busiest season, prompting her to seek hugs and sympathy from everyone in the office. Another time, she cried because Kirstie confronted her about an unauthorised email she had sent out. And then there were moments when her tears flowed because she couldn't adhere to her liquid diet due to our consumption of food in the studio.

Antonio

Antonio, who works at menswear, is the most tastefully stylish, handsome, gay employee at Jim Kendal, yet his demeanor remains somewhat mysterious.

After I approached him for help finding the fabric swatches Jimmy requested, he simply muttered something under his breath and briskly walked away without giving me a moment's attention. I decided to follow him.

"Hey, why are you walking away?" I confronted him, but he remained silent. "Antonio, I'm not here to bother you. Jimmy sent me to ask about the swatches. Do you know where they are?" I continued, trailing behind him.

Suddenly, he turned around and swiftly passed by me, avoiding eye contact as he flew out the door. *What was his problem?* I couldn't fathom his behaviour. Later, when he returned, he dropped a large box at my feet.

"Whatever you're looking for might be in here. If it's not, I have no clue where else it could be," he said, helping me sift through the box's contents.

Amidst our search, he lamented the disorganisation since their recent move and pointed out the team's tendency to misplace items.

"Why are you helping me now?" I inquired.

"These are what Jimmy asked for," he replied, pulling out some silver and orange fabric pieces without directly addressing my question. "I'll take them to him. Just put everything back in the box and leave it on my desk," he instructed.

"Okay," I nodded, complying with his directive.

Fun fact

Antonio is a boy's name of Spanish, Italian origin meaning "priceless one". I read it on namberry.com.

One time, I let slip a compliment about his sharp appearance on a particular day, but his response was to simply turn his back and walk away, once again. It seemed my kindness left him unaffected. I figured that he might either be socially awkward or battled with emotional immaturity. Two weeks later, I discovered that Antonio was leaving for Savile Row, and the reason he had looked particularly sharp that day was because he had just attended a job interview. Ultimately, he would be departing from all of us at JK.

Over the months, I got to know a handful of other employees at the company. Most of them were friendly and dedicated workers. We formed a small international team of around 30 people, with approximately 20 being permanent employees and the rest of us were unpaid interns.

Interns

I share my desk with five other interns: Gracie, Laura, Kid, Vanessa, and Ido. We cram ourselves around two small desks pushed together. Space is tight, and when I start feeling crowded or distracted by the clutter around me, I often migrate to the end of a neighbouring table where the sewing machines are humming away. The seamstress ladies don't seem to mind my occasional presence.

Gracie and Laura

Gracie and Laura are hired by Kamila, JK's in-house textile designer. Both of them are in college, completing a summer internship before their final years. They are eight years younger than me, but since everyone thinks I am 24, they appear to be only three years younger. Despite the age difference, we get along really well. Kamila is super nice, and the girls love working with her. Sometimes, I wish Kamila was my boss too!

Laura lives outside London and commutes to work by train without complications. Sometimes, she isn't in because she also works part-time at a café. And Gracie is originally from Scotland. She rented a cheap bedroom near Alexandra Palace, but it turned out her landlady had a drinking problem that made her feel unsafe. After just three weeks in London, she was looking for a new place to stay. So we made a deal: I shared my room with her until Fashion Week in September, and she helped me out with the bills in return.

The girls ask me every day how I am and what mood Jimmy is in. Often, they can read the answer on my face and forgive me if I don't use words to express myself. They know I am under more pressure.

Because I have access to confidential information and aspects of Jimmy's private life—to a certain level, not everything—they are curious about what I know, but never mean-spirited.

We often laugh at my English towards the end of the day when I am more inclined to speak non-existent words out of exhaustion. Sometimes, I turn to them for help with translation. You have to know that I always have a vocabulary page open on my laptop, from the beginning to the end of the day, next to three other important tabs: Jim Kendal's email, my work email, and Google.

During our internship, I passed some important contacts in the industry to Gracie and Laura, which they might have wanted to use to further their careers after graduation. And, of course, I saved a few (many!) contacts for myself too.

Kid

I don't know if it's his real name or just a nickname, but he's Kid, a very talented menswear graduate from Northern England. He joined us in mid-June as a design intern. Kid is short and fragile-looking, with a Britney Spears face tattoo on his left arm and a stunning portfolio under it. Despite his talent, he is given vapid, small tasks that neither help him gain professional experience nor utilise his exceptional creativity. He sits at our table across from me, and I often see him disinterested. He lights up when we, the girls, chat with him, and for a while, he seems happier as a person. But as a designer, he is so out of alignment that it strains his health. He catches the flu in the middle of summer, travels home to Wales to recover, and never returns.

We became friends on Facebook, and a year later, I saw that he had become the new menswear designer at River Island. I was genuinely happy for him.

Ido

Huh, it's hard to write about someone who I don't want to write about...

Vanessa

Vanessa is the PR intern, but she only stays for a month because of a new law limiting unpaid internships to thirty days. The government's order aims to combat modern fashion slavery in London. Would it work, though? Nicky, the Production Manager, had worked for free at JK for nine months before she finally received a salary. The girls are committed to staying for three months, and I am willing to stay as long as possible. The truth is, fashion thrives on free labor, and companies would rather have new helpers every month than hire someone permanently in a paid role. From the interns' point of view, many one-month experiences don't look attractive on a CV. So, law or no law, if you want to climb the career ladder, you stick around for longer than a month.

Ido

Let me try again...

Ido is like a slug, slithering into everything that isn't his business. He exudes arrogance and superficiality, dishing dirt behind people's backs while pretending to be their best friend.

What really pissed me off was his attitude when he decided he needed to manage me. One time, he instructed me to come to Jimmy's desk to remove the empty mugs and takeout boxes during a break in a meeting. I reminded him that, firstly, we were both interns, and he could ask me to help but not order me around. Secondly, I explained that I was among the last to leave the studio every day and always tidied Jim's work area before going home. If Jim stayed later than me, I cleaned up in the morning before he arrived. This was a routine I followed, which Ido hadn't noticed because he usually went home earlier and came to work later than I did. I was a very good PA, period. Thirdly, I pointed out that Jim would call me if he needed help with cleaning up, so there was no need for Ido to practice his control issues.

So, I told him, "If you're bothered by the takeout boxes, lift them up yourself and chuck them in the bin."

It seemed ridiculous to get worked up over such a small thing, but it was Ido's approach that pulled the trigger, not the mugs. He finally gave me the opportunity to release some of the tension I was holding against his manipulative behaviour. Jimmy overheard my unpleasant tone and asked if everything was okay (no, it was not!). I simply said, "Yes, we can sort it out between us." It was the first time he heard me raise my voice, and he was very surprised, but I knew he was on my side. He didn't like Ido either. *We didn't like Ido.*

At 26, he is the closest in age to me among the interns. An MA student in menswear design from Israel, he traveled to London solely for his internship at Jim Kendal. Apparently Jim Kendal's design is held in high regard in his country, and Ido was thrilled when he received the placement offer. Upon joining us as a pattern cutting intern, he quickly perceived me as the key liaison between the interns and the design team. He started appearing at my desk more often, inviting me to lunch and offering to walk Alba, claiming he loved dogs and wanted to help me. *What made him think I needed help?* Then he pulled up a chair at our table, attempting to integrate into our "tribe" and prying into my work. I gave him brief answers to his nosy questions as the girls and I collectively picked up on his sly tactics. We kept our interactions with him superficial. Soon enough, he realised he was not exactly welcome at our table. Gracie and Laura didn't hold back their feelings, openly expressing their irritation with him. So, he changed tactics and started approaching me when I was alone, attempting to coax me into a private conversation that I kept postponing until he eventually spilled. He wanted me to put in a good word for him with the French team and ask them to move him up to the design team. Kid was gone by this point, much to our disappointment, and Ido knew the "Frenchies" (= people from France according to Catalina) were looking for a new assistant. He claimed he was too shy to ask them directly and suggested that they would listen to me because I was nice. What nonsense! I told him if he wanted something, he had to go after it himself. And he did! Soon after, he became a permanent fixture at our table, much to our secret dismay. From then on, we were careful about the information we shared within our "tribe" until Ido mustered the courage to slide his way over to sit between Cecile and Victor at the big designers' desk. This is when he started to become cockier and acted superior to all the other interns. However, Jimmy remained true to himself and kicked Ido out of meetings where he sneaked in uninvited.

Here's the thing about Jim: he is a Scorpio, a water sign. He is a sensitive man, not comfortable showing vulnerability, and his way of protecting himself includes stinging others who invade his space. He tends to emotionally react rather than consciously respond. His emotions at work are a mix of stress, frustration, anger, and more stress. His language can be very raw and unfiltered if he chooses so. He rarely speaks to the interns, except for me, but there was a time when he unexpectedly thanked the students for their hard work. I don't understand why he is embarrassed about being gentle in front of us. Maybe he interprets kindness a sign of weakness? He is regularly in a mood that makes us, his employees (paid and unpaid), think twice about approaching him. He is good at creating a fight or flight situation.

***

My first month was neurotic. One of the pattern cutting interns leaned over me and whispered "He's coming!" into my ear when he spotted Alba at the door, which meant that Jim was not far behind. It happened on my second day and I didn't understand why he did that. Was I supposed to be intimidated by Jim? Because I wasn't.

As I took over the assistant email account, CVs for the PA intern position were still trickling in, but I quietly deleted them. *Too late, everyone, I'm already here.* Most of my time was spent in front of the computer, sending out emails to key contacts to introduce myself as Jim Kendal's new PA. I diligently monitored Jim's mailbox, filtering out all the spam. He was inundated with sex-related ads—online sex, sex toys, and pharmacy ads for painkillers and Viagra. You have no idea how many messages from Jessica's and Lolita's I destroyed in cyberspace each morning before reading a work-related email.

During the first week, Jimmy gestured towards the seamstress area and mentioned he wanted lights. Initially, I didn't grasp his meaning until I overheard the seamstress ladies complaining about the dim lighting they had to work in. It became clear they needed additional lights to better see their work at the sewing machines.

Just a week before I started working, JK had relocated, leading to the sudden realisation that the new studio lacked adequate lighting despite its decade-long tenure. I was asked to scour the internet for artificial light sources, gathering ideas and price ranges to present to Jim. However, I was unaware of the budget or the specific type of lamps he had in mind—whether desk lamps, floor lamps, or hanging lamps. Jim was willing to review my research but didn't provide any feedback. When I later inquired if he still wanted the lamps, he ignored my question. Assuming he would have responded if he needed further assistance, I didn't press the matter.

Two weeks later, four boxes were delivered to the office that Laoise had ordered. They contained tall floor lamps that bore no resemblance to any of the lamps I had listed. Laoise eagerly began assembling the lamps without checking the instructions, displaying disorganisation as she opened all the boxes and mixed up the parts. Sensing the chaos, I rushed to her side and offered my assistance. After grabbing the instructions to decipher the parts, we managed to assemble one lamp in twenty minutes. And then Laoise left me with "You can finish the rest," and returned to her desk without thanking me for my help or caring if I managed to assemble the remaining three lamps alone.

There was also a stylist with a huge fake smile who regularly showed up at our office because Jim was collaborating with her for the upcoming Presentation. She tried to push Victor and me out to make room for her friends in the industry. "Do you need a new menswear designer? I might know some people. And a PA - also might know someone," she wrote to Jim in an email. Insecurity swamped me at first, then the feeling grew into fear as soon as I read Jim's response later that day, "Hiya. Maybe." I realised that I could be replaced in the blink of an eye.

For the next couple of days, I walked around like a catatonic, feeling sorry for myself and worrying about what the future might bring: losing a great opportunity, the loss of my humility, more job searches, and restarting as a failure. I was deeply disappointed in people and their bitchy behaviour. But then, suddenly, the warrior within me woke up: *I've come far for this! I am staying!* I had endured years of discrimination, being overlooked, belittled, and unpaid in London. I had lowered myself to the level of becoming a recipient of state benefits just to work in the fashion industry, and this girl thought she could push me out? No! I was determined to protect my position. I didn't know how, but I trusted it would work out.

By the way, before you think I used to read all of Jim's emails, I didn't. I did respect his privacy—though, to be fair, he never explicitly asked for it, so I was cheeky at times. Wouldn't you have been? In reality, Jim's email storage filled up within days, and I had to delete his earlier correspondence to prevent incoming ones from bouncing back. I read his emails to make sure I wasn't deleting anything important or unanswered and to remind him about emails he kept postponing. In this particular case with the stylist, the reason I got drawn to her email was the subject line, "BABY XX," and the first line, "HOW ARE YOU SAUSAGE?" in all caps, which made me think her email address had been hacked. So, I ran a quick check to decide whether to toss or keep it.

The stylist, of course, didn't know I had read her message. The next time she came to the office, I restrained my kindness—one of my quintessential qualities. I didn't smile back at her, I didn't offer her a drink, and I certainly didn't lend her my flash drive when she needed to copy some images to print on Bob Marley, one of our perpetually jamming printers.

"Sophie, can I borrow your USB?" she asked.

"Sorry, forgot it at home," I lied.

"Who else has one?"

"Dunno."

***

The studio is in a three-story block above a coffee shop that quickly turned into my favourite place to kill time. It is a really cool place, filled with hipsters, artists, and a creative vibe all around. The smell of coffee in the air, the sound of the espresso machine, the music, and the murmur of people in the background are all things I cherished.

One morning, I waited in line to pick up a soy cappuccino, until someone from the office arrived with the key. Cecile was already there, sipping some green juice while rapidly swiping on her iPhone and talking to someone in French. She waved at me with her bright orange fingernails. I nodded back with a smile and unintentionally started eavesdropping on a conversation behind me.

A girl with a strong Spanish accent was speaking loudly about the mystery of British guys. Her voice danced between drama and comedy as she tried to name things and feelings in English but struggled, so she described them instead and one simple sentence turned into five complicated ones.

Mediterranean people speak with immense passion—truly, a lot of it! In just a few minutes, they can express a full range of emotions that an average British person might take a lifetime to experience.

By the time I reached the counter, I realised I was smiling without even thinking about it. The guy behind the counter smiled back as he took my order. I couldn't help but notice how handsome his arms were when he placed the paper cup of latte in front of me, topped with a chocolate heart sprinkle. And so, our innocent summer flirtation began, marked by countless smiles and blushes every time I passed by the café.

***

Alba presented another challenge for me. Having never owned a dog before, I was given clear instructions on what and when to feed her, but it never crossed my mind that walking her would also be part of my responsibilities. It simply didn't occur to me that she needed to go out several times a day to relieve herself on the grass. So, I learned the hard way, enduring a series of embarrassing pee accidents until I finally realised that when she came to my desk and sat in front of me, it was her way of telling me it was time for a walk. *Why hadn't anyone mentioned this to me?*

She was a quiet, patient dog—I never heard her bark, whine, growl, sigh, or groan. I couldn't be mad at her when she accidentally peed on the stairs as we hurried outside. She just couldn't hold it in any longer, and it happened. Unfortunately, it happened right in front of the handsome barista, who was on his way up to the first floor where the gents' room was. He kindly offered to help clean up, but I couldn't accept. I wiped up the yellow puddle with paper towels I hurriedly grabbed from the ladies' room, praying he wouldn't come back down while I was doing it.

There were many other PAs before me who had already looked after Alba, and at the beginning, I was just another stranger in her life that she was required to accept. Only later did I realise what a precious dog she was, an old wise soul. It was actually me who needed to earn her trust, not the other way around. Soon after the first month of struggles, I started to bond with her. I paid closer attention to her and learned to embrace her personality. I began to enjoy taking her out on coffee runs and "pee" walks. I tried not to rush back to the office and would linger outside a bit longer, playing chase with her in the park or basking in the sunshine. London Fields was just a stone's throw away, making it the perfect spot for our little escapes. However, Alba wasn't as keen on staying outdoors as I was. She was very attached to Jim and preferred to head back to the studio as soon as she was done with her necessary dog things.

Monday, 2nd June

I feel much more confident now that I've survived the first month without being replaced. Still making mistakes, still learning. Most importantly, I'm continuously enriching my vocabulary about professional communication and learning to use new business expressions. I'm also picking up a few words from the textile and production team. Gracie and Laura, for example, introduced me to Mr. "fused" and Mrs. "screen-printed" and explained what happens to the fabric in each process. They even let me cut fabric strips for them. You know, when you run the scissors down lengthwise from the top to the bottom on a large piece of fabric, that feeling is so satisfying! They know I love it, so they call me to do it if I'm around. They're such legends!

Tuesday, 3rd June

In the morning, before anyone else arrived, except for Jim and Alba, I took the opportunity to briefly discuss Jim's plans for the coming week. He agreed to reschedule a few appointments and asked me to block out all-day slots in his calendar for the following week so he could focus entirely on the collection before Presentation Day on the 15th. He emphasised that starting Tuesday next week, he wouldn't be available for anything or anyone. Those dates were now locked in. Period.

It was also a good time to ask him to let me in a little and cooperate with me so I could do my job better. I requested him to give me 5 minutes in the morning and 5 minutes in the evening to run through his schedule, emails, invitations, and anything else necessary. I borrowed the "5 minutes in the morning, 5 minutes at night" strategy from a video featuring Lindsay Lohan's PA that I stumbled upon on YouTube. It's the best advice I've found for dealing with highly occupied power bosses.

Thursday, 5th June

Many of us stayed late at the office, swamped with work. The Presentation was in three weeks, and there was an awful lot to do. Our fitting model had just finished her work for the day and stormed out of the studio, waving goodbye to no one. Then Jimmy called me to his desk.

"Sophie, can you buy me a keychain?" he handed me his credit card.

"Pardon? Buy you a what?" I squinted, trying to make sense of what I heard.

He repeated the question, and this time I heard him say "kitchen." *Buy him a kitchen??* I stood there, dazed and confused for a few seconds, then tried to imitate his dialect. "Kee-tsen?" I was too tired to play the guessing game, so I asked him to write the word down on a piece of paper. Just then, Victor hailed from behind me, "Chicken!"

"You want a chicken?" I asked, eyes wide open.

"Yes!" he responded impatiently.

"What chicken?" Now I was thinking where in the world I was supposed to buy a real chicken. My brain was so fried that I suddenly thought he wanted a living, moving chicken in the studio.

"Chicken to eat," he said, looking at me like I was weird...which I was.

The penny dropped, and I was back on Earth.

"Drumsticks or breasts? Raw or cooked? Or...?" I waited for him to be more specific.

"A whole chicken to cook for dinner."

"The butcher's on Broadway Market is already closed, and the small shops in the area don't sell whole chickens or meat at all. Do you want some cooked chicken from a restaurant instead?"

"No. I'll just call Kevin (his boyfriend) and ask him what he wants. Thanks, Sophie."

He was surprisingly patient with me. I noticed that he was much nicer in the evenings when he could just focus on his design, and the pressure of the day's phone calls and meetings was over.

Friday, 6th June

You're not a true Londoner until you've thrown up in Old Street—or so I told myself to feel better about the puddle of vomit I left behind after a wild night out.

In London, pedestrians have to be adept at slaloming between two things: people and puke. I remember at the beginning, when I first moved to London, I couldn't understand why there were so many puddles of vomit on the streets. It seemed like the Brits were struck by an epidemic. Or was it part of the street art scene? If Brits call chicken tikka masala their national dish, then maybe the puddles of vomit are their national art.

Did you know?

Chicken tikka masala was adapted from Indian chicken tikka and called "*a true British national dish*" by the Foreign Secretary, Robin Cook in 2001.

***

It all started in the restroom. Sometimes I escaped from Jimmy and hid in one of the three toilet stalls where I could find some peace and quiet. I'd shut the lid of the loo and just sit on top of it for a few minutes. We shared the ladies' room with the people from the downstairs co-working space and the café customers. I had no idea whose responsibility it was to clean the loos, but they were always in acceptable condition, and it smelled nice most of the time. To whoever looked after the restrooms: thank you!

It was Friday around 7 p.m., past office hours, which meant no more emails for the day. With nothing sensible to do apart from googling my co-workers' names, I just stuck around in case Jimmy needed another "keychain" or maybe help putting a cigarette in his mouth. Just kidding. To get my body moving, I gave myself permission to leave the hustle and bustle of the office in exchange for the toilet breeze. I moseyed down to the ground floor and entered the restroom. Our fitting model was in there, touching up her makeup in the mirror. A sweet flowery scent hit my nose, though I couldn't tell if it was the model or the air freshener. I went into one of the cubicles, sat on the lid, and buried my face in my hands. The warmth of my breath took me to a safe place. I was so tired.

I was just about to settle in for an imaginary snooze when I heard a squeaky fart. Two seconds later, the door slammed, and my eyes flew open. Was it really what I heard it was? Can models fart at all? I emerged from my cubicle, splashed some cold water on my face, and stretched my body with delight. As I stretched my arms towards the ceiling, my eyes locked onto a small, narrow, white object left on the windowsill. I hoped it was what I thought it was.

Sliding the thing under the sleeve of my jumper—I was wearing leggings with an oversized jumper with no pockets—I rushed back upstairs.

When I saw Jimmy alone at his desk, I went over and asked if he needed me to stay longer or if I could go home. Almost everyone had left by then, which made me confident enough to pop the question.

"No, thank you," Jimmy said, smoking by the window.

"I'll go home in half an hour then," I said.

"You can go now," he approved, and then added, "Do you have my schedule for next week? Can you bring it here before you go?"

"Sure, I'll print it."

Victor and Cecile were back at Jimmy's desk, and I felt I should be nice and ask them as well if they needed anything before I left.

"Do you guys need something before I head home? One last tea or coffee?"

"No, Sophie, thank you," said Cecile.

"Do you really want to make tea?" asked Victor.

"Of course. Do you want one?"

"Yes, I want a thé," he affirmed in a slightly French accent.

"Black tea or herb tea?"

Victor turned toward Jimmy and asked if he wanted some tea too. Jimmy confirmed he didn't want any.

"Can you make a black thé for me?" Victor turned back to me.

"With milk and sugar?"

"Just sugar. Two spoons of sugar." He sounded out "two" with a "d" like in "deux."

I went to the kitchen and made the "thé" for Victor. On my way back, I stopped at the printer to pick up Jim's schedule, leaving it in front of them along with the mug of hot tea for Victor on the wide IKEA table where they were hunching over sketches and fabrics.

"Can you make a thé for me too, Sophie? Please?" Cecile asked unexpectedly.

I could kill her.

"Now you want a tea?" I blurted out, not in my happiest voice.

Jimmy was scanning. Victor was slurping. Cecile was begging.

"I know. I am sorry. Can I have a thé, s'il vous plaît?"

I sighed.

"What kind of tea do you want?"

"The same as Victor's but with a little bit of milk in it too."

"Jimmy, this is your last chance. Are you absolutely sure you don't want a drink?"

"Maybe a glass of water," he responded.

"Merci beaucoup, Sophie!" added Cecile.

I made Cecile's tea and brought Jimmy a glass of water. Before I finally left, I asked them to take the empty cups to the kitchen before they went home. They promised they would.

The oversized jumper, black leggings, Birkenstock strappy sandals, and my no-name backpack with my MacBook (my most expensive possession) didn't actually want to go home yet. I walked from work to Old Street, feeling energised by the TGIF vibe in Shoreditch. I wanted to be part of the atmosphere, but not alone. I called Quinn to see if he was available to meet for a drink. "Just one drink because I work tomorrow," I told him. He said he was still in the office and meeting his friend Esther later, inviting me to join them. He promised to call back in an hour.

What to do for an hour? The cafés were already closed, the streets were busy, and my backpack was heavy. I decided to sit at the bus stop near the roundabout and wait. Quinn called as promised, but it took him almost another hour to actually arrive.

"Zofi works for a famous fashion designer," Quinn said mischievously to Esther as we marched down Old Street toward a new bar run by one of Esther's friends.

"Who's the designer?" Esther asked.

"Jim Kendaaal," Quinn answered on my behalf with an unnecessary gay accent.

"It's no big deal," I shrugged.

"What do you do?" Esther wanted to know.

"She's his personal assistaaant. Now she works long hours like me, lol," Quinn chimed in.

"I'm coming straight from work," I added. You could tell just by looking at me. I felt wanky next to Esther, who was in full makeup, a leather mini skirt, and heels. Why is it okay for men to go out in day clothes while women are expected to glam up? Quinn always wears jeans, sneakers, and sweatshirts, regardless of the time of day. I bet he even goes to bed like this.

"Do you like it?" Esther continued her questioning.

"Yes, I love what I do! It's busy and sometimes overwhelming, but I love it."

My response was shallow as Esther didn't seem that interested at all.

"My boss and Quinn's boss are good friends. Quinn loves to ring me at the office with little nothings," I added, darting a glance at Quinn.

"That's not true! I really needed those samples the other day," Quinn protested.

"But you called *me*, not the PR girl. I had to speak to her on your behalf and explain why you contacted me instead of her directly."

"You're in the same office as her. It's easier like that," he shrugged.

"Not until you feel her disdainful 'tell-me-quickly-what-you-want-then-leave' look on you."

"Lol. I'm sorry. Is she really that bad?"

"She is a mean..." I began, but Quinn finished my sentence with "...bitch."

Quinn then started fiddling with his phone. I turned back to Esther and reciprocated her question.

"What do you do, Esther?"

"I study law."

I didn't expect that.

"Fantastic!" I was glad that one of us was doing something sensible.

"And I work in a nightclub on weekends."

"Are you a bartender?"

"Dancer."

I didn't expect that either.

We arrived at the bar, and Quinn stopped outside the door to light a cigarette. Suddenly, I remembered the rollie I found in the restroom and said, "Wait, let's spark this one!" I pulled it out from the side pocket of my bag.

"Zofi, I didn't know you smoked!" Quinn exclaimed.

"Somebody left it in the restroom, and I took it." Lowering my voice, I added, "Do you think it's weed?"

Quinn sniffed the rollie and shook his head.

"Aww, what a shame!" I voiced my disappointment.

Despite it not being a joint, Quinn lit it, took a drag, and handed it back to me, saying, "This is weak."

"That's good for me, then." I took a small drag and watched the smoke as I blew it out slowly.

Quinn lit one of his own cigarettes instead and most of my found cigarette ended up burning between my fingers because I didn't like the taste of it.

Btw, I don't smoke anymore. Maybe sporadically, when I'm tipsy, I take a hit off a friend's cigarette. That's all.

After we finished smoking, we were ready to enter the bar, a semi-dark hole with loud Caribbean music. Esther appeared in front of us with a look-alike friend and three cocktails. The friend was already drunk and told us to ask his boyfriend if we wanted more drinks. She pointed at an exotic-looking guy in a black uniform, gold watch, shiny rings, and even shinier earrings, who came out from behind the counter and introduced himself.

Suddenly, two lips, swimming in rich pink lip gloss, approached me. They belonged to the girlfriend, who dropped a kiss on my cheek and dragged me into a hug that smelled of almonds—was it her skin or her hair? After she kiss-napped me, we practiced small talk: "How are you? Nice to meet you. You look great! Thank you for the cocktails, etc." I already knew I would never see her, or her boyfriend, ever again after tonight, nor would I remember them at all.

The cocktails were on the house, which was great news because I didn't have an income. They arrived in fancy conch-shaped milkshake glasses with a big chunk of banana inside and whipped cream on top. The cream was so thick that I had to eat through it to reach the liquid. Let's just say these were two-in-one cocktails: dinner and drink. Despite not being a fan of whipped cream, especially not together with alcohol, I accepted the second round. And the third one, too. In the meantime, another girl joined our table with Sinéad O'Connor hairstyle, fully tattooed arms, some piercings, ripped jeans, and platforms. She seemed painfully bored and loudly complained about how much she hated being there. *Then why was she there?* I engaged in a chat with her, and we ended up speaking about her tattoos.

Then Quinn came over and asked what we were talking about.

"Her tattoos," I mumbled, spooning a mouthful of whipped cream. "She's not having a good time."

"Who is she?" Quinn asked.

"Isn't she Susan's friend?"

"No!"

Quinn whisked me away from her, and I snatched my bag from her vicinity. The next time I saw the tattooed girl, she was outside, laughing and smoking with a guy in a studded leather jacket. I guess she was not bored anymore.

Esther's friend confided in me that her ex-boyfriend was trying to win her back. She'd laid down some conditions, though. She told him that if he wanted to rekindle their romance, he needed to buy her the Chanel bag she'd been eyeing. Oh, and she was also angling for a fur coat. Poor guy. Who even were these girls, honestly? I couldn't even find a guy who would buy me a drink. Maybe I should start wearing miniskirts and make-up.

At 11 p.m., Quinn, Esther, and I left the bar. The cocktails were making my head spin as we strolled down the street. It was refreshing to be out in the open air, as fresh as it could be in Shoreditch on a Friday night, with the mix of petrol fumes, taxis darting around, cigarette smoke, and the invisible clouds of perfume that some people seemed to bathe in. I bought a can of beer at the off-license, which we shared. Quinn sprinkled some white powder into it, and we finished it off by the time we reached the club. I hadn't known we were headed to a club, but there we were.

I was drunk enough to slip in behind someone in the crowd while the doorwoman checked the stamps on people's hands. Inside, I lost sight of Quinn and Esther, but I followed some others into a room filled with smoke and muffled, monotonous noise that some might call music. The party smoke was thick, and the oxygen level low, making me feel even more intoxicated. It was like being on a different planet. I could only see a meter or two ahead, so I walked cautiously to avoid bumping into strangers. I noticed that the smoke was thinner above the floor, allowing me to see people's legs clearly if I looked down.

Esther eventually found me and pulled me to a table, where she shared her beer with me. I took a sip, but my stomach told me to stop. They wanted to check out the upstairs room, but I needed to find the bathroom first. I said I'd catch up with them, but I never made it upstairs. The whole world started spinning with me in the bathroom, and I became sick. I rushed outside to take deep breaths of cool air... and Chanel No. 5, a streak in the air left by a woman in a pink suede jacket as she passed by me. By now my vision had turned into a kaleidoscope, and the worst thing happened: I threw up in public. The breathing technique hadn't worked, but at least I was too drunk to feel shame or care about what people thought.

As soon as I started feeling a little better, I navigated myself to the bus stop to catch the N55 to Tottenham Court Road and then from there the N207 to West London. It was a 1.5-hour journey, including a 20-minute wait for the connecting bus—a nightmare when you're alone at night, drunk, and seeing double. I was determined to stay awake on the bus, making sure I didn't miss my stop. Somehow, I also managed to send a message to Quinn, letting him know I'd left. "Hi Quinn, I felt sick and left the cub on my way home.noW. Txt m3 when you get hot." We always text friends after a party to let each other know we made it home safe. I ended the night with a glass of water before collapsing onto my bed, spinning into dreams.

Chanel No. 5 - did you know?

- The world's best-selling perfume and one of the most expensive.
- It was launched in 1921 and was presented on the 5th day of the 5th month.
- The scent was created to describe the new modern, woman that traversed the boundaries between lady and mistress.
- One of its ingredients is civet. Civet is a secretion from the gland of the civet cat.

How do they get it out from the living animal?
"*Allegedly cruelly*" according to an article in The New York Times from 1973. Quote: "... the civet cats were caught in Ethiopian jungles and placed in cages barely long enough for them to turn around in. Musk oil was obtained from an external glandular sac in the genital area with a spoon after the cage door was pressed down on the animal's back to force its legs apart."

"Civet cats, who are rarely bred in captivity, are captured in the wild and held in tiny cages barely larger than their bodies, where they are kept without release in hot, smoke-filled sheds for up to fifteen years. Every ten days or so, the musk is brutally extracted from the glands of the conscious civets."

"Most of the civet now used is synthetically recreated, for ethical reasons—although we have heard that some small perfumers still secretly source the real thing..."

Saturday, 7th June

I came to work voluntarily on Saturday, which I somewhat regretted due to my slight hangover. However, I was also excited to be part of the male model casting. The good news was that I could come to work later today, so I arrived just after half past ten. I began my day by buying a green juice for myself at the café. My usual "flirt" wasn't around, probably off today. My second task was to walk up the stairs, which felt as painful and tiring as taking your first steps after a full-body workout.

As soon as I got in, I took my MacBook out of my bag and turned it on. While waiting for it to boot up, I walked to Jimmy's table to assess the mess left behind from yesterday. *Bastards! They didn't take the mugs out.* I saw a paper cup with some coffee in it, which he had probably bought this morning. I recognised the cup—it was from the coffee shop on Broadway Market. I wondered what time Jim had come to work today or if he had even gone home at all last night.

Only five of us were in the studio: Jimmy, Alba, Nicky, the creative pattern cutter lady, and me. It was a peaceful day. Jimmy acted more like a human than a fashion designer. He was friendlier and more approachable. I think I understood why he loved being in the studio earlier than any of us. The quiet space probably helped him think and see more clearly. That's the same reason I loved arriving half an hour early in the mornings. It gave me time to prepare for the day at my own pace. I tidied Jimmy's work area, emptied his bin (mostly full of crumpled paper and cigarette packs), checked if there were enough cigarettes and dog food for the day, made sure he had pens and pencils on his desk (since he tended to lose them all the time), and sharpened the pencils if they were too blunt.

A bunch of guys came in for casting between 11 a.m. and 3 p.m., slowly, one after the other. Some boys wheeled in on bicycles, others rolled in on their skateboards, and a couple of them just didn't turn up. The latter wasn't unusual after a Friday or Saturday night in London. I almost didn't turn up today either, but psst!

The guys tried on selected designs from the upcoming collection—jackets, shirts, jumpers, suits—and I was asked to take photos of them in front of the wall where I had taped white paper for a plain background. If I had known I was going to take pictures, I would have prepared the camera. Of course, the battery was dead—*Who used the camera last time?*—so I ended up taking the photos with my phone.

All the models were under 25, and while I wanted to say I was turned on by watching them drop their clothes in front of me, I just couldn't see them as sexual beings. Their tall, boyish bodies with long, bony limbs were attached to adolescent faces. There was something gayish about them. No offence! Jimmy, on the other hand, seemed to enjoy the show. He asked me to take close-ups of the models, just their heads and naked chests, which I believed served his entertainment more than the purpose of the casting. I also took a few snaps of Alba, who was watching us while sitting patiently by the side of the desk. Then suddenly, I heard this: "Who is he? Kunta Kinte?" Jimmy exclaimed and laughed, looking uncomprehendingly at a model card. *I wish I hadn't heard that.* He was checking the deck of cards I had requested from the casting director, which had been dropped off by the courier yesterday. He flipped through the cards aggressively. Something had invaded his human demeanor, and as a result, his bad side emerged again. It might have been the coffee. He'd had three cups of the usual large flat white, plus a couple of cigarettes and no food. At least, I hadn't seen him eat anything since he arrived. I hadn't eaten much either: an egg & cress triangle sandwich and a banana.

I took the last shots of a South African model at 5:30 p.m. I was proud of myself for how well I had been coping, staying focused, and looking sober. Although I was getting sleepier by the hour, I was happy that the last model was only two and a half hours late. I just had to download the last batch of photos from my phone, and then I could go home. While I was sitting in front of the computer sorting the images, somebody said "Hi!" to me. It was the model. For some reason, I heard it as "Bye!" and I said, "Thanks for coming! Bye." Then the model leaned over and asked for help with directions on the map. He said it was his first time in London. I asked where he wanted to go and if he was going to other castings. I was just being casually nice, but I didn't actually care what he said because he looked like a twelve-year-old who had lost his mum. Anyway, he said he didn't know about other castings yet but was free today. *Meaning we should go out, or what?* I told him which buses and tube lines he could take to central London. He was uncomfortably close to my face, gazing into my eyes while I spoke to him, which made me think he didn't follow. So, I quickly wrote the info on a piece of paper, handed it to him, and turned back to the computer, pretending to be busy so he would go. I could feel him standing behind me— *Why?*—so I turned around to say, "Bye. Enjoy the city!" He seemed baffled but eventually left.

I was around his age when I moved to the city alone and figured things out for myself. I believe he can do the same. London is the second most populous city in Europe after Moscow, with a little over 9 million people. When you live in a busy city with hundreds of strangers to see and meet daily, you soon start to ignore them and separate yourself emotionally and mentally. You want to save time and energy for yourself and your loved ones. There's no time for sharing yourself with the wrong people. London is about high speed, movement, changes, and power.

I don't know why I found it annoying that he asked for my help, and why I couldn't be friendlier in giving tips and guidance. Maybe because I was tired. Or maybe this is what eight years of living in London has done to me. I've felt invisible for so long that I've forgotten what it feels like when someone shows genuine interest in me.

For ladies. Are you a true Londoner?

- You do your make-up on the tube
- You wear more layers of foundation than clothes
- You go to work with wet hair
- You don't care about the rain (your hair is wet anyway)
- You wear heels and a mini skirt on your night out regardless of the temperature
- You have a gym membership card but you don't use it
- You drink at least one coffee a day from a paper cup
- You carry a Louis Vuitton handbag
- You don't wear socks
- You own a trench coat

Tuesday, 10th June

My sister called me from Hungary, complaining about the sudden temperature rise and her need to buy a new pair of sandals to match her beige linen suit (she's a teacher). It's hard to relate to her complaint when I'm still coming to work in my winter coat. Honestly, it's been winter coat season since late October in London, which means seven months of extra weight to carry on my shoulders in the form of warm layers, and I am so tired of it.

Thursday, 12th June

Nicky booked me an Uber to urgently deliver some buttons to M.E. I love these random tasks that break up the monotony of my nothing-special day! I was excited to peek inside the M.E. office, too. Feeling like I was on an important mission, I enjoyed my midday ride to the city centre. The driver, originally from Brazil, chatted with me and even gave me his cousin's restaurant business card, in case I needed a job after my internship.

When I got back to the office via public transport, I saw Jim outside the café, smoking.

"Where have you been?" he asked.

I explained that I helped Nicky by taking some buttons to M.E.

"Don't go away for too long. What if I need you when you're not here?" he asked firmly.

"You know my number," I replied. He claimed he didn't know it. "I've called you many times," I reminded him and gave him a missed call on the spot so he could finally save my digits. I'm not sure if he did, though.

Saturday, 14th June

We're all in, working from morning till night because tomorrow is the Presentation Day. I made four trips to Broadway Market today to bring coffee.

"Do you guys sleep at all?" the barista asked when she saw me for the third time with my regular order of lattes and flat whites with extra shots.

"I wish!" I exclaimed.

She wasn't there when I placed my final order of eight cups of coffee, which required a bag from the café to carry them all back to the office at once. Miraculously, I made it back without spilling a drop!

LFW Presentation - Resort Collection

We set up the clothing rails and checked all garments and accessory items to ensure they were put together correctly for the look of each model. Jimmy wanted me to be around him, but honestly, I never knew where he was in the 4-storey building, so I just stuck around at the model station with the other interns and let him find me if he needed me. After all, he knew my number now.

"Do you want to eat something before you change?" I asked one of the models because I thought she seemed shy. All the other models were grabbing a bite at the long table packed with freshly made sandwiches, curry, salad, fruits, croissants, and muffins, except for her. During the presentation, the models were going to stand still under a vibrant light installation, and it would be important for them to eat and drink before they changed into JK designs. It was going to be a long day for all of us. Eventually, the model looked at me with an arched eyebrow and said, "Do I look like I eat?" She had a point. And no, she was definitely not shy.

During the presentation, when the press arrived along with the influential and the elite of fashion, cute waiter guys circulated to serve champagne in the crowd. I sneaked away for a few minutes to explore other parts of the building and capture some photos with my phone from abstract angles. This location was really cool! We were in an abandoned wing of a large construction estate in central London.

Light, specifically designed for the show, was only installed in the area where the models were standing and where the samples of the collection were displayed.

When I returned from my little discovery trip, Kid poked me and pointed in the direction of one of the models who appeared to be unwell. And of course, it was the girl who hadn't eaten. I spotted Laoise in the crowd and ran to her for advice. Laoise then ran to Kirstie for advice, and Kirstie went behind the model to check up on her. She gave her some water and a chair to sit down. A few minutes later, Jimmy walked around with glasses of water on a tray to offer to the models standing firm and sweaty under the bright artificial lights, making himself a kind, caring gentleman in the eyes of the media.

When we returned to the studio late afternoon, there were a couple of presents and bouquets of flowers on Jimmy's table from people congratulating him on his new collection. I couldn't help but wonder, how did the flowers get here faster than we did from the presentation?

Thursday, 19th June

I inadvertently directed Jimmy to a 10 a.m. meeting that didn't actually start until 10:30. I must have misread the details in the planning book when I sent him the reminder early in the morning. He didn't bring it up in the office nor did he confront me about what a moron I was making him waste half an hour of his day, much to my relief.

Friday, 20th June

Earlier today as I returned with the collected posts from downstairs, I caught Jim playing with Alba outside on our floor. I smiled at them, but Jim suddenly stopped playing, put on a poker face, and swiftly walked into the office. *Huh?*

Monday, 23rd June

Poor Alba peed on the café doorstep. I had no idea that she was bursting when she sat next to my table, giving me the sign that she needed to go. It took me a while to find her chain behind Jim's desktop, which usually lies on one of the shelves nearby unless he's misplaced it elsewhere. Unfortunately, I didn't make it down in time, and Alba relieved herself at the door of the café, right in front of incoming customers. I apologised profusely, not knowing what else to do, and left the puddle on the stair (sorry!) before continuing our way to the park. Even though Alba was ready to head back upstairs right away, I needed a few minutes to shake off the embarrassment, so I made her follow me to the park with gentle nudges.

The next time the café manager—a young, bearded, soft-spoken but firm man—saw me with the dog, he had a word with me. He's seen me with Alba many times, knows I work upstairs, and is aware that she's not my dog. Plus, as a regular coffee customer, the entire staff has probably noticed by now how fondly we look at each other with the handsome barista. Anyway, we agreed that I'd do my best to avoid another incident and would take Alba out through the other, heavy creaky double door, which is actually the office's main entrance with the buzzers. Although everyone is using the café entrance because it's always open.

The truth about that other door, our official entrance, is that we can open it from inside but can't come back in without a key. I have no idea who has the key, and I don't actually care to find out because it's a nightmare to open that door without collecting minor bruises in the process with a dog and cups of coffees in my hands. So, the new plan is to take Alba out through the office's main door and perhaps walk her back with an empty bladder through the coffee shop.

Paris showrooms

Jim's trip to Paris turned into a whirlwind of chaos. He had already got his Eurostar ticket for 25th June and had asked me to book him a room in one of the boutique hotels in Paris. I tackled an intense, four-day hotel search but unfortunately, most of the boutique hotels I dialled were fully booked. I kept looking until I found new hotels and emailed him the slim availabilities. Then the problems (plural!) began. He didn't reply to my emails, texts, or phone calls. *Oh, his BS behaviour again.* With the departure date looming, Jim still had no accommodation booked. On the day before his planned travel, and even on the day of the journey itself, there was no accommodation in sight. I didn't even see him turn up in the office. Kirstie, from whom I'd have to ask for the company's bank details to complete the booking, was not in the office either. In the end, it didn't matter if he responded or not—I couldn't have booked the hotel without the credit card anyway. Meanwhile, I left the office early on the day of his supposed travel to do my nanny job, where I faced another drama. I got fired.

It was a mutual agreement between the child's mum and me, I guess. She wanted to take a copy of my passport and I told her that I'd only give her my passport copy if she prepares a contract and hires me officially, or she gives me a copy of her passport in return. I have been looking after children for five years and no one has ever asked for my passport details. And now that I work as a personal assistant, again no ID, or passport info were asked from me, despite working for an A-list designer, who gave me his PIN code for his personal bank card and whose office is filled with luxury items from Christian Louboutin heels to Prada sunglasses, let alone the expensive fabrics and the samples of the previous collections. It just felt unfair that I would have nothing to hold on to during this nanny job but the children's mum would get the copy of my passport. I just wanted some kind of an equal give and take. She didn't agree, so we parted.

When I returned to work the next day, I was bombarded with questions about Jim's whereabouts. "Did he go to Paris?" Everyone was eager to know, Victor in particular. I told them that I had no idea. "How come you don't know? You're his PA!" Victor jumped at me. *My question exactly! By the way how rude he was!* Eventually, Jimmy walked in and we found out the answer organically. He called me over to his desk and revealed that he'd postponed his trip to Paris. He added that he didn't need accommodation and asked me to bring him a coffee. Why didn't he go to Paris? We all wondered. I modified his train ticket to the next day as he requested, and left the printed ticket on his desk with an orange post-it writing "EUROSTAR" with bold capital letters.

The next morning, I found the tickets where I had left them: on the desk, decorated with a brown circle coffee cup stain, indicating that he'd at least been in the office. I also discovered his unopened box of food from the previous day, which I decided to have for lunch. If he was indeed in Paris, he wouldn't be needing it anyway.

And then an email arrived that confirmed my intuition about the BS living rent-free in our workplace.

"Dear Jim,

I hope this email finds you well.

I am sorry to inform you that I decided to leave, because despite my numerous efforts and my patience, it became impossible to work with Kirstie.

Kirstie has decided to manage my activity in all areas, and she takes the decisions that fall within my competency and under my missions.

These working conditions are neither productive nor constructive for the business model that we want to create, and more importantly this will not work in cohesion.

I am very sorry because I appreciate and love your work and your personal qualities, but it is also important for me to be respected and to work in a harmonious atmosphere.

I am completely at your disposal if you want to share and discuss about our collaboration.

Kindest regards,

N. S."

Monday, 30th June

I waited in the office until 7:30 pm, hoping to have a quick five-minute chat with Jim before heading home. Most of the team had already left, including Gracie and Laura, leaving me alone at my desk, idly surfing the net. Suddenly, I saw Jim racing past me. Assuming he was just heading to the men's room, I paid little attention. But he shouted, "I'm leaving, bye!" from the door. Alba was at his feet, and they vanished in a second. My wait for him had been in vain.

Tuesday, 1st July

Jim and Kirstie had a meeting with a bunch of business people in one of the meeting rooms downstairs, which I had booked through Lucia, the general manager of the building (she's so fun, by the way!). On my way to work in the morning, I popped into Tesco to buy a few bottles of Evian and San Pellegrino for the meeting, and two cans of dog food for Alba. When I arrived at the office, I went straight to the meeting room and placed the bottles of water on the long rectangular table. Then, I dashed upstairs to our kitchen to grab six clean glasses and brought them down, placing them neatly next to the bottles. I also left a small stack of copy paper and some pens on the table. The latter wasn't requested; I was just being thoughtful. Afterward, I headed to Moses to get reimbursed for my shopping spree, handing him the receipts. Then I heard Jim calling, "Soophiee!" and made my way to his desk. He was busy trying to repair his glasses; it seemed one of the temples had fallen off, and he had probably lost the screw.

"Sophie, could you look for some cello tape for me?" he asked.

"Your meeting is in 15 minutes," I reminded him.

"I know. Please hurry."

I hadn't seen any cello tape around the studio since I started working there, and had no idea where to begin looking. I certainly didn't want to rummage through the entire place. First, I headed to the production desk to ask Nicky. She was always kind and helpful to us interns. Nicky suggested checking the lower cabinets near the

Kirstie-Moses-Laoise desk area. Ugh, my least favourite corner of the office. I opened all the cabinets but only found magic tape. I turned to Laoise and asked if she knew where to find clear cello tape for Jimmy. She pointed at the lower cabinets without looking up from the enormous iMac screen that swallowed her up from the chest up. I opened the cabinets again, moved things around to see better, but still, no cello tape. Resigned, I grabbed a roll of magic tape and delivered it to Jim.

"I said cello tape! This is magic tape," he grunted.

"I know! You may be surprised to hear that there is no cello tape in the studio," I defended myself. "Do you want me to buy some?"

"No. I need it now," he snapped, still fiddling with his glasses.

"Your meeting is in 10 minutes," I reminded him.

"Where's Kirstie?" he asked, getting more agitated.

"She's already downstairs," I informed him. I suspected she had gone ahead to check if I had set up the table correctly.

"Can I do anything else for you?" I asked.

He let out a loud sigh, clearly frustrated that he couldn't repair his glasses. He didn't say anything else, so I took that as the end of our conversation and walked away.

I was sitting at my desk, starting to sort through the mail, when I saw him coming toward me on his way to the meeting. He paused for a millisecond to show me his face with the taped-together glasses, complaining about how ridiculous the frosty magic tape looked on the black frame. I tried not to smile but failed. It was kind of awkward for a business meeting, I agreed, but I found him cute. A bit of vulnerability looked charming on him. By the way, this was the first time I saw him wearing glasses, and he looked handsomely intelligent in them, magic tape or not.

Wednesday, 2nd July

Invitations for summer drinks, restaurant openings, exhibitions, and film screenings from Warner Music, British GQ, LOVE magazine, Royal Academy of Arts, and BOF are all lining up for Jim to be RSVP-ed. One invitation stands out with its fancy envelope and romantic fonts. Can you guess who it is from? I'll give you clues: Don't go breaking my heart, Tiny Dancer, Rocket Man, The Lion King, etc.

"Elton John?"

"Yes!"

Laura and Gracie admired the elegance of the stationery and the fine details of the golden typography.

"Is it for his concert?" asked Gracie.

"No, it's for something called the 'End of Summer Party.' A charity event that celebrates the Elton John AIDS Foundation." I replied.

"Is Jim going?"

"I'll find out soon."

Thursday, 3rd July

I was about to take Alba out for a walk but couldn't find her collar and leash again. Mark, who works in production as Nicky's assistant, picked up a pink tape measure and tied it around Alba's neck. "Voila! You're ready to go," he said, dropping a kiss on top of Alba's head. She led me out of the office. I can't deny that I work for a fashion designer. Not that I want to. I'm actually proud of it. From that day on, I applied this new fashion whenever I couldn't find the chain. I even saw Jim using a tape measure, a blue one, as a leash when I accidentally ran into him at the artisan café on Broadway Market. Has he actually lost the dog chain? I hope not.

Sunday, 6th July

I did a random photo shoot with Mariola, our fitting model from Poland. After chatting with her in the office, I showed her my portfolio and asked if she was interested in a weekend shoot. She happily agreed, so I quickly put together a mood board with ideas for the story. Using my film camera, we shot around my neighbourhood, where there were a few colourful garage doors and damaged wall parts that created the urban feel I wanted. The sun was out, making it a good day for shooting. By the way, had you noticed that in London the sun was almost always out on one of the weekend days, either Saturday or Sunday? If you hadn't, you would now.

Anyway, Mariola was very down-to-earth and easy-going. She didn't mind being barefoot on the dirty ground in front of the garages or leaning her long, silky, brown hair against the dusty doors. She was creative and moved organically in front of the camera, which helped me focus on other details like the lighting and styling. It was a fun shoot, and we got along very well.

Mariola told me that she had wanted to take a photo with Jim Kendal at the studio, but Cecile had talked her out of it, saying Jim wouldn't like the idea and she shouldn't even try to speak to him. Mariola, however, went for it. It was her last day doing fittings, and she had nothing to lose. So, she turned to Jim and kindly asked if she could take a picture with him as a memory of working together.

He posed with her happily, even thanked her for her work, and wished her a safe journey back to Poland.

What's the conclusion? Trust your instincts; don't let others sway you. We often project our fears onto others and give advice rooted in our own experiences. But it's important to remember that everyone has their own unique path and energy, leading to different outcomes in life. If you feel you can do something, you certainly can.

Although, I have to admit—Jim's behaviour can be unpredictable, but if you're sensitive enough, you can pick up on his energy and know whether it's a good time to approach him or not. It's something I've learned to do daily.

Monday, 7th July

I had two adventurous coffee runs today. One before office hours for Kirstie, and another in the afternoon at the downstairs coffee shop.

Kirstie saw me arrive early and immediately sent me to the artisan café, so I didn't get to do the nanny job search I had planned before Jim arrived.

The girl behind the counter was singing along to Ella Fitzgerald's "Cheek to Cheek" when she greeted me with a cheerful "Good morning!"

"Hello, how are you? Can I have a latte with an extra shot? Regular, please," I said.

"You know that all our coffees come with an 'extra shot'?" she asked.

I froze, mouth agape.

"Each cup of coffee contains a double shot. That's the standard. Do you want an extra shot on top of the double?" she clarified.

I was bewildered. My heart nearly stopped at the thought of calling Kirstie to find out the answer.

"That would be three shots in a cup," she explained further.

"Um, yes... I guess. Or no? I don't know... Just do it the way you've always done before."

"I've actually been meaning to ask you about this..."

"It's for my boss... huh, don't make me call her. Um... if double shots are the standard, then she must mean an extra, third shot in the mix...I guess." I hoped Kirstie wouldn't kill me.

"Three shots it is. And a large flat white too?"

"No, just one regular, this time."

I grabbed two sachets of sugar: one brown and one white, to give Kirstie choices. When I turned to pick up the coffee, I realised I had forgotten to say "skinny". I looked at the paper cup with "latte +1 shot" marked on the side and wanted to cry. Then, I had an idea! I borrowed the till guy's pen and scribbled "sk", as in skinny, in front of the word "latte" to complete the line: "sk latte +1 shot". And just like that, problem solved.

"Thanks so much! Bye!" I handed back the pen and made my way out.

"See ya later!"

"I'll be back." I goofed around with a serious Terminator accent.

"I know," they chimed.

Later, when I popped out to buy water for Jim, juice for me, and food for Alba, someone stopped me at the downstairs coffee shop and asked if I was a model who came for the casting. He probably worked for one of the other designers in the block. I could see copy papers with arrows on the wall indicating the direction of the casting from the door of the café to the stairs. I told him I worked for Jim Kendal and he apologised. Why do British people apologise for both good and bad? I was mistaken for a model; what's there to be sorry for? That was probably the biggest compliment I had received in my whole life. Let's celebrate! He totally made my day!

Tuesday, 8th July

Jim was going to Elle magazine's party, and the theme was animal print. I couldn't help but wonder what he was going to wear. He was so not the animal print type.

Wednesday, 9th July

This morning, I saw a woman—one of those office types with slick hair, dressed in Zara from head to toe—with three children at a nearby bus stop. She was raving with fury because she couldn't fit on the bus with the pram. She stomped, hit the lamp post with her bag, and screamed that she had let two buses go already because they had been full, and now her kids were going to be late for school again. She was raging in front of her kids and everyone around. Yep, I could hear her. In fact, the entire city could hear her.

The traffic in London is on another level. I personally try to avoid peak hours because it's so much worse than one can imagine. You can expect the trains and stations to be overcrowded between 07:30 and 09:30 in the morning and between 17:00 and 19:00 in the evening. On top of the inconvenient travel circumstances, you have to pay higher peak fares. Here's something to consider: live close to your work or work close to where you live.

Thursday, 10th July

Jimmy is highly anticipated to attend an event with canapés and drinks alongside important people from the British Fashion Council. I RSVP-ed yes weeks ago with his agreement, and now he's throwing a tantrum because he doesn't want to go. This morning, we had agreed that I would remind him to leave at 4 pm, which I did, yet at 4:30 pm, I still see him constructing garments.

"You have to leave now if you want to be on time," I said.

"Oú? ...Where?" asked Victor with a pin in his mouth.

"Do I have to go?" Jimmy looked at me with puppy eyes.

He asked me like I was making him go, but I was just doing my job. I'm not his mum!

"You don't have to, but you wanted to. We RSVP-ed yes."

"I didn't want to, but I have to," he corrected me. "I'll have to wear a suit. I don't have time to go home to change."

I know he doesn't like social gatherings much. He would much rather stay in the studio working in his black, ripped jeans—there's a big hole on the upper inner thigh area that you can only see if he squats down or bends over—and comfy sneakers. Work was flowing smoothly today, and he seemed very inspired, deeply into working on the collection.

"You can be home in 5 minutes by taxi," I encouraged him.

He looked at the invitation, annoyed, and sighed loudly.

"What is this thing?" Victor continued to be nosy.

"Look, if you decide not to go, at least let them know. They're expecting you," I said.

"Let me speak to Kirstie first." He walked up to Kirstie, waving the invitation in his hand. I saw Kirstie nodding and reading the invitation, then they exchanged a few words. Jimmy returned to his desk and picked up the work from where he left off with Victor and Cecile. He wasn't going for the canapés.

I shared my idea of keeping a smart outfit in the studio in case he needed to attend a similar event in the future, or if he just wanted to look more presentable for a meeting. "A suit at hand can come in handy," I tried to convince him, but my suggestion was not well received. Jimmy scoffed me away.

Friday, 11th July

Gracie accidentally cut her finger with scissors. She couldn't stand the sight of blood and almost fainted. Vanessa quickly pulled a chair under her. We pressed a napkin against her finger until I dug out a plaster from my purse. I always carry plasters because I look after children.

"It would have been so romantic if you had fallen on the pile of fabrics, dripping your blood on the silk," Laura joked.

"The modern Sleeping Beauty. Imagine the stylish death!" Vanessa chipped in.

"If you die here, your soul gets trapped inside the JK studio and you can haunt Jimmy from the other side." That was the best comment I could add.

We all laughed. Then I heard, "Soophieee!" Jimmy was calling me. I walked to his desk with a smile on my face.

"Yes?"

"What's going on there?" he gestured to the interns' desk.

"We're just having a laugh."

"Don't you have work to do?"

"Always."

He didn't say anything else, just stared at me. Was I supposed to do something for him? I didn't get it.

"Um, I'm good at multitasking," I said, though what I was really thinking was, "*Hello, have we met? I'm a Virgo. I created an entire system from scratch and organised the chaos in the storage room.*" But Jimmy just kept staring at me, and I still didn't get it. I flashed a wide smile, hoping to coax one out of him. No luck. Clearly, I need to work on my rapport.

"You can take Alba out for a walk," he suggested.

"With pleasure! Can I get you another coffee or some food on my way back?"

"No."

"A piece of chocolate?"

"I don't eat chocolate."

"Shame. Chocolate increases the levels of happiness hormones, like endorphins, released in the brain," I informed him, but I had a feeling I should stop talking when I saw him tilt his head to the side. Then he scoffed, which he usually does when I say something he cannot or does not want to react to. I took the dog for a walk.

I love going out of the studio to walk Alba or run errands. It keeps me fresh and energised. I really enjoy the movement of the day, going in and out and up and down the stairs, instead of just sitting in one place all day. Alba and I have become best buddies by now. Even Kirstie noticed how well I take care of her. Probably that's why she wanted me to babysit her dog, or I don't know what exactly she wanted the other day, because she wasn't straightforward, but I had a feeling she was looking for a babysitter for her giant schnauzer. She came to me and asked where I lived. I said I lived in the ghetto, in Shepherd's Bush. She let out a laugh and moved on to pop the question to the other interns.

She didn't believe me, but it is kind of true. I live in a ghetto-esque building complex of council flats, with drug dealers, pit bulls, and low-income families as neighbours. Obviously, I haven't met everyone in the block, and believe me, I don't want to. Yellow crime scene tapes regularly decorate our area, and I sometimes hear the police helicopter circling above. My flatmates and I often spot policemen and policewomen around our complex, flitting from different directions with their walkie-talkies. We normally just pass by them minding our business, but I am considering starting to smile toward them as I do with urban foxes when I see them paddling along the pavement—just kidding. Despite its quirks, I have never felt unsafe here, unlike Gracie, who has asked me twice to pick her up at the tube station because she was afraid to come home alone.

One time, I ordered pizza, and the delivery guy rang me on my phone to tell me to come down to the corner of the main road, a five-minute walk from my block, to pick up my pizza because they weren't allowed to bring the food up to the door in council flat blocks. I wasn't delighted by the news. It was raining, which was the initial reason I ordered food, and I didn't want to go down to the street. So, I asked for my money back.

Saturday, 12th July

I have found a new nanny job! Starting next week, I will be looking after the three-year-old Naomi, who needs a nanny only on Wednesdays, as she attends a French pre-school on the other days of the week. I went over for a playdate last weekend and I can tell that she is the most intelligent and sweet-natured child I have known. I am going to love my Wednesdays with her!

Tuesday, 15th July

Jimmy was supposed to start the day at M.E. with meetings scheduled until 1 p.m., but guess what? He didn't show up. I found out because the people at M.E. kept calling and emailing me about Jim Kendal's whereabouts. I tried to reach him over the phone and email, but as usual, he didn't respond. I was torn between worrying and getting annoyed. I asked Libby if she knew where Jim was. "No. Do you?" she responded with a flinch, starting to organise the already organised files next to her desk. She's a bad liar! I knew she knew something. Next, I turned to Laoise with the same question. She whispered to me that Jim was out last night with Kirstie and they got completely wasted. That's when I realised Kirstie wasn't in the office either.

The next day, I cautiously confronted Jim when he called me to his desk and asked me to buy him Solpadeine.

"Are you okay?" I asked.

"Yes," he replied, averting his eyes.

"The staff at M.E. was looking for you yesterday. Did you miss all your meetings?"

"I had a migraine," he said.

"Kirstie didn't come to work either. Did you two accidentally have migraines on the same day?" Silence followed and then I added, "I know you and Kirstie were out drinking the night before." There, I said it. I couldn't pretend I didn't know.

He looked up, clearly unpleasantly surprised by my straightforwardness.

"You don't have to lie to me. Next time you have a 'migraine,' just text me. At least then I can send everyone an apologetic email on your behalf, letting them know you won't be able to attend the meeting or something. I got blamed for your irresponsibility." I spoke calmly and collectedly like an understanding mum would do with her children who misbehaved. He seemed very surprised that I wasn't angry, probably because he would have been.

Honestly, it's hard to respect someone I can't look up to. What's in it for me to learn and grow with a boss who's immature and insincere? I understand that all experience is valuable and that it may appear funny when I look back at it in the future, but right now it's just stressful. The energy I spend on protecting myself and fighting off toxicity could be used for other, more worthy things.

Thursday, 17th July

Today, I handled the coordination between Jim and Julia, the product developer at M.E., regarding flight arrangements for Jim's fittings in Florence. Initially, Julia provided a range of dates for Jim to choose from but Jim wanted control and decided on different dates, thus the back-and-forth communication between Julia and me began.

Upon receiving three new options from Julia with slight differences in the prices, departure times, and airports, I approached Jim to confirm his preference. He was already rolling his eyes because the booking had not been finalised yet. He selected the itinerary that minimised his time in Florence, opting to fly out on the morning of the 23rd and return the same day. I waddled back to my laptop and emailed Julia about it, who raised concerns about the airport arrangements, "Won't it be a problem for Jim to fly from Luton Airport and land at City Airport on his return?" *Don't ask questions, just book it. Please.* So, I went to Jim again and asked him if he was happy to fly out from Luton and be back at London City Airport (LCA). He insisted on departing and arriving from the same airport. He was adamant about LCA.

Back at my desk, I asked Julia if there was a same day itinerary. She replied yes, but the departure would be later in the morning, and Jim would miss his meetings. She offered to book a car for him that would take him to Luton Airport in the morning on the company's account if it helped him. I forwarded the info to Jim, who was stubborn about City Airport. I told him, "Then you'll have to spend more time in Florence. There are no flights from LCA on the 23rd morning. If you want to travel from LCA, you'll have to fly out on the 22nd and spend the night in Florence to be able to attend the fittings in the morning on the 23rd."

"I don't want to sleep over there," he said in a sulky tone.

Jesus, what a baby!

I looked at the paper where I had jotted down the info and reminded him again about the three options. After some contemplation, he decided on the flight leaving at 21:05 on the 22nd, which was actually the cheapest itinerary. I told him this as an interesting fact. Seconds later, I sent the email, hopefully the last one, to Julia about the chosen itinerary when Jim called my name. It turned out he didn't like the idea of flying "cheap," so he asked me the details about the third itinerary again. So here I went again, "The third flight departs at 15:45 on the 22nd, and you come back to London at 21:10 on the 23rd." I read the details slowly and clearly from my note, finishing with a fed-up exhalation.

"Same airport?" he asked.

"Yes, London City Airport." I confirmed.

"And how much is that?"

I couldn't believe he was asking this.

"£249," I rounded up the price from £248.89. "That's the most expensive option out of the three," I added half sarcastically.

"I want that!" he confirmed with a smirk.

"Really?" I blurted out. "Julia has probably completed the booking by now."

"I don't care. I want them to pay more."

If I could blow fire, he would be ash by now.

I rushed back to my computer and started to type to Julia, "The asshole wants the most expensive flight..." Then I took a deep breath, deleted what I'd written, and composed a professional email. I could feel through my computer screen that Julia's head was about to explode.

Friday, 18th July

Jim's iPhone screen cracked, so I started calling repair shops to inquire about the turnaround time for fixing it. While replacing the front glass was a quick process, there was a backlog of iPhones with broken screens at most places. After checking a few options, I found a shop in Covent Garden that offered the fastest repair time. I explained to the shop attendant that I worked for someone important and emphasized the urgency of getting the phone fixed promptly. Unfortunately, they couldn't guarantee a same-day repair, which had been my initial hope. We settled on a plan for me to return the next morning to pick up the phone. Jim had to manage without his phone for nearly a day, but surprisingly, he didn't complain about it.

Thursday, 24th July

Jim sent me to withdraw cash, put it in an envelope, and deliver it to his cleaning lady at his apartment. He entrusted me with the keys to his home, and I was curious to see where he lived. Upon entering the apartment, I noticed that the cleaning lady had already washed the bedsheets, which were now hanging to dry on the doors and along the staircase. The scent of fabric softener filled the air, giving the place a fresh and pleasant aroma.

In the kitchen, I met the cleaning lady amidst a pile of dirty dishes in the sink, a saucepan with leftover food, and unwashed drinking glasses scattered on the table, some doubling as ashtrays. Despite the cleaning lady not speaing a good level of English, she reciprocated my smile when I handed her the envelope of money, likely her wage. With a few missing teeth and a weary appearance, it was evident that she lived in poor conditions, perhaps struggling with alcohol or drug-related issues. It saddened me to see her in such a state, and I hoped that Jim compensated her generously for her work.

Before leaving for the office, I took a quick look around the apartment out of curiosity. The cleaning lady didn't seem to mind. I glanced into a room adjacent to the kitchen, which appeared to serve as either a bedroom or living room. The couch was cluttered with untidy pillows and a duvet, suggesting that someone had slept there. On the table were two beer cans, two coffee mugs, two ashtrays, an unclean plate, wilting hydrangeas, and a rumpled white shirt. The TV remote lay on the floor near the dog bed. The bathroom, which I briefly peeked into, showed signs of neglect, with a peed-on toilet seat and towels strewn across the floor. Okay, I thought, I saw enough. Bye.

Friday, July 25th

I made an entry in my diary: "Victor is a complacent prick." Although I couldn't recall the exact reason for this note, I distinctly remembered an incident involving Victor and a box of chocolates that could explain the above comment.

It all began when Vanessa, our PR intern, completed her one-month internship. She was a lively presence in the office, often working closely with Laoise. Vanessa had a habit of leaving her belongings under our table, including her leather bag, and tossing her denim jacket over the back of a chair piled with folders and magazines. One of her tasks was to archive magazine pages featuring celebrities wearing Jim Kendal designs, and I vividly recalled her excitement over spotting Reese Witherspoon in a JK skirt.

When Vanessa finished her internship, she left a box of chocolates on our table as a parting gift for the staff. Gracie, Laura, and I were sad to see her go. She was a great addition to our intern table with her witty sense of humour. We signed a card for her with good wishes, drawings, and a small piece of fabric of one of JK's trade prints stapled onto the card secretly. However, when Victor passed by our desk and noticed the box of chocolates, he immediately took an interest.

"Whose is this?" he inquired.

I explained that Vanessa had completed her one-month internship and left the chocolate for all of us to share as a goodbye present. Victor seemed oblivious to who Vanessa was, despite her prominent presence during her internship. I clarified that she was the tall girl with Cleopatra-like hair who used to sit with us.

"Where did she go?" he asked, acting difficult.

Which part of my sentences didn't he understand?

"She completed her internship," I told him again.

Seemingly unperturbed by Vanessa's departure, Victor picked up the box of chocolates with a confident move and carried it over to Jim's desk. Then the two of them finished the whole box in one sitting. In fact, Victor must have eaten most of it because Jim was not a big chocolate fan.

Tuesday, 29th July

Ido made an interesting suggestion: "Sophie, you have to be like a mum to Jim."

I couldn't help but quip, "You mean... he's my unwanted child?" The idea didn't exactly thrill me. Ido clarified, "No! Keep reminding him of what he has to do because he's like a child who forgets things." I shook my head, resisting the comparison. "Nah-ah, I am not ready for motherhood. I work for free for the 'child' you want me to mother," I reminded him with a hint of sarcasm.

Saturday, 2nd August

My Spanish flatmate Catalina had an interesting breakfast experience. She emerged from her room at 1 pm, looking a bit disoriented after the night shift she covered at work.

"Sunshine morning!" I greeted her with a smile, munching on falafel.

She responded with a tired yawn and a grumble about being hungry. She retrieved a large bag of muesli from her cupboard section and plopped down next to me on the sofa. However, in her sleepy state, she tore open the bag too vigorously, causing its contents to spill onto the floor between us (btw, she was wearing her snowman socks, which added to the scene). I offered to help her transfer the muesli to a plate, but Catalina was unfazed.

"Tranquila!" she assured me, and proceeded to eat the spilled muesli directly from the floor with her fingers.

"Tranquila" is a popular phrase she uses. It means something like "relax". Every time she says it, I hear *tequila*, not "tranquila", lol. In the beginning, I thought *tequila* was used metaphorically like the Hungarian slang "Hawaii" that translates to cool or awesome.

Later that night, Catalina and I decided to go out for drinks and dancing in Shoreditch. We were both feeling lifeless from our busy jobs and wanted to shake things up. Since Gracie was sleeping over at Laura's, I had the room to myself for the weekend, not that she would have been in the way. Our plan was to start at Strongroom Bar, one of my favourite spots, for drinks and then head to either Cargo or the Joiners Arms to dance the night away. However, our plans changed on the fly, and we never made it to the dancing part. We ended up drinking two bottles of champagne, though sharing the second one with some strangers. At one point, I was tempted to smoke, so I traded a glass of champagne for a cigarette with a guy who also lent me his lighter. However, I was too drunk to light the cigarette properly, and it ended up falling out of my mouth. *Oh well, it wasn't meant for smoking.* We stayed at the bar until it closed, and before leaving, we stopped by the ladies' room. On a whim, I grabbed a jumbo roll of toilet paper and stuffed it into my bag to take home with us. It didn't fit completely, so I threw my jacket over it. Catalina found the whole situation hilariously funny.

After leaving Strongroom Bar, we headed towards Cargo and waited in line outside for a short while. However, Catalina soon realised that the jumbo roll of toilet paper was too conspicuous to take inside without being noticed by the security staff. I had to agree with her. So, we made the decision to skip the dancing and call it a night instead.

Bringing home toilet rolls from public places has become a habit of mine, albeit an innocent one. It all started out of necessity when I was low on funds. I used the toilet paper not only for its intended purpose but also for wiping surfaces and my nose. While my financial situation has improved since then, the habit has stuck. In our flatshare, there always seems to be someone who forgets or neglects to buy toilet paper, choosing instead to use what others have purchased. So, whenever I'm out and about, whether at the mall or elsewhere, I grab a roll or two to bring home. This way, nobody should feel it is unfair to pay more for shared housing necessities.

Sunday, 3rd August

This is the summer I have developed smelly and extremely dirty feet. It seems my faithful Birkenstock sandals, companions of three summers past, are waving the white flag. They've heroically endured the trials of city streets, and now they cry out for retirement. Unfortunately, I don't have enough money to buy a new pair, my housing benefit hasn't arrived yet. My survival depends on my one-day nanny job and the occasional weekend babysitting. While not exactly starving, I am behind with a month's rent.

Monday, 4th August

"Soph, Jim's calling you," Gracie turned to me.

"Jesus!" I sighed.

"It's Jim. Not Jesus," Gracie corrected me.

"At least I got the 'J' right," I called her attention to it, while I was standing up to make my way to Jim's desk.

"If we were in Spain, Jesus would be 'Hesus'." Gracie added.

I think my Spanish flatmate had tainted Gracie's humour.

"And Jimmy would be what?" I wondered. "Himmy?"

Lol.

"Or *Him*. With capital H."

P.S. I remember a Finnish band in the 90's called Him.

Tuesday, 5th August

Jim handed me a Tesco bag brimming with crumpled receipts, a new responsibility to help the accountants track his spending. Flattening these small, creased pieces of paper and deciphering their faded details quickly became my prominent task. Goodness me!

Under the guidance of Vivian, one of the accountants, I embarked on creating an Excel sheet for inputting the data. Unfortunately, my outdated Microsoft Office software couldn't open Vivian's files, which immediately created a problem. She tried to troubleshoot but ended up frustrated. Alison stepped in to help, providing me with the newest version of the software. However, my MacBook, a 2007 model now considered vintage, wasn't compatible with the latest version of the software, nor could it support a newer operating system.

After much effort, we were no closer to a solution. In the end, I created a document outlining Jim's spending, which Vivian then had to retype into her computer before copying the data into the Excel sheet. Not the most efficient process, but it was the best we could manage.

Thursday, 7th August

In the evening, Jim sent me out to buy scrambled eggs. He'd been consuming a lot of eggs lately. Sometimes he'd just ask me to get some protein and I'd then run through the options with him: eggs, meat, or beans? Most mornings, I'd take a slight detour to Pret A Manger to pick up a protein pot for him.

This time, I roamed Broadway Market, searching for a place that might cook eggs. Only the restaurants and pubs were open, and

I doubted their breakfast menus were still available at 7 p.m. I was desperate to fulfill the "egg hunt" mission Jimmy sent me on, so I stepped into an Italian restaurant and kindly asked if they could make some scrambled eggs for my boss, even though their menu mainly featured pasta and pizza. Knowing they'd have eggs in the kitchen, I explained our situation and the chef responded warmly, "I like you! You have a beautiful smile! How many eggs does your boss want?"

I had no idea at first but then I settled on four, hoping it was worth the effort. "10 minutes, okay?" he said. While I waited, I dashed to the mini supermarket next door and bought a bar of chocolate to give to the chef along with the £5 he asked for the meal. True to his word, he presented the eggs beautifully decorated with tomato and parsley in a takeaway box. He even added some thin triangle-shaped focaccia bread, which I knew Jim wouldn't eat due to his strict "just protein" diet. I was contemplating whether to remove the bread before Jim saw it, but the presentation looked so nice that I decided against it. He could simply leave the bread on the side if he didn't want it. And, as expected, that's exactly what he did.

Friday, 8th August

I did my usual coffee run with Alba, using a tape measure as her leash. On our way back to the studio, we had an unexpected and terrifying encounter with another dog. As we passed by the park, an angry, barking pit bull suddenly charged at us. Thankfully, a fence stood between us, stopping the pit bull in its tracks. My heart pounded as I scanned for the owner, but no one was around. I considered turning back toward the café, as the park gates were wide open, presenting a clear path for the pit bull to reach us. I was terrified by the thought that Alba would be attacked. *It can't happen. It can't happen.* Alba, however, had different plans. She stubbornly refused to move. I wanted to pick her up, but I was balancing two coffees. She stood firm like a statue, while the pit bull pressed its nose through the fence bars, growling furiously. I was so scared. Alba remained unmovable. Then suddenly, the two dogs locked eyes, which was followed by five seconds of complete silence, and just like that, the angry pittie let out a whine and ran away. Alba glanced at me as if to say, "Everything's OK, we can go now," and we safely walked back to the office. I was deeply touched.

Later, my flatmate explained that young dogs are less likely to attack senior dogs and that males don't usually attack females. Alba is an old female dog and must have known she could handle the situation. It felt like she was telepathically telling the pit bull off. I couldn't comprehend how she wielded her invisible power and strength so effectively. I realised I should learn from her: (1) trust, (2) face challenges, (3) don't run away. I wish I could understand what she was thinking or feeling in that moment. I don't know if all dogs age the way she does, but Alba seems to be very soulful and wise. I feel privileged to look after her.

Did you know?

8th August is International Female Orgasm Day. It's an unofficial holiday that began in Brazil, aimed at encouraging men to satisfy their wives. The day has since gained international recognition and is celebrated to raise awareness about women's right to sexual pleasure. Interestingly, it follows shortly after National Orgasm Day, which is celebrated on 31st July. Ladies, prepare to come twice!

9th - 17th August – House sitting

Jim is on holiday in Ibiza, and I volunteered to move into his apartment to look after Alba. I figured a change of scenery would be healthy for me too.

It's a slow-paced week, and the studio is much quieter. Everyone is allowed to arrive at work later in the mornings. Gracie is in Scotland for the week, and many other staff members and interns are on break too. I talked to Kirstie, and she let me work from home—I mean, Jim's home. This way, I can answer emails and manage the calendar from the comfort of his sofa with Alba gently snuffling next to me.

Jim's flat in East London is very basic. He doesn't live in luxury. However, having the entire two-bedroom flat to myself for a week feels like a luxury to me.

As soon as I arrived, I waltzed through the place. I love the charm of the black stairs that lead up to the first floor, where the kitchen, bathroom, and small living room are. The living room has a wide bookshelf, a flat-screen TV, and a shabby couch, which is definitely Alba's favourite spot. The character and even the smell of the split-level flat remind me of my old Hackney Road flat. Oh, I love it here! From the first floor, white-painted stairs take me up to the roof room that Jim uses as his bedroom. He sleeps on a mattress on the floor and stores most of his clothes on clothing racks. There is a Helmut Newton DVD next to the iMac on the desk under the roof windows. It is a simple home with minimal decoration, such as some photographs, magazines, and framed collage artworks on the wall. The place is not too personal, not too artsy, and not at all what you'd expect an A-list designer to own or rent.

Having seen how messy Jim could be, I asked him to have the flat thoroughly cleaned before I arrived. He confirmed that the cleaning lady had prepared the place, scrubbing the sink until it sparkled. Thank you for that!

I invited my two favourite flatmates for a sleepover on Saturday, and no, Jim didn't know about it. Our bathroom was being renovated in Shepherd's Bush, so I let the girls shower here over the weekend. During the week, they showered at work or at the gym, while our third flatmate stayed at her boyfriend's place, where she could use the bathroom comfortably.

We went to Camden for a gig—it's so much more convenient to reach Camden from East London than from West London—and we came back to the flat later with a pizza and dog treats for Alba. My flatmates love dogs and spoiled Alba with cuddles. They were also a bit disappointed with the flat because they expected more from a fashion designer's home. However, I had told them it was a pretty average East London home with no signs of a prestigious person living there. Anyway, they made jokes about the condition of the place and the random stuff lying around, like the three-legged chairs in the kitchen. Yep, three-legged chairs. How did that happen? And why? It just made no sense. It seemed like someone grabbed a leg on each, otherwise four-legged wooden chair, and tore them out. But why? We created a list of ideas to console our minds with silly reasonings. You don't want to hear them, trust me.

We heard the downstairs neighbours "Woohoo"-ing, and my Spanish flatmate got excited.

"They probably think we are fashion models," she said.

Lol. I highly doubted that anyone in the building knew who Jim was, but I didn't interrupt Catalina when she began entertaining us with a series of poses imitating fashion models from magazines. She was hilarious!

While we were eating pizza, I remembered something Jim had told me at the office: "Open the bottom drawer and help yourself to clean bedding." I had told him I wouldn't need it because I sleep in my sleeping bag—I don't like sleeping in strangers' bedding; it's a thing I have. Yet, he sounded persuasive, almost plotting, when he repeated that I should definitely open the bottom drawer if I needed clean bedding. I'm good at perceiving non-verbal cues, something was suspicious about the way he said it.

I told the girls I was going upstairs to open the drawer because I was curious. I instructed them to run after me to save me if they heard me scream. In the roof room, I saw Alba napping in Jim's bed (on the mattress) with only her nose visible under the duvet. She might have gotten a bit overwhelmed from the attention she received tonight, or maybe she was missing Jimmy.

So, I opened the bottom drawer, and there it was... a huge black silicone dildo. *Why did he want me to see it?* I went back downstairs and Flora asked me, "Was something in there?"

"Nothing.. just a BBD," I said.

"A what?"

"Big Black Dildo."

"You opened his goodie drawer?" Flora jumped at me.

"It is not a goodie drawer."

"It seems it is, for him."

"Gay people have the worst sense of humour. It's all about their penises," Catalina said.

"I guess it's generally true about all men. Sometimes they make fun of the penis, and sometimes they put it on a pedestal," commented Flora before she drank her Coke.

"And apparently, they get offended if women joke about the penis and leave you for that," Catalina added.

"Are we talking about Jean again?" I asked.

Catalina shrugged her shoulders.

"Come on! He was so immature!" I said with pain in my voice.

"Was it the guy who sculpted a penis in the snow during his ski holiday and sent you a photo of it on WhatsApp?" Flora turned to Catalina. "And how old was he... 33? It's so good for you that he left."

I was nodding in agreement.

"Does anyone want the last slice of pizza?" Catalina asked, trying to change the subject out of embarrassment.

"No, you can have it," we both said, shaking our heads.

We all slept on the mattress, which was very uncomfortable. I could feel the springs in my back. When we woke up at around eleven the next morning, we grabbed some coffee and cakes for breakfast and took Alba for a long walk in the park. It was lovely to spend a few hours outdoors in the green.

On Monday, I woke up to a constant pounding that I just couldn't identify. It was five or six in the morning, and I struggled to fall back to sleep. I sat up in the bed, moving my head around to listen and figure out where the noise was coming from. I thought it might be coming from the roof. Looking at the roof windows, I realised it was raining. The windows were slightly open, and I had left them like that to let some fresh air in. Thankfully, the rain didn't fall inside.

Sometime later, I woke up to a different noise. I heard steps on the roof. The sluggish movement and the short slap sound were accompanied by an occasional deep honk. What the hell? Still half-asleep, I couldn't recall hearing anything like this before. The steps grew louder, making me jump out of bed and rush to the window to shut it. I waited, listening. The thing was still waddling around up there, right above my head now. It had to be some kind of animal. A squirrel? A cat? A mouse? No, they don't honk, and their footsteps aren't this loud. What else would parade on the roof? When I looked up again, I saw two duck feet on the roof window. "A wild goose!" I slapped my forehead. How could I not think of that? London parks are loaded with wild geese, though I had always seen them by the lakes, never in residential areas, and certainly not on rooftops.

On Tuesday, one side of the towel bar in the bathroom fell out of the wall. Despite my attempts, I couldn't screw it back in, so I left it hanging. The numerous marks on the wall indicated it had been fixed countless times, so I didn't bother too much.

Jim's bathroom was an interesting mix: a collection of Aesop toiletries, a nearly empty bottle of Chanel perfume, baby shampoo, and a framed black-and-white photo of a nude woman's body on the wall. Although the toilet was clean, I still wiped the seat with antibacterial wipes before using it, just in case. And as a small act of revenge for how he treats me at work, I started peeing in his bathtub during my evening showers.

I didn't cook much in the kitchen. Most days, I ate porridge, fruits, and roasted veggies unless I picked up ready-to-eat meals from one of the nearby cafés. I didn't eat a lot but drank plenty of water and green tea those days.

On Friday, I met up with the seven-year-old Lily, whom I used to look after before I moved to West London. She was thrilled to walk Alba in the park and blow bubbles for her. After our doggy adventure, we dropped Alba back home, did a bit of colouring at Jim's coffee table—I found a set of colouring-in placemats on the bookshelf and helped ourselves to a page—and headed to Franco Manca for a pizza.

Lily's reaction to Jim's flat mirrored that of my flatmates. She'd imagined a fashion designer's home would be glamorous—her mum works at Glamour magazine, after all—and was quite disappointed by what she saw. I might be the only one who loves the flat. Probably because I didn't have any expectations and I know from experience that the fashion industry isn't as glamorous behind the scenes as it appears in front of the public.

Later, after returning to the flat, I did some work on my laptop, took Alba out for a quick wee, and then watched "The Red Shoes", the 1948 movie. I had discovered more DVDs in the flat that day. "The Red Shoes" was my sister's favourite Andersen fairy tale that our grandmother used to read to her from an ancient book. The pages were dark brown, the illustrations were fading, and the binding was so loose that the pages were falling out.

The last weekend dragged on slowly. With the weather being dismal, I spent most of my time reorganising folders on my desktop, reading some of Jim's books, and indulging in more colouring. I also had a spider fright incident in the kitchen. My hands started shaking when I spotted a big, fat spider on the wall. Dealing with it alone was terrifying. I hate getting close to big spiders. I never intend to kill them, but I don't know how to catch them from a safe distance. More often than not, I end up killing them out of fear. This one got sprayed on first with an air freshener I found in the bathroom and then hit by a heavy book. I'm sorry.

Monday, 18th August

Jim returned from his holiday and arrived at the office at 10 o'clock, much later than usual.

"Julia from M.E. is coming over for a meeting at 10:00," I rushed to remind him as soon as I saw him.

"She's already here," Jim replied.

"Oh. You?" I turned to the woman in the yellow dress, surprised. "I'm sorry, I didn't see you walk in. Nice to finally meet you!" I introduced myself and shook her hand. Then, without warning, Jim announced he had something for me and immediately tossed a large black and white heap in my direction. My brain hadn't yet registered his words, so my instinct was to step to the left to avoid being hit. It reminded me of secondary school volleyball when some guys hit the ball with such speed that I found it safer to jump away rather than attempt to hit it back. I guess my reaction was as unexpected to Jim as his sudden action was to me. It was awkward, but I maintained my composure. When I looked at the stripy pile on the floor, it clicked that this was a canvas bag. I reached down to pick it up.

"It's a present for you," Jim said, looking a bit nervous. "Why didn't you catch it?"

"I'm not that sporty," I lied.

The truth is, I love sports, but I don't have much free time to pursue physical exercise. Playing chase with Alba at the park, walking up and down the stairs in the building, and lifting coffee cups are part of my current workout routine.

"Thank you, that's kind!" I smiled at him gratefully.

So, he gifted me a bag because I looked after Alba in his absence. He could have just handed it to me instead of throwing it at me, but never mind. I forgive him; he's not that artful in his communication. I know he meant well.

At home, my flatmates and I searched for the label inside the bag to find out where it was from.

"Is it a Birkin?" Silvia asked half-humorously, half-seriously.

I told her it wasn't. I'm ashamed to admit it, but I did the same—I checked the label despite it clearly looking like a woven beach bag. Not that luxury brands don't sell woven beach bags—Chanel, D&G, Loewe, Dior, Fendi all do! But you have to admit, if you work for a well-known fashion designer, you'd expect a well-known designer's bag. Gracie even examined the lining and the craftsmanship, lol. In the end, we all agreed it was a good-looking bag—we loved the black and white stripes—that was probably picked up at a local market on the island. Although I appreciated the gesture, my practical side kicked in. I mean, where am I going to use a beach bag in London? I ended up giving it to Gracie because she loved it more than I did.

Tuesday, 19th August

Gracie and I went to work together in the morning. Bus, tube, bus, walk. On most days, I leave earlier, but today I allowed myself to sleep in a bit longer so we could go together. First, we took the bus to Shepherd's Bush station, then the Central line to Bethnal Green, and from there, caught one of the buses toward Hackney Central. We stayed in the buggy area, standing, for only a few stops on the last leg of our journey. Just as we pulled out into traffic, the bus hit a cyclist and came to a sudden stop. I just heard a bang, didn't see the cyclist, and lifted my sleepy head at the unusual sound. For a second, I thought a bird had flown into the window, but then I realised the bang was too loud for a small, innocent bird. So, I came to an 8 a.m. conclusion: the victim was either a fat goose (that goose again?!) or a human. I looked at Gracie, who was turning white rapidly and seemed about to faint.

"What happened?" I asked.

Gracie trembled, unable to speak, just looking at me, freaked out.

"Did we hit someone?" I popped the question.

Gracie nodded. The black ladies sitting at the back of the bus—coming from work? Going to work?—were screaming and praying.

"Driver, YOU killed her!"

"Murder!"

"Oh Jesus Lord...!"

Then more screaming.

I located the blood strip on the wide window while turning my head toward the screamers. Gracie started to fall. I grabbed her arm, "Hold on to me! Don't fall!" I stepped closer and enveloped her arm to save her from a possible collapse—*who needs another accident?*—and tried to calm her down.

"Take some deep breaths, look at me, everything's okay—*is it?*—breathe," I told her.

Within a minute, she looked healthier and was able to speak. We watched the cyclist, a young woman, get up off the road with the help of two people who probably jumped out of the cars behind us. They helped her shattered body across the road. A third person carried the deformed bike behind them. The driver ordered everyone to leave the bus and wait for the next one. What an exciting start to the day! I love London!

Sunday, 24th August

Seeing my handsome barista crush walking down Oxford Street with a girl brought me face to face with reality: he's got a girlfriend. Or maybe a sister? Nah. We exchanged an awkward glance as we passed each other, but neither of us said hello. Any hope of him ever asking me out evaporated. After this, I started to see him less frequently at the café because I stopped glancing over the counter to check if he was there. He sprinkled one last cocoa heart on my coffee foam when I stopped by at the café, and I didn't blush when I thanked him for my drink. After that, our eyes never really met again.

Monday, 25th August

My housing benefit has arrived! I am so relieved. Thank you xx council & London for supporting me and my dreams!

Thursday, 28th August

For two weeks before his holiday, Jim had been on a protein kick and hit the gym every day. It just dawned on me that he did it all to look good at the beach. By the way, he didn't even bother to tell me he'd be away for a week. I only found out a few days before his trip when he was scrambling to find someone to look after Alba.

Anyway, about the gym... Jim asked me to block out-of-office slots in the calendar for his gym sessions and to keep his whereabouts a secret. Victor and Ido—who's basically become Victor's sidekick—came by a few times asking where Jim was, but I lied and said I didn't know. Everyone else either respected his privacy or didn't notice his absence for that hour.

It was amusing when he asked me to buy him a body wash. I popped into the nearest supermarket, a Costcutter, and found only two options for men. I sniffed both bottles and picked the one I'd prefer on my boyfriend... if I had one. Back at the office, Jim wasn't at his desk, so I placed the body wash on top of his gym bag, which he'd left behind when he went to work out.

"Why didn't you take the body wash with you?" I asked when he returned.

"I don't like it," he simply replied.

"You use baby shampoo at home. Look at this as an improvement!" I suggested with a grin.

"Soph! Ssh!" he shushed me, even though I hadn't spoken loudly. "What are you talking about?"

"I saw a big bottle of Johnson's baby shampoo in your bathroom," I whispered loud enough for him to hear it clearly.

"That's Kevin's, not mine," he denied.

He was lying; he looked away when he said it. I don't understand why he denies the cute things about himself. Is he really that insecure? Or is it something else?

Friday, 29th August

"I don't like this coffee!" shrieked Kirstie after taking a sip from the cup I brought her from downstairs.

I stood next to her, confused. Did I forget to say skinny again? Did it have too much sugar? Too little? What did I do wrong?

"Is this coffee from downstairs?" she asked, her tone dripping with disdain.

"Yes," I replied, innocently.

"Whyyyy? I hate that coffee!" she yelled toward the ceiling, drawing the attention of everyone in the office. I couldn't believe her behaviour.

"I didn't know... that... um... You've had coffee from downstairs before. I didn't expect it would be a problem if I hadn't gone to Broadway Market," I explained.

The reason I bought the coffee at the downstairs café was that I had a lot of work to do, helping both Jim and Alison, and wanted to get back as quickly as possible.

"Do you want me to go to Broadway Market to get the coffee you like?" I offered.

Kirstie puffed and made faces, clearly showing her disappointment and irritation, then waved me away from her desk.

"That was quite a show!" Gracie turned to me as I sat down at our desk.

"Honestly!" I sighed, shaking my head in astonishment. "Why did she have to humiliate me?"

"She humiliated herself, not you!" Gracie reassured.

"What's her problem?" Laura jumped in.

"She doesn't like the coffee I brought her from downstairs. I've seen her buying coffee there before. Never thought it would be a problem," I complained in a low tone.

"She's so ungrateful!" muttered Laura.

"Whatever," I whispered, staring at my screen.

"Maybe she's on her period!" Gracie tried to lighten the mood.

"T.O.M.?" asked Laura.

"Who's Tom?" I wanted to know.

"Time Of the Month," Laura explained.

Lol, okay, then all women know Tom.

"Do you think she still...? How old is she?" I wondered.

"Dunno," said Laura.

"Or menopause!" guessed Gracie.

"Does menopause come with tantrums?" I asked.

"It comes with mood swings and like twenty other symptoms," Gracie informed us.

Why is she an expert on menopause, by the way?

"Good for her. Does it come with memory loss too? Maybe she could delete the idea of disliking the downstairs coffee."

"Let me check." Gracie turned to her laptop and typed "symptoms of menopause" into Google. She started to read the 34 symptoms listed: "Hot flushes, mood swings, headaches, electric shocks... what?... irritability, weight gain, memory lapses... there you go!"

"Really?"

"...hair loss, bloating, depression, body odour... does she smell?"

"Stop it!"

Lol.

September 2014

The first half of the month was a whirlwind. Fashion week loomed just two weeks away, and the pressure was palpable. Gracie was in Scotland for university, but she'd be back just in time for the weekend when the show was scheduled. Victor had developed an obsession with Rihanna's "Man Down," and sometimes I couldn't resist joining in for an impromptu sing-along when I was called to Jim's desk.

Jim and I sat down with the creative team to hammer out the schedule for the next two weeks. He became a fortress of focus, blocking out anything and anyone not directly tied to the show. Meanwhile, Kamila was at her wits' end, venting to me about how Jim had repeatedly cancelled their scarf meeting. Her sketches were ready; they just needed Jim's approval. She demanded a 30-minute meeting with the power boss.

I felt for her, but I couldn't make Jim prioritise her if he didn't want to. Determined to help her, I got creative. I started peppering his weekly schedule with red-highlighted reminders of Kamila's request, hoping it would catch his eye and prompt him to address it. It took some time, but my strategy finally paid off. Jim eventually sat down with Kamila to discuss her sketches, and the crisis was averted.

The stylist Jim's collaborating with now—different from the one we had in June—has already begun pulling looks together and is actively involved in model casting. She's no-nonsense, with a clear vision and a straightforward communication style that garners respect from everyone. Her presence feels like a breath of fresh air in the team.

Anthony, one of our creative pattern cutters, is officially off until after the show. I ran into him outside the café one morning when we both arrived too early to get into the building. Anthony, a middle-aged East Londoner, explained that he always takes the last two weeks before fashion week off because the stress level is too high for him. I'll miss his infectious laughter. Anthony, along with two other senior pattern cutters, works at a wide wooden table near the entrance. Their hearty laughs often spill out, brightening my day. The vibe at their table is fantastic—they're such lovely people.

From now until the show, work consumes us. Everyone is so busy that simple things like grabbing a meal or chatting about the weather are often left until the end of the day—if we have the energy. Kamila, however, wasn't too drained to share with us her traumatic encounter with slugs crawling happily on the walls of her apartment. *Yuck!*

Whenever I can, I walk around collecting bins, especially in the pattern cutting area, where paper waste overflows daily. I sweep the waste into a pile, squeeze it into recycling bags with the help of another intern, and store the bags in the kitchen temporarily until we take them down to the collection point at the end of the day.

Tuesday, 2nd September

Jimmy disappeared, and his phone was unreachable. I tried calling Kevin, who might have been at Jim's apartment, but he didn't pick up either. I was at a loss about what to do with Alba. Jim had left for a meeting in the afternoon, promising to return later, but he hadn't shown up before Moses shut the office for the night. I asked Moses for the keys so I could stay with Alba in the studio until I heard from Jim, but he refused. *He trusts me with the credit cards but not with the keys?*

I could have gone home like everyone else, but I didn't want to leave Alba alone. Nobody wanted to, and since I was Jim's assistant, everyone assumed she was my responsibility. I didn't mind looking after Alba, but I did mind being locked out of the office, wandering under the black sky until whenever Jim decided to show up. After sending numerous texts and making countless unanswered calls to both Jim and Kevin, I surrendered and just waited. I sat on a bench in the park for a while, then moved to the stoop of Jim's apartment block. I was exhausted and starving.

After an hour, Jim finally called me back. He showed up at 9 p.m. and mumbled a sorry, but I didn't care. If he were truly sorry, he'd have sent me home in a cab. Then, without thinking, I blurted out, "Fuck you, Jim Kendal!" It came out naturally, and I wasn't sorry. That "Fuck you!" encapsulated the five months of nonsense I had endured as his unappreciated assistant.

Wednesday, 3rd September

I didn't go to work.

Wednesdays are usually my day off because of my nanny job, but I normally pop into the office for two hours in the morning before I start looking after Naomi at noon. Today, I didn't even bother to get out of bed.

"*Words are not needed to teach a man how to treat you. A little bit of silence or distance will often do the trick.*" Sherry Argov

Although Jim was gay, he was still a man and no one describes men's behaviour more than Sherry Argov in her book "Why Men Love Bitches".

Thursday, 4th September

Jimmy and I weren't talking. I didn't bother to say hello when I arrived at the studio, and he didn't ask me to bring him coffee. Instead, he stepped out and fetched a flat white for himself while I kept busy, working independently without interacting with him.

At the end of the day, as almost everyone was gone, Jim walked out of the studio, leaving me with the fear of having to look after Alba until late again. *Please, don't be an asshole!* But then, 25 minutes later, he came back with flowers, placed them in front of me without a word, and raced back to his desk. I presume it was his way of saying sorry. I have to admit, it helped de-ice the situation.

P.S. Today is the Elton John party, and yes, he's going.

Friday, 5th September

I had an early morning conversation with Jim. As soon as I walked in, I heard him calling my name and asking me to sit down at his desk. What's going on? He seemed slightly nervous, which made me nervous too. Still, I sensed something good was coming.

"Sophie, what are your plans?" he asked in his deepened boss voice.

It seemed we weren't going to talk about why I didn't come to work on Wednesday, or about the flowers he gave me yesterday.

"You mean... um... what do you mean?" I was confused.

"Until how long are you here working for me?" he clarified.

"I am doing the show with you, as you know. Then I'll be away for a holiday and... um... when I'm back in London I'll have to look for a paid job."

While gathering my thoughts, I felt something was cooking in the background. I was apprehensive about being told something I hadn't prepared for. There was something inside me that held me back from expressing myself authentically about discussing the topic of continuing to work for him—and asking to be paid—which I believed he was hinting at. In my head, I could hear the song "You Can Get It If You Really Want" by Jimmy Cliff. I was feeling somewhat insecure, and Alba came to my rescue. She left Jim's side, crawled under the table, and climbed into my lap. Jim and I looked into each other's eyes, and I could tell we were thinking the same thing: Alba had left his side to come to support me. What a precious dog, OMG!

If I read him well, he wanted me to stay and work for him, but he didn't say it explicitly, and I didn't say it for him, although I would have been happy to receive the offer. His closing words were: "Alba likes you very much!"

Later that same day, Jim wanted me to post a parcel to his family and told Alison to give me the address. Alison suggested I leave the parcel on her desk, and she would address it later, but Jim asked her to copy the address for me because I would need it in the future. I thought, "What future?" My future here lasts for two more weeks. Unless he wants me to stay... and expects me to read his mind.

Monday, 8th September

Jim's sister and niece were coming to the show, so I had to book a train for them. On top of that, I needed to run to Argos to buy an inflatable air mattress and take it to Jim's flat.

Later, I helped Alison with some Photoshop work, which I quite enjoyed for a change. Then Jim kept me busy organising his desktop folders, printing a ton of model cards, and sending me to buy more whiteboards for him and the stylist to pin images on.

Drew, one of the new interns, a sweet boy in his second year of menswear design, kept asking when Cara Delevingne would come and if it was true she would walk for JK. There was a rumour in our office that Cara Delevingne was doing the show, but honestly, I hadn't a clue.

Cecile pulled the hair tie out of Laura's hair without asking. Laura was colouring digital sketches for Kamila when Cecile turned up looking for a hair tie for the model at the fittings. When nobody had a spare one, she stepped behind Laura and, with a sudden movement, pulled the tie out of her hair and went back to the model saying, "Found one!" *Honestly? What a bitch!* Laura went after Cecile to give her a piece of her mind, but got intimidated by Jim's presence, thus staying quite moderate with her language. Cecile didn't apologise, making it sound okay to do such things in emergencies, and reassured Laura she would get her hair tie back.

Jim decided to leave earlier than usual and, without a word of warning, switched off the lights on us. The office went dark, and we were all startled. He sent everybody out. In record speed, I saved the changes I'd made in the calendar, logged out of the email system, shut down my laptop, grabbed my bag and jacket, and scooted out of the office. I finished packing on the waiting sofa in the corridor. Moses was extremely furious—his face was red, his eyes were glassy, and his hair looked like he'd been trying to pull it out. None of us could finish our work.

Jim went too far.

Tuesday, 9th September

"Where are my Ray-Bans?" Jim asked while rummaging through the stuff on his desk, clearly agitated.

I had a feeling I might have boxed them away with the sample sunglasses we are using for the S/S show. JK is collaborating with a new accessory brand that makes some really cool and edgy sunglasses. We have about 50 pieces to choose from for the catwalk. Until yesterday, they were all laid out in rows on the white paper-covered desk. I had cello-taped white paper to cover the surface of the desk and also taped a large piece of white paper on the wall where I sit, which is now the backdrop where the models are photographed.

Anyway, I was more than sure that Jim's sunglasses got mixed up with the brand's sample glasses. So, I rummaged through the storage box, unwrapping each pair from their individual packaging until I finally found his Ray-Bans. I decided not to give them back to him until the end of the week—my little punishment for his selfish act yesterday.

Thursday, 11th September

Laura asked me to fetch her phone charger from Jim, clearly too scared to approach him herself.

"I love you, Laura, but no. It's your charger, you get it back," I replied, feeling cranky and snowed under with work.

"Pleeease!" she pleaded.

"No. Just go and ask for your charger back. He has no reason to be mad at you. Chill. Be firm and KISS," I suggested.

"What??" Laura exclaimed, eyes wide with confusion.

"K-I-S-S. Keep It Simple Short. You'll be fine. Go!" I encouraged her.

Laura had been snubbed by Jim when she was dyeing fabrics because she used the wrong colour. It wasn't her fault; she just followed Kamila's instructions. Jim lost his temper in the moment, and the monster within him came out. Poor Laura! I think that's why she's afraid of meeting him eye to eye again. I'm sure the incident has already paled into insignificance for Jim, or he wouldn't even remember who he yelled at. But the experience is much harder for Laura to move on from.

Friday, 12th September

"What's that noise?" Laura grumbled, lifting her head as Laoise walked away, having just yanked the desk out from under us because apparently, she *needed to* make more space by the wall for the upcoming photo shoot.

First of all, it was straight-up rude. She barged in without warning and started moving the desk we were sitting at. I was actually standing over my laptop with one knee on the chair when the desk began to tremble. I instinctively picked up my MacBook, clueless about what would happen next. She's such a bull in a china shop sometimes! How does she even work in PR with such terrible communication skills?

"Her infamous nylon trousers," I responded to Laura's question.

Laoise was wearing her black, wet-look nylon trousers again, the ones that make noise whenever she moves. Paired with a loose T-shirt, she looked like a log. I don't get why anyone would wear those trousers—they look hideous unless, maybe, they're a designer brand. Even then, labels don't excuse bad style. But what do I know? I'm just an intern in a Sesame Street hoodie that says, "I was raised on the street."

Saturday, 13th September

Early morning at my laptop I started the day with a mini video of vibrating dildos in various colours and shapes that unexpectedly popped up in front of my eyes after I had accidentally clicked on one of the sex toy ads. I was mesmerised by the dildos, which had little to do with my non-existent sex life and everything to do with the five hours of sleep I'd had four days in a row. I was, by then, the slow motion version of my normal self. After a minute of being hypnotised by disco dildos, I disciplined myself and closed the pop-up window, deleting the email. But then Jennifer's chat window popped up, saying, "Hello, do you miss me?" I decided to rest my head in my hands for a while, exhaling loud and long. Breathed and exhaled. Breathed and exhaled.

"Sex ads again?" I heard Mark's voice as he was passing by.

"Yep," I mumbled.

"How many?"

"Not enough."

Then Jim's voice shook me out of my coma "Where's my schedule, Sophie?" I told him it was on his desk. *It's always on his desk.* He was inquiring about the schedule for the following week when I wouldn't be here anymore. He looked down at his iPhone's screen and started to walk away from me toward the door which was in the opposite direction from his desk. I pottered over to his work area to check where he had misplaced the print. It was in the window, next to his desktop. Even the blind could find it.

Later...

Jimmy lit up his twentieth cigarette of the day, but surprisingly, he hadn't had any coffee yet. Instead, he kept two bottles of still water on his desk—one of them from yesterday, half-empty. I suspected he was on something else to keep him going. He was making last-minute changes to the designs, driving the seamstresses into a frenzy with their sewing machines. The models lined up outside in the corridor for fittings, with an average waiting time of two hours. Some left for fittings with other designers and either came back later or not at all. I occasionally checked on them, offering drinks or fruit from the kitchen.

Alba was hiding in the storage room again, as she had been all week. For a moment, I panicked when I couldn't find her. Mark and I searched the building up and down, while Jim didn't even notice her absence. I eventually found her curled up in the back of the storage room. Dogs can sense human emotions, and Alba was definitely picking up on the stressful vibe in the studio. I stroked her wise little head and thought leaving her alone would be the kindest thing right now. I printed a note, "ALBA IS INSIDE. KEEP THE DOOR

OPEN," and taped it to the storage room door for everyone's consideration.

I took a few minutes to stop and look around the studio at its busiest time, appreciating what I was part of. I inhaled deeply, soaking in the atmosphere and saving this moment. My internship would end with the show, and I was already feeling nostalgic.

Jim's sister and his 16-year-old niece spent the afternoon in the office. They had been out and about in London earlier, shopping, and now they were just chilling and finding comfort next to Kirstie. They probably knew each other for a long time. Moses ordered pizzas for the team, which we devoured with our hands in minutes before everyone returned to their stations to continue working.

At 8 p.m., Jim called me over to his desk and asked me to find someone to walk his niece home. I offered to drop her off, but he said he needed me at the office. He also pointed out that it was dark outside, we'd have to walk across the park, and I wasn't a boy. *So what? I've been walking myself home at night forever. Park or no park.* Besides, we could walk around the park, it's well-lit and safe by city standards. But he wanted one of the male interns to escort his niece, leaving the choice between Ido and Drew. All the other interns were girls. Ido, tall and masculine, was needed next to Cecile and Victor, so it had to be Drew, a skinny young man resembling Howard Wolowitz from the Big Bang Theory.

I gave Drew the address and told him Jim's buzzer didn't work, so they'd have to call Jim's sister on her cell once they arrived. She was already in the flat and would come down to open the door.

"Call me if there's any trouble," I added, giving him a missed call so he could save my number.

He put on his denim jacket and walked out the door with Jim's niece, a full-figured young girl almost three times his size. If anything, I believed the niece would be the one protecting Drew, not the other way around.

Half an hour later, I was in the kitchen making myself a cup of tea when my phone rang. It was Drew. I tucked the phone between my ear and shoulder as I poured hot water into the cup.

"Hi, Drew, what's up?"

"Sophie! We can't get in the house."

"What do you mean you can't get in?"

"The niece's mother isn't answering the phone."

"Maybe she's in the bathroom. Keep trying. There's no other way to get in."

"Okay."

I returned to my desk. Meanwhile, a few more models had arrived. I took their names and informed them they'd be in for a long wait. Then Drew called again.

"Any success?" I asked.

"No. She's not picking up the phone. We're trying from two different phones, but no response."

"Is she home at all? Can you see if the lights are on at the top of the house? That's Jim's flat. If she's home, the lights must be on."

"Yes, the lights are on."

"Why can't she hear her phone? Do you think something has happened to her?"

"I don't know, but it's getting cold."

"Then shout. Shout, scream, yell her name as loud as you can. She might hear you through the windows."

"Are you serious?"

"Do you have a better idea?"

"Okay, we'll try," he sighed.

I went on my business and ten minutes later, Drew called again. His voice was croaky and exhausted, probably from all the yelling.

"Hey, Sophie. We're still outside...," he sounded like a drunken sailor.

"Oh, Jesus," I exhaled loudly.

"...we're trying everything but nothing works," he cleared his throat.

"Let me think. Maybe I can ask Jim to call his sister... or you know what? Try to buzz in the neighbours and see if they're willing to let you in."

"You said the buzzer didn't work."

"Jim's buzzer doesn't work, but I have no idea about the neighbours' buzzers."

"Okay."

Drew was clearly fed up. I could tell.

"Then try calling her again, and if she still doesn't answer, walk back to the studio. We'll figure something out from here," I advised.

Drew went quiet for a worrying amount of time, so I texted him to find out what was happening. He texted back saying, "Niece is inside the flat. Her mum's phone was on silent mode. On my way back. Cu"

It was 11 p.m., and one of the models approached me, visibly exhausted. She had been waiting for three hours and insisted on leaving. Understanding her fatigue but knowing Jim's determination to include her in the show, I hurried to the stylist. I asked if there was any chance they could see the "it girl" now. They assured me they could fit her in within twenty minutes. Relaying this to the model, she reluctantly agreed to wait a bit longer.

Twenty minutes stretched into thirty, and she grew increasingly impatient. Glancing at me with frustration, she declared she was leaving. Hastening back to Jim's desk, I urgently informed them of her imminent departure. The stylist immediately called the model's agent, pleading for him to convince her to stay. Despite their efforts, the model abruptly walked out without a farewell.

After midnight, we were finally allowed to go home. JK arranged Uber rides for everyone. Gracie and I shared a car, she was back in my room for the weekend. We had hardly spoken to each other since her return to London; it had just been too crazy in the office and I was too washed to care to chit chat. Exiting the building at 1 a.m., I noticed a girl jumping out of an ELITE car (the chauffeured car service) parked on the pavement, rushing to ring our office doorbell—the last model for fittings.

Upstairs, Jim, the stylist, Cecile, Victor, Laoise, and others were still working hard while Gracie and I relaxed in the car on our way home. Utterly spent, I leaned my head against the window, closing my eyes during the ride.

London Fashion Week

I overslept in the morning, and when I finally got up, Gracie was nowhere to be found. *Why didn't she wake me up?* I arrived at the studio an hour late, but it didn't matter—no one seemed to notice in the midst of the chaos.

The show went incredibly well. It was held in a private location in Central London, a beautiful building rich with history and art. All the models were on time, lined up for hair and makeup before the rehearsal. A photographer was hovering around, capturing candid backstage moments and distracting the girls. Kamila had taken over coordinating the models, so I wandered around, looking for anyone who needed assistance. Meanwhile, I snapped photos with my phone. The photographer struck up a conversation with me, and we exchanged numbers.

In the audience, I bumped into Lee. It was a pleasant surprise. He mentioned he hadn't known I was working for Jim Kendal, or perhaps he was just pretending—I couldn't tell. He asked what I thought of the collection, but I honestly had no opinion. I had been so consumed with work that, despite being surrounded by the designs and photographing the models, I hadn't really seen the garments. All I could recall were the floral elements and some bright colours.

Ido approached me during the lineup, visibly upset about our falling out. He told me that he was hurt by the fact that we were no longer friends. *When were we friends? I didn't even realise we had ever been close.* He still hadn't gotten over our verbal spat and the way I distanced myself afterward. His eyes welled up as he confessed that while he didn't care about what the other interns thought of him, my opinion and friendship meant a lot to him. He couldn't return to Israel without knowing I had forgiven him. I was staggered. Even now, in 2020, as I edit these lines, I still can't tell if his apology was sincere or mere theatre.

After the show, everyone quickly dispersed. I found Moses in the crowd and asked, "Where's everybody? When are we going back to the studio?" He informed me that the van had already left and there was no need to return to the studio. Kamila and enough others were there to tidy up, and I was free to go home. I told him "Okay, I'll come to pick up my laptop tomorrow". He replied that the office would be closed tomorrow—everyone had the day off after the show. *How could they neglect to tell me this? I need my laptop!*

I called Kamila immediately and asked her to wait for me. She told me to hurry up as they had already unloaded the van and would soon lock the office door. I hurried. Bus, tube, bus. I arrived after forty minutes, flushed from the rush. I quickly picked up my things, tidied my desk, and scribbled a note for Laoise that I left on top of the planning book on her desk for handover to the future PA, if there would be any.

My to-do list for Monday, my perceived last day, ended up in the trash:

- Double-check events in the calendar
- Send thank you & goodbye emails to my liaisons at M.E.
- Say goodbye to Lucia (the studio manager)
- Print weekly schedule
- Buy dog food, cigarettes, and water to stock up for the first week in my absence
- £33.25 petty cash from Moses
- Try passion fruit smoothie from the café downstairs
- (Card for Jim?)

I still naively hoped to speak with Jimmy about whether I'd stay on after the show when the burden was off his shoulders. However, another part of me believed the bullshitting would just continue in the office, and I wasn't sure I wanted to be part of it any longer.

> "*Leadership which lacks integrity can bring down an entire corporation. The lack of integrity leads to distrust. When you question someone's trustworthiness, they will not retort back by accepting that you should not trust them. The dishonesty in people is mostly hidden.*" Shankar R. Santhiram

I got home after the longest week of my life. I was d.e.a.d. t.i.r.e.d. I washed the stress off my skin and hair in the shower and lay on my bed, naked. And now I am just resting in the quiet room, bathing in the warm orange light of the sunset. I could fall asleep... Maybe I will.

Monday, 15th September

When I finished my internship, I received no thank you card, no goodbyes, no hug, nothing. Not from Jim, nor from anybody else. I expected some form of gratitude for my work but got nada. When Gracie asked if I was going to miss the place, I said I would miss belonging. It was a disorganised workplace, but I created a system and a routine that provided the structure I needed to function. I spent most of my time there over the past five months and grew to love the place with its ups and downs. I finally figured out Jim's behaviour, earned his trust, and Alba's love. I had a job I loved in a creative atmosphere I had always wanted, and then it was suddenly over.

Tuesday, 16th September

I met up with the photographer, thinking it was a date, but it was hard to tell. Is it a date if I pay for my own coffee? It was my birthday, but I didn't tell him. We popped into some art galleries around New Bond Street and chatted the hours away about our work and how we got into fashion. It didn't seem like he wanted to get to know me; he asked a lot of questions about the people I work with, leaving me with the feeling that he was more interested in my contacts than in me. The next day, I went away for my holiday and never heard from the photographer again.

***

After the internship, I don't find myself for months. I am off track with my life and live with heartache. I really loved my PA job and hoped Jimmy would call me back. Instead, the only person I heard from was his new assistant, who asked me about the photos I took of Jim's clothes to list them on eBay. I miss Alba and worry she won't be taken care of lovingly by the new assistant.

I find it harder and harder to re-enter the job market. I crave stability and predictability for a change. I am tired of the constant job hunt and the uncertainty of my future. But I have to keep going. I aim to nurture my personal assistant aspirations, sending out job applications and emails to creative professionals whom I'd be happy to assist. At the same time, I need to take another part-time job to continue receiving housing benefits. I am juggling again. I believe I have been juggling since I entered adulthood.

Then, on top of everything, my beloved Spanish flatmate decided to move back to Spain. She can't feel it in London anymore. No more "white bitch". At least not in London.

I'm so heartbroken.

December 2014

A rich Asian guy named Li, a sharp-witted Iranian girl named Giti, a well-connected British guy (Quinn), and an innovative Hungarian girl (me) gathered in a pub to discuss the idea of launching a fashion magazine. The meeting was brief and filled with more laughter than actual work. Honestly, I don't remember anything important happening during our get-together.

For our second meeting, we visited the Photographer's Gallery to check out the Viviane Sassen exhibition. By some twist of fate, we all wore black and looked like a creative gang fresh from a funeral. I wore black leggings, a black oversized sweater dress, and a self-made Versace badge pinned above my chest. Giti had a black dress and black Dr. Martens on. Li sported a black shirt paired with tailored navy wool trousers, and Quinn put on a black sweatshirt with a graffiti print on the front, which he had secretly kept from an up-and-coming designer who had sent his samples to The Magazine, along with a K-pop baseball hat and extra-wide sunglasses.

"Howdy, partner," I greeted Quinn with a cowboy accent.

"Lol! Zofi, you're funny!" he chuckled.

"We have something in common."

"Oh yeah? What's that?"

"Your dark shades."

"Do I look funny or what?" Quinn seemed mildly offended, trying to catch his reflection in the glass of an exhibited photo.

"Nope. It's just that the paparazzi didn't follow us here," I teased.

"They're part of my image."

"You might regret missing out on the original colours of the Sassen photos."

"Hmm, you've got a point," Quinn mused, swapping his sunglasses for reading glasses from his bum bag belted across his chest. He then asked why I had an American accent.

My accent was a chameleon. It shifted between British and American English, and if I spent a lot of time with my Spanish and Italian flatmates, I'd start sounding like them too.

"I was binge-watching Sex and the City all weekend," I confessed.

"Didn't you have better things to do?"

"Um, let me think... nope. I also baked banana bread."

"You should come to a party with me and Susan."

"I will. On New Year's Eve. Not sooner."

"You're such a weirdo, Zofi!"

"The music at those parties is too monotone. It's the same beat for nine hours."

"Of course! You have to take drugs."

"No thanks!"

After the exhibition, we settled at the gallery's café to brainstorm our first editorial. Giti and I were buzzing with ideas, showering the boys with creative suggestions. After half an hour, we had the story sketched out in my palm-sized notebook, complete with details and quirky touches.

Our third meeting never happened. Quinn continued to slave away with endless hours at The Magazine, struggling to find time for anything beyond work. Giti, caught in the throes of a breakup, froze us out. Li's whereabouts became a mystery. The four of us never met again; only Quinn remained my fashion buddy and occasional Sunday roast companion.

Sometimes, he calls on weekends with an unrecognisable husky voice, after partying until dawn and riding the comedown from whatever drugs he's taken. The little boy in him needs reassurance that the world is still intact, that there are still good things in it, even if he feels pain and depression. His synthetic bliss has the lifespan of a shooting star, falling into the Earth's atmosphere and transforming into [3]"Gloomy Sundays". I wished he didn't take drugs, but he likes them. They are his escape from the roles he plays for others in his daily life.

---

[3] Hungarian suicide song Gloomy Sunday by Rezső Seress (Billie Holiday version was released in 1941)

February 2015

One evening, I popped into The Magazine's office to fill my two shoulder bags with issues from the towering stacks of previous editions. Quinn, ever the jokester, signed the latest issue under his name on the credit page, proudly pointing out that his title had changed from Junior Fashion Editor to Senior Fashion Editor, and he now had a decent salary. The wheel turned in his favour when the Fashion Director had resigned, and Lee had stepped into the role. As Lee had previously worked as the Senior Fashion Editor, they promoted Quinn to take Lee's title, but his responsibilities hadn't changed much. He was still the one pressing the button to open the door, sorting the post, and tying up loose ends after everyone else had gone home at 5.

Quinn then casually mentioned that Lee had asked about me, saying, "We should get a job for Zsofi at The Magazine." *He wants to bring me onboard? Yes!*

> "*Titles mean absolutely nothing. Fashion hierarchy is bizarre and totally unfounded on any rationale. You may be given a place on the masthead of a magazine you've never even heard of, while slogging away for 10 years in the hope of an unpaid Junior Fashion Editor credit which you will never, ever receive.*" Bertie Brandes

When I was ready to leave, I found myself standing still. The bags were too heavy to lift. I had to leave a few copies behind to manage carrying the rest. My shoulders ached, but as they say, what doesn't kill you makes you stronger. And somehow, I survived another winter in London.

March 2015

I flew to New York for a portfolio review event in Brooklyn. I had saved enough money for the flight and stayed with acquaintances for free. I bought a refurbished iPad to showcase my portfolio, only to realise they required prints. *Bummer.* I scrambled to print a selection of my artwork and factored in the extra weight of the portfolio book when packing my suitcase.

At the event, there were gallery curators, designers, agents, creative directors, photo editors, publishers, and other representatives from established powerhouses like Vice, CNN, BuzzFeed, New York Magazine, and W Magazine that made me feverish with excitement.

Coming to New York is a dream come true. I'd wanted to visit New York ever since I watched "Taxicab Confessions" on HBO in my early teens. My mum's childhood friend lives in New Jersey, where Jon Bon Jovi also resides, and I would beg her to take me to the continent whenever she visited us in Hungary. Now, after almost 20 years, it was finally happening—I was going to the USA! Awesome!

The flight across the Atlantic was pleasant and peaceful. I spent my time editing photos on my phone and watching in-flight entertainment. Sleep eluded me, so I meditated through the night hours instead.

The portfolio event was a so-so experience. I didn't meet anyone interesting, but it didn't matter because I WAS IN LOVE WITH NEW YORK! Despite a snowstorm, I walked for hours, breathing in the city's atmosphere. I visited [4]Patricia Field's boutique, a four-level bookstore that felt like a library—so cool, OMG!—the MoMA, Times Square, Trump Tower, 5th Avenue, Studio 54, Central Park, the Brooklyn Bridge, and various art galleries in Brooklyn. The list went on.

Before flying out from London, I tracked down Lina Plioplyte, the director of "Advanced Style", and sent her an email asking if she was interested in teaming up on a video project. She replied the next day with positive news. Now that I was in New York, we tried to meet up, but time was tight, so we arranged a video chat instead. Even though we didn't meet in person, she made my day! She loved the project idea, adored the video I made for the Miami Fashion Film Festival, and was eager to collaborate with me. The rest will follow.

I came back to London with:

- Two books
- A New York postcard (I had to!)
- Two NY fridge magnets (I collect them)
- A Polaroid photo taken by a guy on the Brooklyn Bridge
- A curator's contact who was interested in being my mentor
- A breathtaking experience of watching the sunrise from the plane above the clouds
- Mild jet lag

---

[4] Patricia Field is the costume designer & stylist who worked on movies like Sex and the City & The Devil Wears Prada

- The completion of 4 out of the 5 things on my NY wish list from 2012:
    1. Wandering the city and taking pics with my Smena film camera
    2. Sitting in a yellow cab
    3. Walking the High Line
    4. Visiting family friends in New Jersey

It was a trip to remember!

May 2015

I went to see Bradley Cooper in "The Elephant Man" at the Theatre Royal Haymarket after hearing him talk about bringing the "handsome but underpowered production" to London on the Howard Stern Show. The reviews weren't convincing, but I wanted to see Bradley Cooper on stage!

The play turned out to be boring and sluggishly directed, and it was hard to hear from the cheap seats in the back. However, the actors were all great in it!

P.S.
The interval with the theatre staff selling ice cream... I mean, why? I was watching a rather dark and dramatic play, and then, in the middle of it, the lights turned on, and staff members appeared with wide smiles, trying to lure the grown-up audience into buying cool refreshments. I was busy digesting the emotions of the play—how on earth was I supposed to make space for ice cream?

June 2015

I asked Quinn if he wanted to come to the Tony Bennett & Lady Gaga show at The Royal Albert Hall, but he wasn't interested. I wasn't entirely sure if I should go either because the tickets were a bit too pricey for my wallet. Quinn, however, tried to use his new title as Senior Fashion Editor to snag me a press pass. Unfortunately, the gig got cancelled because Bennett came down with the flu, but I did manage to watch the full concert on the plane when I flew to New York the second time.

In June, I also visited the V&A to check out the Alexander McQueen: Savage Beauty exhibition. I was mesmerized by the Kate Moss hologram video, watching it many times from beginning to end. The entire exhibition was breathtaking, and I couldn't get enough of it. I stretched my time there by walking back and forth between the rooms filled with masterpieces.

Did you know?

Alexander McQueen died on 11/02/2010. If you add up the numbers, the result is 7.

> Number seven in numerology:
> "*Seven is a magical, sacred or Divine number. Seven is a "perfect number", an emblem of the totality of space, time and the movements of the universe. As well as change and evolution. It is also the number of completed cycles, death and rebirth. It takes Saturn (The Planet of Karma) seven years to revolve around the sun.*" Federico Raffo, "The Numbers Man"

Fun fact:

The opposite sides of a dice always add up to seven.

Summer 2015

This summer, I start working on getting my driving licence and move to yet another house in West London—my seventh move in nine years.

Life in London is becoming less fun. I feel like I'm stuck in a loop, facing the same struggles over and over, unable to break out or break through. I'm torn between seeing this experience as growth or loss.

Some emotional support would be nice. Magic would be appreciated too.

November 2015

Lee and I found ourselves at a private studio in East London, shooting for H. magazine. Our models were a blonde lesbian and a high school-aged girl, chaperoned by her mum who sat through the entire shoot on the sofa outside the studio. The models didn't need to be particularly beautiful; their faces were painted, and their hair was styled into voluminous shapes, making them unrecognisable in the photos.

Lee brought along Soner, a tall guy with dark hair and dark eyes, as a second assistant. He was fun to work with, and we shared responsibilities on set, chatting away the empty hours. It was clear he was experienced, and I later found out he had been assisting Lee at The Magazine. I couldn't help but wonder what had happened to the "We should get a job for Zsofi at The Magazine" idea?

That day, we worked with high-end brands like Miu Miu, Fendi, YSL, McQueen, Dior, Kim West, Balenciaga, Prada, and Dries Van Noten. Soner and I were dazzled by the outfits hanging neatly on the rack. We couldn't stop "ooh-ing" and "aah-ing" as we touched the delicate fabrics and picked our favourites from the carrier bags before placing them on hangers. The silver, crocodile leather boots from Loewe totally stole my heart! They were beyond stunning—my gosh, I wanted them! We also had unique headpieces from new designers and one-of-a-kind costume designs. My imagination was already crafting edgy looks for the pages, and I was over the moon with excitement about the shoot!

We spent two days in the studio with a team of 15 people, including an agency-signed makeup artist and a set designer. Their assistants were just as amazed by the stunning outfits as we, the fashion assistants, were.

After Soner and I set up the stylist station and finished steam-cleaning the creased shirts, one of us had to go pick up a bag from a distant showroom. Lee sent me, which made me realise I was the second assistant, not Soner. After many years by Lee's side, I felt officially replaced. I fought a sinking feeling in my stomach.

Just give me a moment...

I was disappointed—dammit, it hurt—but I didn't show it. Someone once told me, "If you react emotionally, you're not a professional." So, I remained myself—enthusiastic and dedicated—throughout the weekend. By the end of the shoot, I felt somewhat relieved that I didn't have to deal with returns now that I wasn't the stylist's right hand anymore.

Later, Soner and I added each other on social media, and he sent me the photos he had secretly snapped with his phone of the last look we both loved. For the final shot, the high school model wore a stunning white haute couture dress that sparkled in all shades under a special light effect, transporting us into a surreal world somewhere between disco and fairy tale.

This shoot marks my last professional gig in London. Although Quinn tries to keep me in the loop by texting me if I am available to assist some no-name designer or stylist he met at The Magazine, I quietly walk away. I am not aligned with the unpaid opportunities anymore. I've changed. I have grown into my worth, without needing a title to tell me so.

I am of service to people as a QUEEN and not as a slave.

***

Two years later, I heard that Lee got fired, and shortly after, Quinn celebrated his new title as Fashion Director at The Magazine.

As for me, I won a photo challenge, revisited New York, and even sold pieces of my collection in three little East London boutiques. But eventually, I stopped pouring my time and money into a dream that no longer felt alive. I was tired of running in circles. I needed a change. And honestly, I was dying to see blue skies and live in a healthier environment. Remember when Catalina said she wasn't feeling it in London anymore? It finally got to me, too.

After months of careful consideration, and a lot of mental and emotional preparation, I packed my bags and left to travel, armed with my brand-new driver's license and every penny I had saved. It was terrifying at first. I kept asking myself—what if I missed a big opportunity? I'd spent years building my contacts and my experience. Was I really ready to throw it all away? But I knew it was time. I'd chased my dreams in fashion for seven years—seven, the number of completed cycles.

And after 11 years, I finally said goodbye to London—the city that had shaped me, tested me, taught me resilience, pulled me into its chaos, and, in the end, released me into a new chapter of my life. Eleven—the number of ascension. In numerology, it's a Master Number, a gateway to awakening and transformation, urging you to trust your intuition and embrace new paths. For me, it was the sign I needed.

References

Sargon

1. The 22 season retail calendar by Apparel Resources, 2012, link https://in.apparelresources.com/business-news/retail/22-season-retail-calendar-know/

OCTOBER 2011, Writer's note

1. Quoted from the article *Britain not sunny enough for healthy vitamin D levels, say experts*, 2015, link https://www.theguardian.com/lifeandstyle/2015/aug/02/britain-not-sunny-enough-healthy-vitamin-d-levels-supplements

Thursday, 6th October, Did you know?

1. www.npr.org

2. www.guardian.com, link https://www.theguardian.com/cities/2016/apr/12/why-cant-french-cities-clean-up-after-their-dogs-montpellier

July 2013

1. *Ego* as described in vocabulary.com

Shoreditch House with Isa

1. Shoreditch House: The private club for hipsters, article by Rebecca Magniant at www.doitlondon.co.uk http://www.doitinlondon.co.uk/en/culture/shoreditch-house-le-club-prive-des-hipsters-19383

Friday, 06th June, 2014

1. Quoted from wikipedia, *British cuisine,* link https://en.wikipedia.org/wiki/British_cuisine

2. Chanel No. 5 - did you know?

Chanel no 5: The story behind the classic perfume", 2011, link https://www.bbc.com/news/world-13565155

For the full article read '*A Boycott of Chanel No. 5 Urged by Humane Groups*', link: https://www.nytimes.com/1973/04/15/archives/a-boycott-of-chanel-no-5-urged-by-humane-groups.html

Animal Musks: The Dark Secret of Perfume, 2019, link: https://purrfumery.com/pages/animal-musks-the-dark-secret-of-perfume

The Perfume Society, 2020, link: https://perfumesociety.org/ingredients-post/civet/

Friday, 8th August, Did you know?

1. Quoted from the article *8 August is Female Orgasm Day, Thanks to Brazil,* link http://rabaah.com/international-female-orgasm-day-8-aug.html

Sunday, 14th September LFW catwalk

1. Quoted from the article *Work Matters! The consequence of having no integrity* by Shankar R. Santhiram, 2020,link https://www.nst.com.my/opinion/columnists/2020/03/572105/work-matters-consequence-having-no-integrity

FEBRUARY 2015

1. 35 realities of working in the fashion industry by Bertie Brandes, link https://i-d.vice.com/en_us/article/7xvekx/35-realities-of-working-in-the-fashion-industry

Printed in Dunstable, United Kingdom

78751366R00198